PROFILES IN JUDICIAL EXCELLENCE

Wilbur S. Shepperson Series in Nevada History
Michael Green, University of Nevada, Las Vegas, Series Editor

Nevada is known politically as a swing state and culturally as a swinging state. Politically, its electoral votes have gone to the winning presidential candidate in all but two elections since 1912 (it missed in 1976 and 2016). Its geographic location in the Sun Belt; an ethnically diverse, heavily urban, and fast-growing population; and an economy based on tourism and mining make it a laboratory for understanding the growth and development of postwar America and post-industrial society. Culturally, Nevada has been associated with legal gambling, easy divorce, and social permissiveness. Yet the state also exemplifies conflicts between image and reality: It is also a conservative state yet depends heavily on the federal government. Its gaming regulatory system is the envy of the world but resulted from long and difficult experience with organized crime. And its bright lights often obscure the role of organized religion in Nevada affairs. To some who have emphasized the impact of globalization and celebrated or deplored changing moral standards, Nevada reflects America and the world; to others, it affects them.

This series is named in honor of one of the state's most distinguished historians, author of numerous books on the state's immigrants and cultural development, a longtime educator, and an advocate for history and the humanities. The series welcomes manuscripts on any and all aspects of Nevada that offer insight into how the state has developed and how its development has been connected to the region, the nation, and the world.

Charcoal and Blood:
Italian Immigrants in Eureka, Nevada
and the Fish Creek Massacre
Silvio Manno

A Great Basin Mosaic:
The Cultures of Rural Nevada
James W. Hulse

Gambling With Lives:
A History of Occupational
Health in Greater Las Vegas
Michelle Follette Turk

The Sagebrush State:
Nevada's History, Government,
and Politics, Sixth Edition
Michael Bowers

The Westside Slugger:
Joe Neal's Lifelong Fight
for Social Justice
John L. Smith

Monumental Lies:
Early Nevada Folklore
of the Wild West
Ronald M. James

Profiles in Judicial Excellence:
Territorial and Supreme
Court Justices of Nevada
David A. Hardy

PROFILES IN JUDICIAL EXCELLENCE

Territorial and Supreme Court Justices of Nevada

David A. Hardy

UNIVERSITY OF NEVADA PRESS | *Reno & Las Vegas*

University of Nevada Press | Reno, Nevada 89557 USA
www.unpress.nevada.edu
Copyright © 2024 by University of Nevada Press
All rights reserved
Manufactured in the United States of America

FIRST PRINTING

Cover design by Louise Ofarrell
Cover photograph © by Kit Leong/stock.adobe.com

Library of Congress Cataloging-in-Publication Data

Names: Hardy, David A. (David Allen), 1964– author.
Title: Profiles in judicial excellence : territorial and Supreme Court justices of Nevada / David A. Hardy.
Other titles: Wilbur S. Shepperson series in Nevada history.
Description: Reno, Nevada : University of Nevada Press, [2025] | Series: Wilbur S. Shepperson series in Nevada history | Includes bibliographical references. | Summary: "Until the publication of Judge David A. Hardy's Profiles in Judicial Excellence: Territorial and Supreme Court Justices of Nevada, there has been no single source containing biographies of these influential figures from the state's history from 1861 to 1997. Hardy curates various sources and presents profiles of these judges in sequential order of their service. He also examines the influence of territorial judges in the 1864 vote for statehood. The Nevada judiciary has played an integral, but often unrecognized, role in shaping the unique character of the Silver State"—Provided by publisher.
Identifiers: LCCN 2024032537 | ISBN 9781647791858 (hardcover) | ISBN (ebook)
Subjects: LCSH: Judges—Nevada—Biography. | Nevada. Supreme Court—Officials and employees—Biography. | Nevada—History. | LCGFT: Biographies.
Classification: LCC KFN1125 .H37 2025 | DDC 347.793/140922—dc23/eng/20240716

LC record available at https://lccn.loc.gov/2024032537

ISBN 9781647791858 (cloth)
ISBN 9781647791865 (ebook)
LCCN: 2024032537

The paper used in this book meets the requirements of American National Standard for Information Sciences—Permanence of Paper for Printed Library Materials, ANSI/NISO Z39.48-1992 (R2002).

Contents

Preface   vii
Introduction   1

NEVADA TERRITORIAL SUPREME COURT

George E. Turner   23
Gordon N. Mott   28
Horatio M. Jones   33
Powhattan Locke   39
John North   42

NEVADA SUPREME COURT

James F. Lewis   51
Henry O. Beatty   56
Cornelius M. Brosnan   59
J. Neely Johnson   64
Bernard Crosby Whitman   69
John Garber   73
Charles Henry Belknap   78
Thomas Porter Hawley   81
Warner Earll   84
William H. Beatty   87
Orville Rinaldo Leonard   92
Michael Augustus Murphy   94

Rensselaer R. Bigelow	96
McKaskia Stearns Bonnifield	98
William A. Massey	101
Adolphus Leigh Fitzgerald	103
Thomas Van Camp Julien	105
George Frederick Talbot	110
Frank H. Norcross	112
James G. Sweeney	115
Patrick A. McCarran	117
Benjamin W. Coleman	119
John Adams Sanders	123
Edward Augustus Ducker	125
Erroll James Livingston "E. J. L." Taber	128
Willian E. Orr	133
Charles Lee Horsey	138
Edgar Eather	143
Milton B. Badt	147
Charles M. Merrill	152
Frank McNamee	156
Miles N. "Jack" Pike	161
Gordon R. Thompson	166
David Zenoff	172
Jon R. Collins	177
Cameron M. Batjer	183
Thomas L. Steffen	190
Sources	195
Acknowledgments	219
Index	221
About the Author	231

Preface

INSCRIBED ON THE FAÇADE OF the National Archives are the words, "What is past is prologue." This phrase from Shakespeare's *The Tempest* describes what we all know intuitively: the past helps us understand the present and can be an inspiring influence for a transformative future. Thus, biography is more than entertaining.

As will be seen, the justices profiled in this book are homogenous; reflective of the judiciary of the time, they are all men. Although it was not until Justice Miriam Shearing's election in 1992 that Nevadans elected their first female justice, the Nevada judiciary now recognizes the power of diversity, particularly in appellate courts where jurists deliberate the law through the lens of their own individual circumstances. In this important way, the modern supreme court reflects a richness and diversity so obviously absent in the past, and so critical for the future.

Historical biography is the work of dedicated scholars who triangulate original source materials and present their subjects without personal preference or agenda. Professional biographers develop their subjects as they unfold from the historical records—regardless of the complexities that emerge. This is not a book of historical biography; it is hagiographic and devotional; the subjects are presented as larger than the lives they lived. The sources for this book are primarily memorials and tributes, written for post-mortem honor. On occasion I have excerpted news accounts and other secondary sources, but always with the purpose of portraying the justices positively. I have done so intentionally and acknowledge that this book presents only a partial portrayal of its subjects. I have included some critical material about the territorial judges, not for the truth of the criticisms, but to demonstrate the territorial judiciary's influence on statehood.

Post-death memorials are historically difficult because death invites reflection where the positive is accentuated and the negative is concealed. Memories and records of the deceased become one dimensional as time passes. Good qualities grow to great, while flaws are soon forgotten. But this is appropriate—particularly because none who precede us is binary; each has inspirational qualities to emulate, even though each also fell below the highest standards of their time and the highest expectations of our modern time. Therefore, whether exaggerated or incomplete, honorific themes teach those who live about how to live. For example, one tribute to Justice Benjamin Coleman is a template for how we may choose to live: "laughing freely, thinking deeply, and working hard—dying rich in the golden opinions of those we serve."

As I compiled these brief profiles I began to see common threads woven throughout the lives of the justices. Among these threads are public spiritedness, intellectual honesty, courage, endurance, resilience, magnanimity, social progressivism, commitment, and scholarship. Several of the justices survived their own failures before realizing great success. Each is inspiring in his own way.

There is no single source location for biographical information about the justices who have served on the Nevada Supreme Court. This book is my attempt to compile the first volume of hagiographic biographies of those who have served on the territorial and Nevada supreme courts. I hope others will continue this work as time passes. There was no objective standard for including or excluding justices of the modern era. I chose not to profile any living justices and I passed over a few who were recently deceased. Writing about deceased justices nearer to our time is challenging because there are more resources and the subjects remain known to many who still live—including family and friends. Throughout this work I attempted to quiet my voice and resist the personal narrative.

The justices profiled in this book are more important than their individual lives. Together they are the authors of Nevada jurisprudence. Their work composes a system of laws that bind our communities through interpreting and enforcing contracts, defining property rights, assembling and disassembling families, seizing and awarding money, protecting victims and punishing predators, giving voice to the vulnerable, and ensuring equal protection and civil liberties for all. Through the work of the Nevada Supreme Court, the citizens of our great state may anticipate their affairs, be confident in the independence and integrity of judiciary, and enjoy public safety and social order. Nevada governor Paul Laxalt emphasized this unique role of the judiciary in his remarks to a special session of the Nevada Supreme Court on October 2, 1967, during the investitures of Justices Mowbray and Batjer, whom he appointed when the court expanded from three to five justices. He encouraged all in attendance to:

> once again, for a few moments... dwell upon the increasing importance of our judicial system in preserving our cherished American way of life and the freedoms upon which it is based. The efficient administration of justice is the bulwark of these freedoms and the keystone of the arch of the many liberties upon which our free society rests. Let us then always be keenly mindful that the effective administration of our judicial system in turn depends upon the judges. Judges who must dispense justice and in doing so must make the machinery of the judicial system operate not only smoothly, tirelessly, and continuously, but of even more importance fairly, promptly, and justly. We cannot possibly have justice fairly unless we have judges whose integrity is beyond question, whose abilities are of the highest, whose dedication for public good motivates them always, and whose every action instills in the public respect for our courts and our system of laws and complete confidence that these laws are being administered by our judges and our courts with complete impartiality and without fear or favor.

This book is my attempt to illuminate Governor Laxalt's idealistic words through the lives of justices who have contributed to the remarkable institution of the Nevada Supreme Court.

PROFILES IN JUDICIAL EXCELLENCE

Introduction

Nevada became a state to escape the dead-fall of her Territorial courts. Her Temple of Justice had been transformed into a den of iniquity.
       Nevada attorney general Robert M. Clarke, 1867

THE NEVADA SUPREME COURT SPRANG into existence on October 31, 1864, when Nevada was admitted as the thirty-sixth state. But it was not created without context or controversy; it was born of circumstances that directly influenced statehood and indirectly influenced the work of its early justices, who inherited a failed judicial system that had lost public confidence. Thus, any review of the Nevada Supreme Court justices best begins with the territorial courts and judges that preceded statehood.

Nevadans popularly believe Nevada became the "battle born" state to increase the number of votes in Congress to pass the Thirteenth Amendment; obtain three additional electoral votes supporting Lincoln's reelection; strengthen the political power of legislative postwar reconstruction; create a Republican advantage in the House of Representatives if third-party candidate John Frémont prevented the other two candidates from receiving a majority of electoral votes; and fortify the Union army as it marched toward victory over the Confederacy.

While each of these influences contributed to statehood, they compose an incomplete story of how Nevada transitioned from territory to state in less than four years. Statehood required more than the desire of the federal government because consent from territorial residents was also required. The journey of Nevada statehood began with a popular vote by a four-to-one margin in September 1863 to convene a constitutional convention. Yet just three months later, in January 1864, after the first constitutional convention adjourned, territorial residents *rejected* statehood by a four-to-one vote margin. Nine months later, in September 1864, they *approved* statehood by an eight-to-one vote margin.

The shifts in public sentiment in the twelve months preceding statehood are traceable to a series of events involving judges who were perceived as corrupt and unaccountable, delivering judgments to the highest bidder, when they could be persuaded to perform their duties at all. But judges were not the only problem; lawyers, witnesses, and jurors were also susceptible to the corrupting influence of shadow money in the courts. Mining and other commercial endeavors became paralyzed in populous Virginia City during this time, and discontented residents agitated for statehood, in part, to restore judicial normalcy.

Records from the second constitutional convention in July reveal a deep distrust of territorial judges appointed and imported from afar. Statehood was the antidote because judges would be elected and accountable to the citizens they served. Statehood also provided a constitutional template for constructing a judiciary system that balanced independence with accountability.

While convention delegates debated statehood within the halls of government, several newspapers urged statehood in the halls of public opinion. On August 22, 1863, just sixteen days before the vote on statehood, all three judges of the territorial supreme court resigned their offices. And because these judges also served as trial judges in their respective districts, the entire territory was left without a judicial system. Residents reversed course and voted in favor of statehood, at least in part to rid themselves of a judiciary they perceived as corrupt.

The most reliable description of the judicial environment preceding territorial status and statehood was written by the Nevada Supreme Court in 1865, shortly after statehood:

> This being the first volume of Nevada State Reports, we have deemed it advisable to state a few facts in relation to the organization of the Territory, adoption of the State Government and the laws under which these reports are published. . . . In the years 1859 and 1860, the silver mines of this region began to attract attention, and population to pour into those portions of the present State which were known to possess valuable mines.

Besides those who crowded around the principal mines then discovered, a sparse population began to settle in those valleys and favored spots along the eastern base of the Sierra Nevada Mountains which were suitable for grazing and agricultural purposes.... [T]he inhabitants who came to work in the mines found themselves in a country, the only written laws of which were the United States Constitution, and such statutes enacted by the congress or the United States as might be applicable to their situation, and the statute laws of the Mormons. The latter were not calculated to inspire much respect in a free and enlightened community. There were no statute laws of the United States applicable to the wants and requirements of the people. It was difficult to determine what system of laws were in force among the mining population and what was then Carson County. By some it was contended that civil law was in force here, because when the Mormons settled the Territory of Utah it was within the Mexican Republic, where the civil law prevails. By others it was contended the common law was introduced into Utah because the Mormons generally came from countries where the common law prevails. And more especially did they contend that the common law must be held to have prevailed in Carson County because the entire population of miners coming from California, settling in a country then almost a desert, and without written law, must be held to have brought their own laws and customs with them.

NEVADA TERRITORIAL SUPREME COURT

Creation of the Nevada Territory: 1861

President Buchanan signed An Act to Organize the Territory of Nevada on March 2, 1861, at least in part to quell disorder and lawlessness in the area. National interests also influenced the creation of the territory. Jefferson Davis had been inaugurated president of the Confederacy just twelve days earlier, and southern members of Congress had abandoned their offices to join the secessionist government. Creating the Nevada Territory was one of President Buchanan's final acts, as Abraham Lincoln was inaugurated just two days later.

The act organizing the territory provided for a supreme court consisting of a chief justice, two associate justices, and three judicial districts in which "one of the justices of the supreme court" would preside. The composition of the court is unusual in modern times because the justices served as individual trial judges and then sat together as appellate justices of the territorial supreme court. Thus, the very judge challenged by appeal was one of three judges considering the allegations of error.

President Lincoln commissioned James Nye as territorial governor and Orion Clemens as secretary. (Clemens was the older brother of Samuel Clemens, better known as Mark Twain.) President Lincoln appointed George Turner as chief justice and Horatio Jones and Gordon Mott as associate justices on March 27, 1861. When Governor Nye arrived in the territory, he wrote to Secretary of State William Seward that "no such thing as law or order exists." He issued a proclamation defining the three judicial districts and appointing Judge Mott to the First Judicial District (comprising Carson City and Virginia City), Judge Turner to the Second Judicial District, and Judge Jones to the Third Judicial District. The proclamation establishing the judiciary was the first important order of business because lawlessness demanded court action, and "the absence of legal authority was the major reason the settlers had lobbied for separate territorial status."

Endless Litigation

Not surprisingly, litigation began almost immediately after the Comstock Lode was discovered in 1859. It is estimated that litigation cost approximately $10 million and consumed 20 percent of all mining revenues between 1860 and 1865—which adjusted for inflation would exceed $300 million in modern times. One scholar suggested "the first result of the opening of the Comstock mines was wild speculation, and the second almost endless litigation."

The litigation was grounded in the geological uncertainty of where the subsurface quartz veins began and ended. The predominant legal fact litigated between 1860 and 1864 was whether the rich veins emanated from a single ledge or whether there were multiple narrow ledges, separated by walls of barren rock. The respective geological theories were referred to as single-ledge and multi-ledge, and there was no conclusive science underlying either theory. Unlike the shallow placer gold mining in California, silver mining involved subsurface horizontal moves and vertical depths of thousands of feet. The miners simply needed to mine downward and laterally to determine the vein's origins. Because the original locators were allowed to follow "all the dips, spurs, angles, and variation of the vein" wherever the vein went, they claimed ownership to all outcroppings, regardless of where they arose. Thus, the Comstock claims had no definite and measurable surface boundaries. By the summer of 1860, the resulting "mess of confusion" was that "everybody's spurs were running into everybody else's angles."

The epicenter of mining litigation was Virginia City. By the time Judge Mott opened court in 1862, "the multitude of suits which had been accumulating during the past twelve months were eagerly pressed for trial." Virtually every claim of any value was in litigation and the competing ledge theories were "passionately combated; rights of rival locators were hotly asserted, and the confusion was worse confounded by the vagueness of the notices of location and the lack of trustworthy records."

Judge Mott was not equipped to manage the litigation, but in fairness, no single judge could have been successful. He confronted a volume of valuable litigation without the benefit of commensurate staff, infrastructure, or established law. He was also overwhelmed by the legal teams advancing their respective clients' ledge theories. One prominent lawyer, William Stewart, who later served as a US senator for Nevada, reportedly earned $500,000 between 1861 and 1864, and earned as much as $200,000 in his most lucrative year. Mott resigned during the fall of 1862, with a conflicted reputation, and was replaced by Judge North. Judge Jones also resigned in 1863 and was replaced by Judge Locke. Judge Turner served for the duration of the territory.

During the spring of 1864, the endless litigation and uncertain results began to show in declining mining productivity. Fault was placed with the judges, and Judge North in particular. To illustrate, a speaker before a "miners' league" in Storey County suggested "a most potential cause of the present depression of mining industry, is the universal distrust of our judiciary." A newspaper reported: "It is possible—barely possible—that [the territorial judiciary] may be above reproach. But enough has been brought to light to destroy all confidence in their integrity. [Nevada] never can prosper while the judiciary is suspected. Capital will refuse to go there for investment unless at heavy premium for risk, and men of families will decline to make a spot for their homes where vice instead of virtue reigns."

First Constitutional Convention

The act creating the Nevada Territory authorized territorial citizens to seek statehood. In 1862, the territorial legislature passed the Act to Frame a Constitution and State Government of the State of Washoe. In September of 1863, Nevada territorial voters *authorized* a constitutional convention by a four-to-one margin. Yet four months later, these same voters *rejected* statehood by a four-to-one margin.

Historians have ascribed the electoral defeat to an unpopular mining tax provision and dissatisfaction with the single slate of Union Party nominees (including judges) who would be elected concurrent with the vote on statehood. These explanations are initially persuasive, yet they do not explain why William Stewart campaigned for statehood despite the constitutional mining tax provision he opposed, or the extent to which the statehood vote was a referendum on Judge North and a repudiation of Stewart's attempt to reshape the judiciary. It appears the territorial judiciary was *the* divisive issue underlying the statehood vote.

A record of the 1863 constitutional convention exists in limited form. The *Reports of the 1863 Constitutional Convention of the Territory of Nevada*, published in 1972, was assembled from the notes taken by Andrew Marsh, Samuel Clemens, and Amos Bowman for the *Virginia Daily Union*. The delegates met for thirty-two days, beginning on November 3, 1863, and one of their first acts was to elect Judge North as convention president. Judge North had been known in the territory for two years before his appointment to the bench just a few months earlier, and his election as convention president reveals the confidence he still enjoyed as the newest territorial judge.

The delegates patterned their constitution after the California constitution, which is not surprising as thirty-four of the thirty-nine delegates had come from California. The delegates were aware of the litigation challenges of the time. They debated about the judiciary: the percentage number of jurors necessary to reach a civil verdict, the size of the judiciary, how to increase the number of supreme court justices in the future, the lengths of judicial terms, the manner of selecting judges, and whether district judges should also sit on the supreme court. One delegate argued that judges should enjoy longer terms so they would be "removed from any of the baneful influences surrounding elections—enabling them to discharge their duties faithfully, without reversing decision, and changing doctrines to catch popular favor." He continued that when judges "yield to popular prejudice—then it is the mob, and not the law, which decides upon our causes."

In addition to the spirited judiciary debate, the delegates also disagreed about how mines would be taxed. A majority of the delegates proposed the legislature impose taxes on all mining shafts, drifts, and bedrock tunnels regardless of productivity. In opposition, William Stewart and others sought to exempt unproductive mines from taxation, proposing that mines be taxed on net proceeds because an unproductive mine was nothing more than a "hole in the ground." Although Stewart represented the largest mining interests financed out of San Francisco, he fashioned his argument in favor of the individual prospector who worked every day with the hope of success and ever-present risk of failure. In contrast, Judge North argued that a tax on net proceeds would allow the largest companies to escape taxation altogether through creative "sleight of hand" accounting practices. Although Stewart lost the argument, the convention ended in December with "kindly feelings" and all delegates announced their support for statehood, which was scheduled for vote more than a month later on January 19, 1864.

Stewart had supported North's appointment to the bench and election as convention president. But shortly after the convention ended—and before the vote on statehood—North issued a decision favoring the multi-ledge theory against the powerful single-ledge interests Stewart represented. The ensuing battle between Stewart and North became the dispositive issue underlying the vote on statehood.

While statehood initially seemed inevitable, public sentiment quickly changed because of perceptions that Stewart was advocating for statehood to enrich himself and his wealthy clients against the interests of the individual miners. Stewart was distrusted because of fears that (1) statehood would strengthen his mining clients through control of the legislature, which in turn controlled taxation, and (2) statehood would remove territorial judges, who would be replaced by popularly elected judges favorable to the single-ledge theory.

Through proxies, Stewart challenged North's integrity and fitness to serve as a judge. Stewart accused North of being favorable to black suffrage; being placed on the bench by the multi-ledge mining companies; accepting loans from litigants to build a sawmill and quartz-crushing mill; and accepting bribes to render certain opinions. In contrast, others asserted Judge North was "too honest to be bribed; too intelligent to be hoodwinked, and too firm to be driven." North announced he would sue Stewart, who responded on December 22, 1863, by inserting a card in the newspapers acknowledging the bribery allegations could not be proven. Nonetheless, Stewart's public retraction did not end the dispute and the two men remained publicly critical of each other.

On December 28, 1863, just three weeks before the vote, Stewart packed the Storey County Union Party convention with supporters and was elected chair of the committee on nominations. He successfully passed two resolutions: (1) the power to control the taxing of mines is conferred upon the legislature and the legislature should "only subject to the burdens of Government such claims as yield net profits to their owners"; and (2) the Storey County delegates were "to oppose by all honorable means the nomination . . . of John W. North to [gubernatorial] office by said State Convention." Thus, Stewart gained control of who would be nominated for state office and appear as a single slate and be voted on at the same time as the vote on the proposed constitution. Accordingly, upon statehood, several state officials would owe their positions to Stewart and the large mining interests he represented.

Opposition began to mount because the area had come under "a base and unparalleled submission of imposter leaders . . . whose effrontery and heartlessness impel them to infer that *their* rights are the first rights to be known and guaranteed in all this part of Nevada." The *Virginia City Union* reported:

> William M. Stewart played a leading part in our [Storey] County Convention, and was successful in the State Convention to a very great degree. He succeeded in defeating Judge North for Governor. . . . It was stated weeks ago, that Mr. Stewart's sole aim was to defeat Judge North and secure a District and County Judge for Storey County, and a Supreme Bench for the new State of Nevada of his own choice. . . . It is a notorious fact that Mr. Stewart had the reputation of dictating the decisions of the District Court, to a very great extent, previous to the time at which Judge North took his seat. . . . Why does he want North removed? Because he cannot be used as a tool. . . .
>
> Stewart and Company want a state government because they have come to the conclusion that our present judiciary care more for the people and for justice than they do for the influence of improper

combinations; and there are several legal gentlemen who like to have an opportunity to try the "one-ledge" theory before new and different judges. All the representatives of these private interests would like a State Government, and if they can obtain one, and thereby achieve their personal ends and advancement, it matters but little to them how immeasurable the disaster which would be inflicted on this Territory.

On January 15, 1864, just four days before the statehood vote, Stewart published a newspaper challenge to Judge North to appear for a public debate. North accepted and the two met at Maguire's Opera House in Virginia City before a large group of voters. It was generally reported that North acquitted himself well. A newspaper wrote two days after the debate: "The defeat of the constitution is a foregone conclusion." Indeed, it was. Newspapers that had previously supported statehood now changed their positions. A newspaper in Aurora reported: "The constitution would have been adopted had it not been for riding Stewart and his Clique into power." The *Virginia Daily Union* similarly reported:

> The UNION was in favor of a State Government when it supposed that the people would be protected; it opposes a State Government now that it discovers that under a State Government the people would be hopelessly subject to a very mean kind of "one man power." We prefer that the people should elect their own officers rather than those officers should be appointed at Washington. But as it stands, they are appointed by one man, and as the people have no choice anyhow, we prefer Uncle Abe to Bill Stewart as an appointment power.

Stewart's political calculation backfired. Many perceived his attacks to be spurious and self-serving because he had supported Judge North until North's decision in favor of the multi-ledge theory. The vote was a crushing defeat for statehood and a validation of North and the smaller mining interests who were dependent on the multi-ledge theory. Nonetheless, the statehood question would soon arise again with a much different answer.

Second Constitutional Convention

The first battle for statehood left political and personal bruises that would take some time to heal. One newspaper suggested that any future statehood attempt be delayed for at least a year. But President Lincoln and Governor Nye had other plans. A mere twenty days after the failed statehood vote in January, Senator James Doolittle from Wisconsin introduced a bill to allow the territories of Nevada, Colorado, and Nebraska to hold constitutional conventions and establish state governments. President Lincoln signed An Act to Enable the People of Nevada to Form a Constitution and State Government, and for the Admission of Such State into the Union on an Equal Footing with the Original States on March 21, 1864.

On May 2, 1864, Governor Nye proclaimed that elections of delegates to a constitutional convention would occur in June. The delegates were to be elected by county, according to county population. Voter turnout was low, probably because "the people generally felt no interest in the matter. They care but little who goes to the convention since they are determined to vote down the constitution anyway."

Storey County had twice the population and double the number of delegates of the next most populous county. Of the thirty-nine delegates elected to the convention, ten were from Storey County, which is significant because the First Judicial District was essentially vacant because of an ailing Judge North, hundreds of cases were pending without hope of resolution, the devastating mining recession was ascribed to judicial impotence, and there were widespread stock failures, bankruptcies, and a collapse in capital investments.

The convention began in Carson City on July 4 and continued until July 27. Unlike the incomplete notes from the prior constitutional convention, the second constitutional convention is reported in the *Official Report of the Debates and Proceedings of the Constitutional Convention of the State of Nevada*. The delegates began with the unsuccessful constitution from earlier in the year. Their primary disagreements were grounded in mining taxation, courts and judges, loyalty to the Union, and a railroad subsidy. A recurring theme was the judiciary's impediment to the mining industry. The delegates were aware of the ineffective territorial judiciary, and their experiences with the courts informed several constitutional features, such as the composition of civil juries, the preference of district courts over county courts, the election of judges, the size and composition of the supreme court, the propriety of civil filing fees, and most notably, the provisions for impeachment and removal of judges from office.

The chairman of the convention was J. Neeley Johnson, who had previously served as governor of California. (Johnson later served as a justice of the Nevada Supreme Court from 1867 to 1871.) During the first minutes of the convention, the delegates discussed whether county delegates should sit together. One delegate, "with great amusement from the larger body," suggested the delegation from Storey County was a "litigious group" and should be scattered among the entire group. This lighthearted moment revealed a truth known to all: Virginia City was defined by its interminable litigation and a crisis in judicial confidence.

The first resolution offered was to permanently adjourn the convention without action. It quickly died on the floor. The second proposed resolution revealed that judiciary reform was an underlying and important purpose of the convention. One delegate suggested the statehood question be postponed and, instead, the delegates petition "Congress to give us a change in our Judiciary," and "if this change is granted us, we think it better for the present to remain as we are, under a Territorial Government."

Charles DeLong was an active and influential delegate. He argued that "if the recommendation could be carried into effect immediately, and we could be assured that the desired change in our judicial system would be effected in that mode, I would certainly favor it, and it would be all I should ask." He further explained that although he voted against statehood eight months earlier, he had since seen in the judges

> such an extraordinary lack of ability to come up to the requirements of our condition . . . that I have come to the conclusion that some remedy is absolutely demanded. Nor is it alone a lack of ability on the part of our judges. Of our three judges a nisi prius, at this time, one is sick and the others have absented themselves, and thus blocked the wheels of justice; so that in reality we have no Courts at all; although I know, and every lawyer knows, that we have interests in litigation so vast in importance that the parties interested in them could almost afford to pay the expenses of a State Government for one year if by that means they could have their rights judicially determined. That is what impels me to favor a State organization. It is to obtain the power of electing our own judges, and just as many of them as we want, to transact our criminal and civil business.

Other delegates joined DeLong and expressed concern that Congress would not act quickly to reform the territorial judiciary and that statehood was the fastest and surest way to be liberated from the existing judges and courts. The resolution was postponed "indefinitely," although it was unsuccessfully renewed six days later.

Throughout the convention the delegates expressed frustration with the judges and territorial courts. Themes of corruption, accountability, and judicial independence are woven throughout the deliberations, and at one point the judiciary was referred to as "the great evil" and judicial reform the "most important business to come before the convention." One delegate summarized the sentiment against the judiciary, and of statehood as the antidote for judicial impotence, as follows:

> I am tired of this rat-trap of a Territorial Government, sir. I want a government of a more substantial character—one which will encourage the development of our rich mines and all our resources. I want to see the numerous valuable mines which are now locked up by litigation, unlocked, and developed as they should be, in order that their hidden stores of wealth may be brought forth and cast upon the commerce of the world. I want to see the two thousand men now idle in Storey County . . . and scarcely possessing the wherewithal to obtain a living, once more in constant employment, and to accomplish that end I desire to see the Judiciary so reformed that the numerous cases now in litigation may be promptly disposed of and the mining claims unlocked, and allowed to be developed. Then those strong men, now idle, can be put to work in the mines, earning their four dollars a day, and so obtaining an honest and honorable livelihood.

The outcome never seemed in doubt, and at the conclusion of the convention only two delegates voted against the proposed constitution. Unlike with the earlier vote in January, statehood and state officers would not be voted on at the same time. The vote on statehood was scheduled for September 7, and the election of state officers was scheduled for November 8, 1864.

Newspapers and the Summer of Discontent

While the delegates were in convention, several local newspapers engaged in a relentless attack on the judiciary, and ultimately called for all three territorial judges to resign. The *Territorial Enterprise* and *Gold Hill Evening News* published articles against the judges, whereas the *Virginia Daily Union* generally defended the judiciary. These newspapers provide a glimpse into the passion and depth of the public's sentiments toward the judiciary. There were more than seventy articles published in July and August 1864, condemning the judiciary with scandalous and sensational language. The newspapers spared no detail when writing about the judges, and their conflicting content reveals the truth was fluid and only a minor part of the story. All judges were accused of being carpetbaggers, legally inept, and morally corrupt.

Judges Mott and Jones were rarely named, as they had previously resigned. Judge Locke had been severely criticized a few months earlier and was not a primary target of the press. Judge Turner was accused of arriving in the territory as a poor man and immediately acquiring wealth well beyond his annual judicial salary. His wife and brother-in-law were also named as co-participants in specific bribery allegations. Judge North received the most scrutiny, partly because he was the presiding judge in the First Judicial District (encompassing Virginia City), and partly because he had the highest public profile and was inclined to defend himself. Among other criticisms, he was accused of conflicts because he owned a processing mill that received preferential, profitable material to process, and he purchased the mill with loans from mining entities that appeared before him.

In addition to outright corruption, the judges were accused of being absent from their districts, whether to the Atlantic states or California. Even though approximately four hundred cases were on calendar in the First District in 1864, only three civil cases had been submitted to a jury and only one of those resulted in a verdict. Judge North had become increasingly absent in the "trees and mountains of California" because of poor health, and his "calendar is crowded to an extent that would require three years of ordinary court routine to clear, and some measures for a very general reference of cases must be adopted or the business of the territory must suffer beyond computation." Judge Turner was also reported to be in California. He opened court on July 5 but was in session only seven days during the previous four months. In one case he granted a preliminary injunction "but did not hear the case himself within a few days, but appointed his clerk to hear the testimony and submit it to him for a decision. The mining company who obtained the injunction hopes to call one hundred witnesses to delay, freeze, or starve out it[s] opponent. Meanwhile it furiously works the mine. The other side is totally deprived by the caprice of the court." Judge Locke's location was unknown, though "it don't make any difference. He has not got either of his accomplices here to tell him what to do, and he does not know enough to hatch up any deviltry himself."

In August, one newspaper reported "unanimous dissatisfaction with the present condition of our judicial affairs" and "an absolute loss of all confidence in the Courts so long as they are presided over by the present judges." The *Territorial Enterprise* prepared a resignation petition and announced, "let every man who feels and believes that the broad charges of corruption and incapacity made against these judges to be well founded, boldly, honestly and fearlessly record that belief, upon the petition." The petition was circulated the next day with the solicitation: "It is a matter that interests every citizen who has a dollar's worth of property in the Territory, or who breathes the air polluted by this judicial corruption, and it is the duty of every citizen, by signing the petition, to affix the seal of his condemnation upon this official rottenness."

Judge North responded to the petition by denying the charges and denouncing his critics. He wrote: "I not only challenge, but invite the closest scrutiny into my official conduct. If respectable men will make definite charges that can be met, and let their names be known, so that I can know who is, or who are my accusers, nothing will give me greater pleasure than to meet the issue promptly and boldly." He also separated himself from Judges Turner and Locke, for whom he seemed to have little regard: "*Let no other Judge suffer for what I have done; nor let me be held responsible for the acts of others.* Let the question be upon my conduct as a Judge, and let the allegations be made definitely and distinctly." A few weeks later, Judge North published a lengthy defense of his judicial work.

Several lawyers defended the judges, arguing that "not one in ten of the prominent business men have signed" the petition, asserting it was the result of "workingmen which paraded our streets a few days ago," soliciting signatures from many who were unsophisticated and easily influenced. Nonetheless, the tide of public sentiment had crested against the judges and the relentless public campaign had its intended result. The judges could never recover from the stain on their work. Whether accurate or not, the accusations created a public perception that demanded change. The judges resigned on August 22, 1864, a mere sixteen days before the statehood vote, which left the territory without any trial or appellate courts. For Justice North, the resignation was at least partially the result of his declining health, while his colleagues' motives are less known.

The statehood vote on September 7 was an anti-climactic, foregone conclusion. In total, 10,375 residents voted for statehood, whereas only 1,184 voted against. In the two most populous counties the vote was 5,448 to 142 (Storey) and 1,055 to 115 (Washoe). Only Humboldt County voted against statehood (544 to 320). While statehood would have occurred at some point, and President Lincoln's supporters were agitating for statehood for other reasons, the absence of any judiciary, combined with the insatiable demand for judicial services, undoubtedly contributed to the popular support for Nevada's admission as the thirty-sixth state.

The first election after statehood was held on November 8, 1864. Voters elected the three Republican Party candidates to be the first justices of the Nevada Supreme Court. The new justices took their oaths of office on December 5. To ensure the justices served staggered terms, the new Nevada constitution provided the justices would "draw lots" to determine who would serve an initial term of two, four, or six years. Thereafter, each justice would serve a six-year term. The justice who drew the two-year term would also be designated as Nevada's first chief justice. The office of chief justice would be subsequently decided by seniority in commission, that is, the justice most senior in the term being served, as opposed to the justice with the most aggregate service on the court. (If two or more justices shared the same seniority in term, the chief justice would be chosen by lot unless the judges agreed to divide the two-year terms as chief justice.)

Through a Modern Lens

History has not been kind to the territorial judges. They were among the highest profile public figures during territorial times and the subject of deep and divisive public sentiments. It is largely assumed they became corrupted along with other legal participants during the frenetic litigation years between 1861 and 1864. Historian Hubert Howe Bancroft was more generous in 1890:

> Probably the first federal judges would have been able to hold their own against the criminal element in Nevada; but opposed to the combined capital and legal talent of California and Nevada, as they sometimes were, in important mining suits, they were powerless. Statutes regarding the points at issue did not exist, and the questions involved were largely determined by the rules and regulations

of mining districts, and the application of common law. Immense fees were paid to able and oftentimes unprincipled lawyers, and money lavished on suborned witnesses.

Judge North's own words were telling when he wrote: "It is generally conceded . . . that there is no place in the United States where a judge has so difficult and responsible duties as at Virginia [City]. . . . Judges Mott and Jones who preceded me had got the whole community by the ears, and had allowed a large amount of business to accumulate on the calendar. The difficulties they encountered caused them to hesitate and delay until they were overwhelmed."

Determining the legitimacy of the corruption claims is complicated. Judge Mott appears to have been disengaged and frequently absent, but the evidence that he accepted a significant bribe to resign was made by proponents of the single-ledge theory he ruled against. There is insufficient evidence to condemn Mott and it is difficult to reconcile his election as a territorial delegate to Congress with the suggestion that he was corrupted by bribery during his brief service on the bench. There are subtle indications that he left the territory with financial resources beyond his meager salary. Additionally, his unsteady service as a delegate to Congress suggests his engagement as a territorial judge could have been better.

There is no known evidence linking Judge Jones to financial corruption. He was frustrated by his colleagues' pedestrian approach to juridical work and is best known through his appellate decisions, which he laboriously researched, and which demonstrated his commitment to the courts and rule of law. His private correspondence confirms this commitment.

Judge Turner's place in history is uncertain. He was a proponent of the single-ledge theory, which was not grounded in geological certainty. This alone is insufficient to criticize him, as many judges reach the wrong result with good intentions. Turner could have been more engaged in defending himself. This is particularly true because of the specific bribery details alleged against his wife and brother-in-law. Turner did not answer the charges publicly but defended himself in private communications. For example, after reading in the *Sacramento Union* that he would be removed from office, Turner wrote an impassioned letter to President Lincoln defending his work and honor.

Many lawyers offered their public support to Judge Turner two days after he resigned. The *Carson Weekly Independent* reported that a "Meeting of the Bar and Citizens of Ormsby County" resulted in resolutions that read, in part:

> Whereas, The Hon. George Turner has for over three years acceptably served as Judge of this District, and as such, having himself held every term of court provided for by law, having also held sundry courts in other Districts, having disposed of all the business as fast as it matured, and having so fully and satisfactorily transacted the same that to-day the public business of this District is completely done, and no causes at issue anywhere are awaiting trial on account of any delay of the court; and our said Judge having himself performed a very large majority of the labors of the Supreme Court, as is well known to all our people; and. . . .
>
> Resolved, That we tender our thanks to Judge Turner for the industrious, impartial and able manner in which he has discharged his judicial labors.

Judge Locke was widely known as indecisive and susceptible to external influences, including money and alcohol. At best, he misunderstood the word "judge" as both a descriptive noun and an action verb. At worst, Locke rendered inconsistent decisions because of external influences, which is the hallmark of judicial misconduct. Locke also appears to have left Nevada with wealth incommensurate with his salary. Years after statehood, William M. Stewart wrote in his autobiography that "[Judge Locke] was too ignorant for denunciation," and after he resigned he "imbibed so freely that he became more stupid than usual [and was] probably the most ignorant man who ever acted in any judicial capacity in any part of the world."

Judge North was likely a worthy jurist overtaken by the unique circumstances of territorial litigation and politics. He was a man of conscience who cared deeply about slavery, suffrage, and sobriety. He wrote to his wife on December 1, 1864: "I long more and more to escape from a life of strife and conflict, and go where I can indulge my tastes in labors of love. . . . I long to go down [to Tennessee], after the war is over, to help build up good society . . . to heal the wound the war has inflicted." North did just that for the duration of his life. His primary effort was to colonize areas for newly liberated slaves to enjoy the opportunities of freedom.

His pre- and post-judicial conduct was consistent with his social conscience, and it seems unlikely that he suspended his conscience during his eleven months on the bench.

Judge North did rule in favor of the multi-ledge theory in December of 1863, after carefully considering the evidence and conducting his own site visit. The mines were still relatively shallow, and the geographical source of the quartz veins could not be determined. Judge North included a caveat in his decision that "at the depth where the controversy arises the evidence on both sides shows that there are several and distinct ledges. *If at a greater depth there shall be found conclusive evidence that all these are blended in one, when that depth is reached and that evidence is adduced, then will be the proper time to determine what ledges run out and what continue*" (emphasis added).

Ironically, on the day before he resigned, Judge North affirmed a referee's decision that the various quartz veins all emanated from a single, geological source. He changed his previous opinion and concluded the single-ledge theory was correct. His decision was grounded in empirical evidence that required a "long, anxious, and laborious examination." This is critical when reconstructing his service on the court. He essentially reversed himself. He demonstrated that doing right was more important than being right. He issued an order that aggrieved his supporters and emboldened his enemies. In so doing, he vindicated a contemporary ethical imperative that judges not be "swayed by public clamor or fear of criticism."

The US Sanitary Commission was a private relief agency founded in 1861 as the precursor to the contemporary United Way. Its first president, Massachusetts clergyman Henry Bellows, traveled the country raising money to provide temporal aid to wounded Union soldiers. Bellows visited the Nevada Territory in July 1864, and wrote a letter to US Attorney General Bates that was critical of Judges Turner and Locke. Regarding Judge North, however, Bellows wrote:

> Judge North is spoken well of in proportion usually to the intelligence, moral worth, and standing of the speaker. He seems to me a man of inviolable truth, self-respect and dignity of character—a man of settled principles of conduct from which nothing could drive him. I have met no man on the whole coast who has inspired me with greater respect, and such is his personal impression, that a

dozen witnesses swearing to his hurt, would not move my conviction of his purity and truth. He, however, does not escape the bitter suspicion and serious charges. Every definite charge he scatters to the winds—but what reply can be made to mischievous rumors?

Finally, Judge North aggressively defended himself in the court of public opinion. He offered detailed retorts to the charges of bribery and self-dealing, which appeared adequate to the people at the time. More than thirty lawyers publicly supported North against the newspaper crusade in July and August 1864. He sought to clear his name after he resigned by suing Stewart and the *Territorial Enterprise.* The lawsuit was referred to a three-referee panel who censured North for poor judgment (apparently related to his quartz mill) but ultimately exonerated him from the more serious corruption charges. For these reasons, North's position in history should not be undermined by the sensational reporting and superficial accusations from those with specific litigation interests. The reflection of time reveals that Judge North may well have honored the judicial office he held.

NEVADA TERRITORIAL SUPREME COURT

George E. Turner

1861–1864

CHIEF JUSTICE GEORGE E. TURNER was born in Ohio in 1828, in a family of ten children. He learned of faith and politics from his parents—his father was a part-time Methodist Episcopal minister. He attended college at Ohio Wesleyan University but did not graduate. He acquired property early, as suggested by an 1851 loan from his grandmother in the amount of $1,100. His grandmother's will indicated the loan was secured by property likely purchased with loan proceeds. He married sometime between 1848 and 1850, when he was studying law with W. V. Peck, "Portsmouth's able jurist." The Turners' only child was born in 1850.

Turner enjoyed quick success in the law. During his ten years in Portsmouth, Ohio, he was described as a "prominent figure" in politics and "an energetic lawyer, and being full of push and alive to all that was going on, in politics, business, or society, he was especially much in people's minds." In addition to the private practice of law, Turner was also the county solicitor.

In 1861, President Lincoln appointed him as chief justice of the Nevada Territorial Supreme Court. The appointment is traceable to Ohioans Salmon Chase, Lincoln's secretary of the treasury, and Senator Benjamin Wade. Turner immediately set out for Carson City, and when he arrived he took his oath before territorial secretary Orion Clemens. Justice Turner seemed to enjoy his public role. Mark Twain described him as a "small man, but what he lacked in height he made up for in oratorical vim and egotistical demeanor." Twain's observation is consistent with an Ohio newspaper's

George E. Turner

description of Turner as "a man of audacity and self-possession, perfectly free from embarrassment." Also, a record of the investiture ceremony of his judicial colleagues describes him as "a small man in size, but chock-full of patriotism, as was evinced by the immense vim and relish [with] which he read the oath of the Councillors."

Judge Turner's outsized personality continued to be a theme in the months following his arrival in the territory. In characteristically creative prose, Mark Twain reported a July 4 speech Judge Turner gave and suggested Turner had been "foisted on the new Territory by President Lincoln" and "had earned a reputation for being the shallowest, most egotistical and mercenary occupant of the supreme bench. It was known that when he signed his name on a hotel register it was invariably as 'Honorable George Turner, Chief Justice of the United States.' . . . It was known that when he delivered a lecture in Carson on some apparently important subject, it turned out to be merely a rehash of his own vainglorious achievements." Whether fair or unfair, Turner was given the appellation of "Professor Personal Pronoun."

Regardless of personality, the assignment to create a judiciary in a lawless area was difficult and the judges struggled to define their roles. Early after his arrival, Judge Turner found a California judge from Mono County presiding over cases he thought were within the jurisdiction of the Nevada Territory. Yet, "neither judge interfered with the other" and "litigants took their cases to the court they preferred." As noted by the press, "the novelty was presented of two courts sitting concurrently, exercising jurisdiction by virtue of authority derived from distinct sources."

Jurisdiction among the Nevada territorial judges was also undefined. Judge Turner presided over a murder trial and sentenced the defendant to be hanged immediately. When he refused to grant a stay of execution, Judge Mott intervened and granted a writ of habeas corpus, staying the execution for several months. This and other examples reveal "anomalies in juridical affairs." And as one observer noted, relentless litigation was grounded in incomprehensible wealth—thus, "no decision . . . is made that does not create virulent enemies, who use the local press to blacken the character of the judges."

Almost immediately, Judge Turner was accused of corruption. He was portrayed by the more sensational press accounts as debased, mostly interested in his own wealth. One example illustrates the fevered tone of the criticisms: "No one had ever spoken well of Turner; his very presence was suggestive of flattery, fawning, treachery, and dishonesty. 'For Sale' is written on his countenance as plainly as on a house, and he has grown wealthy by virtue of that sign." Despite the hyperbole of the time, some of the bribery allegations are detailed and included Turner's wife and brother-in-law. Though the truth is lost to history, Turner arrived in the territory without means but within a few years owned mining interests of substantial value.

In 1863, Judge Turner wrote directly to President Lincoln in response to one particularly cruel newspaper allegation:

> Now I have labored hard here, drawn most of the laws, prepared union Resolutions, attended public meetings and made speeches in defense of the Government and in support of the Administration. Furthermore I have held court almost monthly for two years here and [all this for small pay] and I know that no federal officer here is more acceptable to the people, none have been endorsed more fully by the press and Legislature, nor the population generally and while I would not have lost much to have remained in my own good home in Ohio in full practice and prosperously pursuing my profession yet now after leaving there and bringing my wife and family here to discharge the duties of my office, I could not sit lamely by and be decapitated and disgraced without notice or cause. . . . I ask it of you as one who is every way entitled to it that any charges made against me may be treated with the scorn they deserve or notice given me before any action is taken."

Another side to Judge Turner emerges from the historical records. In a charge to the grand jury, Turner cautioned against "the knife and the pistol," advocated protection of social rights and privileges, deplored recklessness and disorder, saying, "Our citizens have trusted more than was necessary to ideas of self-protection by their own weapons, and thought far too little of the efficiency and majesty of the law." One newspaper reported that "Judge Turner is entitled to public gratitude for his noble and patriotic conduct. Every true man will applaud him and welcome his views, not only as the expression of judicial propriety, but as a faithful indication that the reign of order will henceforth prevail throughout the limits of Nevada." After one absence, a newspaper reported that he had returned "with renewed health and vigor, and we congratulate him on his reappearance in our midst. He enjoys a large measure of public confidence, and is well worthy of it as a citizen and a judicial officer."

After statehood, Judge Turner placed an advertisement in the newspaper announcing he would open a law office in Carson City. It appears his priority was to publish three hundred copies of the sixty-nine decisions issued by the territorial supreme court, for which the first Nevada legislature appropriated $5,000. However, Governor Blasdell vetoed the appropriation because he believed the records were incomplete and available through other means. One newspaper applauded the veto and posed the question, "If the judges were so obnoxious as not to be tolerated, how much respect will their book of decisions command?" Governor Blasdell's veto is significant because whatever original records Judge Turner possessed have now been lost to history.

Judge Turner left Nevada soon after statehood and settled in San Francisco. On September 1, 1865, he wrote a letter to his friend and political benefactor Senator Wade, which selectively recounts his time in the territory. He boasted about the appropriation to publish his records, which he "regarded as a kind of endorsement after four years labor among them in trying the most bitterly litigated suits in the world to wit mining suits." He indicated he would stay in the West to try some "heavy suits in which I have been recently employed" but intended to return to Ohio in the future.

Judge Turner began practicing law in San Francisco, but he also traveled extensively through Europe. The ensuing years were not kind, particularly as his resources decreased. In August 1885, while in the bathroom of his boarding home, Turner shot himself with "an ivory-handled, silver-plated XL five-shooter, which was found at his feet." He was fifty-seven.

Documents found on his person indicated he had been contemplating suicide for several months. One letter addressed to Governor Leland Stanford, written five months earlier, revealed he had no money, and he asked the governor to care for his wife, whom he described as "noble, KIND and GOOD, and in all the world you could not find one more worthy of your care." He also wrote a farewell letter to his wife identifying a small sum of money with instructions for how she should pay his final debts. He included many statements of faith that reveal his despondency, such as "God bless you and Nellie [his thirty-five-year-old daughter that he referred to as an "invalid"] and grandson and all. You were always a good and loving wife. . . . [W]e shall all be soon together. Believe me this is best. I am so very, very sick. Christ died for us, and must love and deal gently with his own children. . . . That is all. Your loving husband, George Turner. I am very sick. . . . Also thank God for last Sunday's sacrament. Tell Nelly and the boy to serve the Lord. God is love, and I feel sure he will receive his own child, who is too sick to remain longer here." Thus, Judge Turner's life ended in tragic circumstances likely influenced by his years in the Nevada Territory.

Gordon N. Mott

1861–1864

Gordon N. Mott was born in Ohio in 1812 to a pioneering farm family. He had limited public education and began studying law in Sydney, Ohio. Despite completing his education at the age of twenty-two, he traveled throughout Indiana, Kentucky, Tennessee, and Alabama before settling into his legal career. His wanderlust and desire for adventure overshadowed his law practice, and the next year he enlisted with his two brothers to fight for the Republic of Texas when it seceded from Mexico. He was "inclined toward military ideas" and enjoyed drilling and other military activities but was discharged early because he had "become so ill as to render him unfit for the remainder of his term of enlistment." He then returned to his law practice in Ohio.

In 1840 he was recognized as a lawyer "of worth and ability," and he sponsored his younger brother's legal education in his law office. He married in 1844, but once again dreamt of military service. So, in 1846, he raised a company of volunteers to fight in the Mexican-American War. He was awarded the rank of captain for his efforts. It was during this time that his politics became known. He and most of his company were Democrats, and when asked how his company would vote he replied he would support any candidate he regarded as most competent—regardless of party. His reply was not well received by his superior officers, who were members of the Whig party. "This honest response deprived [Mott] of the glory of leading his fine company into battle. There being three more companies than were called for, his company was rejected and disbanded." Still seeking adventure, he became a sutler and followed a regiment of regular soldiers to Mexico. He never realized his dream of battle but returned with a $3,000 profit and an experience he described as "a most disagreeable, vexatious and dangerous year's work."

Mott used his profits from Mexico to buy a large stock of hardware, groceries, iron, steel, glass, and nails, which he traded for real estate. He remained in Ohio during 1848 but again longed for adventure. In 1849 he joined a wagon train for California, arriving in Sacramento before moving to Auburn to become a miner. He did mine a little but was soon transporting goods through mountains and engaged in a "bushwacking law practice." By 1850, he settled in Sutter County, just north of Sacramento. He practiced law and was appointed judge to fill a short-term vacancy. He hoped his term would continue until the election two years later, and he resisted the appointment of a permanent judge to replace him. The dispute between Mott and his successor was resolved against Mott by the California Supreme Court. Mott also served for a short time as the Sutter County recorder.

Though on the frontier, Judge Mott held to the concept of gentlemanly honor. He participated as a second in at least three duels, one between judges who felt dishonored by the other. Later in life, the *San Francisco Daily Evening Post* described him as follows:

> The Judge is a man of very positive convictions on questions touching religion, politics and society. He was strictly reared in the Puritan faith, but has departed from his early training. He is a freethinker. He was taught that dueling was murder, but he believes that dueling is the proper way of settling serious disputes. He declares that war is only dueling on a large scale. He has never fought a duel, but has several times acted as second. He is an accurate shot. His sense of honor is very acute, and his nerve and count undauntable. He has no patience with cowardice, but he says that the suicide is not a coward.

Mott practiced law in Sutter County for almost a decade. As a sign of his legal ability, he was counsel in eight appeals to the California Supreme Court. Alas, his wanderlust returned, and in 1859 he began building roads and operating a mule and stage service between Sacramento and the area soon to become the Nevada Territory. His preferred route was through the Yuba Gap, past Downieville, and over the Beckwourth Pass in the Sierra Valley.

Gordon N. Mott

In January 1861, he traveled to Washington, DC, for President Lincoln's inauguration. Shortly thereafter, he applied to Attorney General Edward Bates for appointment to the Nevada Territorial Supreme Court. He was appointed on March 27, 1861, at age forty-eight. His appointment was well received by some because he was generally known through his time in Northern California. One newspaper wrote:

> Judge Mott is really the pioneer judge of this District, being the first Judge properly assigned to this part of the Territory. Our people we hope will properly appreciate him, and recollect that he has done more upon former occasions towards establishing law and order here than anyone else. The Judge's advent into the territory was by

no means flattering. There was no court, no court house, no office appropriate to his use, whether by the citizens here or of the General Government, and no building could be procured without an advance in money of rents. The Territory has no credit even with her own citizens. Judge Mott struggled through all of this, receiving a salary of only $1,800 a year.

Judge Mott's district included Virginia City, the epicenter of mining wealth and litigation. He favored the single-ledge geological theory and was viewed as hostile to the substantial interests advancing the multi-ledge theory. He was also occasionally absent from duty; one newspaper wrote: "The good Lord deliver us if we are to wait for justice until the return of Judge Mott; for no one knows whether he intends to return, and a great many entertain very serious doubts as to whether he will be very instrumental in administering *justice* if he does return."

A year after his arrival in the territory, Judge Mott was elected to be the territorial delegate to Congress. A newspaper reported that he consented to be a candidate "after urgent solicitation by his friends. He is popular, and the people say of him: 'in gaining an able Delegate we lose an excellent Judge.'" Even though the election was in September 1862, Mott did not leave immediately and there were questions about if and when he would resign his judicial position. The Nevada Territorial Legislature ultimately assigned his judicial responsibilities in the First District to Judge Jones, but despite his absences and diminished role, Mott did not formally resign until 1863, and then was accused of resigning in exchange for a large payment from mining interests aligned with the multi-ledge theory. Statehood was on the horizon and lawyers in the Virginia City Bar debated if they should petition President Lincoln to postpone appointing a successor "in order that the people might, after formation and ratification of their contemplated state constitution, elect their own judges."

Judge Mott's service as a delegate to Congress was unremarkable. He talked of resigning before ever leaving for Washington, DC, and when he arrived he stayed only a few months before leaving to visit Ohio. One newspaper reported, "We understand that considerations of health had something to do with his excursion, but it is to be hoped that he has now fairly recovered and resumed his seat, where the interests of his constituents demand his close attention, and watchful care." Mott's lackluster efforts were noted by a group of Virginia City miners who opposed a gross mining revenues tax being considered in Congress. They forwarded their resolution to Senator Conness of California because he was "for the present, at least, the only champion upon whom we can rely."

Judge Mott's term ended when Nevada became a state, and he moved to San Francisco to practice law. He became a court commissioner and was briefly considered for county judge by the Republican Party in San Francisco. Described as a "feeble old man" in 1884, he died in San Francisco in 1887, at the age of seventy-five.

HORATIO M. JONES

1861–1864

HORATIO M. JONES TRACED HIS family's arrival in America to the 1600s. He was born in Pennsylvania in 1826 and attended Oberlin College in Ohio. He met a young woman who was also studying at Oberlin with the patriotic name of America Strong. He and America both graduated in 1849, the first year Oberlin conferred degrees upon women. He became a teacher and was married to America in 1851. America was ahead of her peers and gender for the time, and the same resolve that led her to a college degree in 1849 helped her sustain Judge Jones later in life as he struggled with insolvency, depression, and poor physical health. She was his life partner and, at times, his protector.

Jones was intellectually gifted and inclined to the studious life of a gentleman. He was moved by abstract ideas and scientific theories throughout his life. Subjects of interest to him were education, mesmerism, spiritualism, Hegelianism, phrenology, speculative psychology, philosophy, and logic. He enjoyed reading monographs on a variety of subjects and was described as "a man of unusual culture, an acknowledged connoisseur, and a discriminating collector of prints." Jones was a frustrated scholar: brilliantly moved by ideas, born without affluence, and incapable of commercial success. He is consistently described as detached from the labors that lead to wealth. One family member wrote about him after his death, "Judge Jones was a mere child in the matter of making and holding on to money."

After teaching school for two years, Jones attended Harvard Law

Horatio M. Jones

School and graduated in 1853. He first attempted private practice in St. Louis, but his efforts were unremarkable. One St. Louis newspaper wrote about him: "He seemed unable to turn his talents and his really valuable services into money. . . . At last a lawyer has been found who took a $3,000 fee when he might have asked $10,000. . . . He was the type of man who was lost when not on a salary." Jones was soon drawn to the intellectual work of compiling laws and volumes of decisions as the reporter of the Supreme Court of Missouri. He was well suited for the work and remained with the court until his appointment to the Nevada Territorial Supreme Court on March 27, 1861. He was thirty-five at the time—well educated in the law and skilled in appellate concepts—but unprepared for the rough-and-tumble realities of frontier lawyers competing for vast wealth within a primitive judicial system.

Judge Jones arrived in the territory in September 1861 and was assigned to the Third Judicial District, where he was not besieged with the volume of litigation under way in Virginia City. Nonetheless, he was criticized for a poor work ethic and for "damaging business interests by failing to hold court while litigation involving large amounts is pending." One newspaper reported, "He had become unpopular from inaction and wrong headedness, and although no one ever charged him with corruption, many accused him of legal incompetency." This criticism may be unfair, as several of his appellate decisions reveal him to be a thoughtful and articulate jurist capable of resolving the more complex legal issues of the time.

Later in life he was described as "an unusually high-minded man and had no part in, probably knew but little of, the political chicanery going on about him [in Nevada]." This is likely inaccurate, as he undoubtedly knew of the problems besetting the territorial courts. In November 1862, slightly more than a year after he arrived in the territory, Judge Jones wrote a letter to US Attorney General Edward Bates regarding the appointment of a successor to Judge Mott, who had recently been elected to Congress. He asserted:

> A great deal of anxiety exists among the members of the legal profession and the public at large on the subject. Suspicion also exists that moves have been made to secure the appointment of a successor entirely unacceptable to the people here. . . . Nothing whatever has been done here touching the securing of the appointment of anyone in Judge Mott's place that represents the wishes of anyone but schemers and plotters. . . . Nobody has been recommended by persons in this territory who is not expected to act in the interest of those recommending them. *I mean precisely what I say. Intrigues are going on, of which the public know nothing.* (Emphasis added)

Judge Jones ended his letter by suggesting it would be best to appoint a disinterested person from the Atlantic states "who would be entirely uncompromised of any business or professional relationships with the [Nevada] territory." He repeated this theme when later giving a speech for statehood, saying he "seldom knew of a case that was considered thoughtfully and carefully, and free from partisan influence."

Judge Jones resigned by letter to President Lincoln, dated July 20, 1863, asking Lincoln to "accept my thanks for the honor conferred upon me in appointing me." The reasons for his resignation are unknown, but a letter he wrote to Attorney General Bates reveals his dissatisfaction with his salary. He wrote that carpenters get paid three dollars more per day than he was paid, and "no person can live here with a wife on the salary allowed."

After his resignation, Jones practiced law in Austin, Nevada and was a vocal advocate for statehood. In early 1864, he allowed a committee of several lawyers to advance his name as a possible judicial candidate when Nevada became a state. However, his public profile plummeted when he campaigned against President Lincoln, whom he had "soured" on because "for a peace man, he was terribly violent." Jones announced he would vote for a secessionist candidate "cordially and cheerfully" because he was "one of the purest, bravest men, and one of the maturest intellects on this coast." Some described his comments as treasonous and had "sealed his political doom. A renegade is despised by all honorable men. Go and hang yourself, Horatio, as Judas did of old."

Jones returned to St. Louis shortly after statehood, where he again struggled in his private law practice. He was elected judge of the St. Louis Circuit Court in 1870 and served a six-year term. At the end of his term a newspaper reported:

> Judge Jones should be considered more in the light of a jurist than as a lawyer; and although but few men are more thoroughly conversant with the practice of our courts, yet it is upon the bench that he rises, as it were, superior to himself. . . . A man of remarkable clearness of perception, his decisions and rulings are ever characteristic of fairness and equality, and are delivered in such a clear and minute manner as to seldom fail in giving satisfaction to all parties concerned.

Despite these platitudes, Jones was unable to create a profitable law practice. His physical and mental health began to decline, and he was distracted by his nonlegal interests. He left Missouri a final time in 1884 when he went to Michigan to board in his sister's summer home. From there, he returned to Philadelphia, where he had been born. Unable to "make a lodgment," he became despondent and quit corresponding with friends.

In 1890, his wife America stepped in to help him help himself. She relocated to Riverside, California, to prepare for them to live near her nephew. She had visited California a few times, and instead of spending money her husband had given to her "for a vacation at some fashionable resort," she stayed with her nephew, "saving money thereby" from Jones's profligate spending. Her nephew later remembered that she knew "her husband was not going to succeed as a practicing attorney, and she began planning for a home in California near us where she and the judge could become self-sustaining." She identified several acres to purchase so she and he could sustain themselves growing oranges. In time, Jones sent his "books and bookcases . . . carpets, chairs, and other personal effects" including "his collection of engravings, expensively crated for shipment by express."

When Jones finally arrived in California, he did not even have money for "the price of [a] meal." To America's dismay, he "had spent the $1,500 he had received from the closing of his business in exchanging some of his old prints for new ones that made the collection he was shipping a better illustration of the development of copper plate engraving." Though America still had some money, without the $1,500 her husband promised to bring, they were unable to purchase the land America had identified for their future. Instead, they moved into their nephew's home and stayed seven years. During this time, Jones provided some assistance on the nephew's farm and assisted the nephew's work as a local superintendent of education.

Jones's health continued to decline, yet he occasionally found energy to resume correspondence with a longtime friend, William Torrey Harris, the US secretary of education. In one letter, he confided that "since I left St. Louis I have felt almost as if my life were ended." As a sign of his interests, the next year he requested that Harris send various census records, legislative records, public surveys, geological surveys, and Civil War charts for his personal study.

In 1893, he was becoming lost to despondency, writing to Harris, "There is nothing to say about my life. I doubtless have a good deal of work in me yet, yet there are few persons so weak in the matter of getting the work to do. I wish I could be in Chicago next summer for a week at least. But I cannot afford it." Later, he asked Harris for help in obtaining a job in Washington; his sadness is palpable: "I need [help]. The agony of saying this at this moment you cannot know."

It was during this time that America increased efforts to help her husband. She privately wrote to Harris on her husband's behalf, emphasizing she had always admired her husband's ability and intellect, and imploring Harris for work that could draw Jones out of despair. In another letter she told Harris that her husband was so despondent he could not write. Harris responded with suggestions for how Jones could improve his circumstances, but in response Jones indicated he was "utterly destitute" and did not even have funds to get himself to Washington to proceed with the course of action Harris proposed: "I appealed to you as a sort of last desperate chance. . . . I know the difficulty, I may say the impossibility, of doing anything without my presence in Washington."

In 1896, America facilitated her husband's move to Washington while she remained in California. He was then seventy. She recommended to Harris "some simple work each day, occupying six hours of his time," and added that he was mostly healthy, and "when he is happy mentally, his body always responds quickly to any call." Jones lived in a home owned by Harris in exchange for nominal research assistance. America attempted to pay room and board, but Harris would not accept it. In 1898, Jones was injured when he fell off a streetcar and became unable to live independently. He moved to Vermontville, Michigan, to live with his niece. He wrote that he had been very sick "and was scarcely able to sit up. . . . I have suffered a great deal, been in great pain." He devoted the last of his time visiting the local library and died in 1906 from "hemorrhage from the bladder."

After his death, a local newspaper reported that Judge Jones had a "strikingly attractive personality, even in his old age. . . . So much so was he that one wishes that he might have been so fortunate as to have known him when he was in his prime. . . . His bright, genial, hearty presence will be missed on our streets and by none more than by the little children, whom it was hard for him to meet, and not stop for a cheery chat and hand out pennies to them."

Powhattan Locke

1863–1864

Powhattan Locke was born in Kentucky in 1830. His father, David Locke, was a veteran of the War of 1812. Little is known of his education, as he first emerges as a lawyer in the census of 1850 when living in Caldwell County, Missouri. He was named in the newspapers as a delegate to several Whig and Constitutional Union Party conventions between 1852 and 1860, and described in one announcement as "a gentleman of fine ability, and a true Union man." He was elected mayor of Savannah, Missouri, in 1854 and reelected in 1855. The 1857 census listed him as an attorney in St. Joseph, Missouri, and the *History of Buchanan County* reports his anti-slavery efforts in the area. For the next several years he practiced law in Buchanan, Platte, Clinton, DeKalb, Andrew, and Holt Counties.

It appears that Locke began his judicial career in 1862, when he and two others were appointed as temporary county judges for the wage of $5.00 per day. During this time, he volunteered as a member of the Board of Curators, the governing agency of the University of Missouri. He also formed a law practice with his younger brother Morris, pledging in an advertisement "prompt attention given to procuring of pensions, back pay, and bounties and the prosecution of claims arising out of the war." His interest in politics increased as he explored a campaign for the legislature. He decided against the campaign and was later an unsuccessful candidate for judge in Buchanan County.

On August 31, 1863, President Lincoln appointed him to the Nevada Territorial Supreme Court to fill the vacancy created by Judge Jones's resignation. He was thirty-three. The local Missouri newspaper described him as "a man of fine general information, a good lawyer and a courteous gentleman, and the people of Nevada have been fortunate in his appointment." He soon left for the Nevada Territory with his wife, three sons, and brother Morris.

Judge Locke was assigned to the Third District and soon appointed Morris to be the court clerk. He was warmly welcomed with high expectations that he would immediately begin resolving disputes "among our rich mines." One of his first cases involved a duel and witnesses who conveniently "forgot" everything they observed when summonsed to court. He demonstrated judicial courage by sending the recalcitrant witnesses to jail for contempt. In another early case, he sentenced a manslaughter defendant to three years in the territorial prison. His first few weeks were difficult, but within a few months he had earned the respect of lawyers who appeared in front of him. The local newspaper explained:

> It is not to be denied that a strong feeling was engendered against him [Locke] during the first few days of the court, occasioned by what were considered arbitrary proceedings. These prejudices were gradually worn away by the urbanity of manner, the learning, dignity and firmness displayed as a presiding officer, and the uprightness and determination displayed in bringing criminals to justice. With such an officer as Judge Locke there will never be the need of a Vigilance Committee in this district.

If nothing else, Judge Locke was holding court, "taking care of a considerable amount of business [which had] accumulated on the calendar on account of the former judge showing no disposition to clear it." The compliments continued into the early spring of 1864, when the newspaper reported the "new judge" was "an affable gentleman, socially sound. From the Bar we hear but one opinion as to his qualifications for the position he occupies and that is a perfect indorsement [sic]."

Public sentiment shifted in May 1864, when Judge Locke was required to leave his one-judge district and sit as one of three judges on the territorial supreme court. The seminal appeal was between two large mining companies who asserted competing geological theories about the subterranean ore veins. Fortunes were at stake, and the parties enlisted competing newspapers to advance their positions. Locke was excoriated by the newspapers when the court announced its decision. There may be some truth to the criticisms, as Locke first sided with Judge North, then filed an addendum to the opinion shifting his position to that of Judge Turner (who concurred in the addendum), before finally withdrawing his addendum and restoring the first decision by realignment with North. The most critical voices alleged he was persuaded by alcohol, money, and physical escorts provided by the competing litigant companies as he rendered different opinions. Locke responded by claiming to be unwell and leaving the territory for a short time to recuperate.

Locke relocated to Missouri after statehood and died of "consumption" in 1868 while visiting his father in Louisiana. He was thirty-eight. The newspaper reported he left a "bereaved widow and desolate orphans" when he died. The local bar association published a resolution of condolence upon Locke's death for "a brother, who was cut off in the prime of manhood, whose fine social qualities, whose correct moral bearing not less than the profound morality and intellectual powers, endeared him to us all."

John North

1863–1864

A REVIEW OF JUDGE JOHN North's entire life reveals a man of depth, principles, and conviction; much different from the judge who was mercilessly criticized in the last days of the territory.[1]

North was born in New York in 1815 to parents devoted to their religious faith. His father was a traveling preacher, inclined toward Wesleyan Methodism and Unitarianism. While young, Judge North worked on the family farm and, like many of his time, was schooled at home under the tutelage of parents. At thirteen he had a religious conversion that remained with him throughout his life. At fifteen he attended a three-month training school to qualify as a teacher. When he moved with his family to Cortland County at age seventeen he accepted a teaching position near Albany. The next year he registered as a lay minister.

North enrolled in the Seminary of the Genesee Conference in Cazenovia, New York, at age twenty-two and Wesleyan University at twenty-four. During his three years at Wesleyan he became an abolitionist, speaking publicly against slavery and attending several abolition conventions. He was also a member in the student literary debating society and Missionary Lyceum, an organization devoted to foreign ministries. After graduating in 1841, he worked full-time for the Anti-Slavery Society as an organizer and lecturer. He began a "pilgrimage" to speak in every city

---

[1] Some of the information in this profile comes from Merlin Stonehouse's 1965 *John Wesley North and the Reform Frontier*, published by the University of Minnesota Press.

and town in Connecticut. He described his activities as "going to-and-fro as a flaming firebrand."

Choosing the law over ministry, North began studying in 1843 with several abolitionist lawyers, including John Jay, the grandson of US Supreme Court justice John Jay. The atmosphere was a "happy combination of law and reform." He was admitted to the New York Bar in 1845 and began his legal career in Syracuse. That same year he married his first wife, Emma Bacon, who, tragically, died of tuberculosis two years later. He was deeply grieved and received care in the home of abolitionist Dr. George Loomis, who allowed his dairy farm to be a waystation on the underground railroad for twenty years. Nursed by Dr. Loomis's daughter Ann, North slowly recovered. Not surprisingly, North and Ann developed a relationship and later married. They had six children, naming their first daughter Emma Bacon, after North's deceased wife.

An activist and risk-taking speculator, North moved with Ann to the Minnesota Territory in 1849. He began practicing law, and they were instrumental in settling St. Anthony, which still exists today. North was a successful land speculator and accumulated wealth of some substance. He was also elected to the Minnesota House of Representatives. There, he proposed a university and argued "it was none too soon to provide for 'liberal, scientific and classical education.'" The university bill passed, and the legislature chose St. Anthony for its location. North raised money for construction of the two-room university and contributed one-third of the cost from his own resources. He also hosted the university's first professor in his home. For reasons not discernible from the historical records, and despite being described as a "man with a golden voice," North was defeated in his campaign for reelection, though his social views may have been a contributing factor. He was opposed to slavery, a vocal and public leader of the temperance movement, and moved by his religious beliefs.

North continued speculating on land, a toll bridge, various mills, and the railroad, but he leveraged himself too far and lost everything when the area suffered an economic recession. Undeterred, he turned his attention to politics. He and friends organized the Republican Party of Minnesota. He hosted its first convention in his home and ensured passage of a resolution to abolish slavery in Washington, DC, the territories, and all new states. The party also called for the repeal of fugitive slave laws and for complete prohibition of alcohol. In 1857, North led a Republican delegation to the Minnesota constitutional convention and was elected

John North

president. He strongly advocated for voting rights for women and African Americans.

North was an early supporter of President Lincoln's 1860 election. He traveled to New York to raise campaign funds and was chairman of the Minnesota delegation to the Republican National Convention in Chicago that nominated Lincoln for president. After Lincoln's nomination, North traveled with a small group by train to Springfield to notify Lincoln he had been nominated. He tirelessly campaigned for Lincoln and traveled to Springfield again, shortly after the election, to visit with Lincoln in his home. It was there that he first requested an appointment as superintendent of Indian affairs. Lincoln did not make a commitment, but he invited North to travel with him on a train to Chicago, where

Lincoln introduced North to Vice President-elect Hannibal Hamlin. President Lincoln also invited him to attend his inauguration. Encouraged, North later met Hamlin in New York and traveled to Washington, DC, in Hamlin's private rail car. Shortly after the inauguration, North called on President Lincoln in the White House and renewed his request to be appointed superintendent of Indian affairs. He did not receive the appointment, but President Lincoln did appoint him to be the surveyor general of the Nevada Territory.

North arrived in Carson City in June 1861 and settled into his work as a surveyor. He also opened a law practice and built a quartz mill with borrowed money. The "Minnesota Mill" was completed in 1863. His ownership of the mill would haunt him throughout his judicial service, as he was accused of receiving preferential rock to process and being a debtor to some litigants who appeared before him. As he had shown in Minnesota, and would later demonstrate in Tennessee and California, North was a city builder. He began mapping out the development of Washoe City, which later became the first seat of Washoe County. He also returned to his passion for education when he was appointed superintendent of schools; the appointment was later confirmed by election. Consistent with his earlier positions in Minnesota, he opposed segregation in public schools.

Shortly after Judge Mott's election to Congress, North sought appointment to Mott's position. He wrote to Secretary of State Seward: "Though my salary was cut off just as I got my family into the Territory I have not troubled the President or any of my friends with complaints. Being accustomed to rely on my own energies, I have done so here, and with success. My law practice is now worth much more than my salary as Surveyor-General. I stand in no need of an office. But the late election of one of our Judges as Delegate to Congress creates a vacancy which I am desired to fill." In December 1862, several members of the territorial legislature and lawyers telegraphed petitions and letters supporting his appointment, and territorial governor Nye personally lobbied for him when he was in Washington. On August 20, 1863, President Lincoln appointed North to the territorial supreme court. He was forty-eight at the time.

Judge North was initially praised for his industry and decorum. He was recognized for his tireless work on the backlog of cases that had accumulated over the prior two years. In addition to the volume of mining cases, he also presided over criminal and civil cases. He issued a warrant for Mark Twain's arrest after hearing of a duel between Twain and a rival newspaperman. (Twain reportedly fled the territory before the warrant was served.) He also balanced his judicial duties with personal compassion. He was troubled when a jury convicted a woman of manslaughter because he thought she had presented evidence of "extreme provocation." After sentencing the woman to territorial prison, he signed a petition seeking her pardon.

Judge North reached his public zenith during the 1863 constitutional convention, when he was elected president and named a leading contender to be Nevada's first state governor. However, his public battle with William Stewart and others took its toll on his health, and he was periodically absent from service during the spring and summer of 1864. He was also in frequent conflict with his judicial colleagues; one newspaper reported that "[Judge North] begs that no sins of Turner or Locke be visited upon him. It is sad to behold this lack of harmony, of confidence among the brethren judges. It is evidence tolerably strong that all is not right with the bench; that North reviles Turner, Turner recriminates on North, and North and Turner never concur, except in adjudging Locke to be an ass."

The relentless workload involving large fortunes came with a cost. Judge North's daughter remembered how he would return to Washoe City on the weekends, "his tall, spare figure bent, his face white and worn." He was advised to carry a gun or be escorted during his travels between Virginia and Washoe Cities. His wife was his most ardent supporter, though she acknowledged he suffered a form of nervous breakdown during the worst of times. She wrote in a private letter, "No one can know the real beauty of his character <'>til they have lived with him and see him under all circumstances." In 1864, before the second vote for Nevada statehood and when political pressures were at their worst, his wife wrote to her parents that North was so exhausted from his court duties that he fainted at the breakfast table.

His health became a public issue in the spring and summer of 1864, and his critics were not kind. One newspaper editorialized about his health and wrote that the sooner an unwell official "dies or resigns, the better it will be for the Territory." Another newspaper quoted the editorial and expanded, "We know nothing of the facts alluded to, but we do know that the manner in which the affairs of that court have been conducted, or rather not conducted, is an outrageous wrong, an inexcusable disregard of the rights of the people and an irreparable calamity to the country.... Whether Judge North is an invalid from overwork and too close attention to his judicial duties, or from some other cause, is a matter of total indifference to the community. He is confessedly unable to fill the position and transact the business of the court; he has no moral right to retain his office of Judge, to the damage of the vast and vital interests of the public."

In early August 1864, Judge North communicated to California governor Frederick Low, US senator from California John Conness, and California Supreme Court justice Stephen Field that he intended to resign. His knew his successor would be appointed by President Lincoln if statehood was unsuccessful, and he asked them to ensure that Stewart and other local lawyers involved in mining litigation not be allowed to influence the president's appointment.

When the judges took the bench on August 22, 1864, North announced he was "compelled by severe and protracted illness to relinquish the office of Associate Justice of the Supreme Court and Judge of the First Judicial District of this Territory." He therefore resigned from the bench, effective immediately. His resignation letter to President Lincoln is revealing; it reads in part:

> All agree that I have done more business in court during the past year than all that was done in the three years preceding. Yet there are about 450 cases now on the calendar; and scores of them are suits on the decision of which millions are turning. Everything is intensified to the highest degree, and corruption has to be met with a firm hand. To hold the helm in these troubled waters is like navigating a whirlpool continually.

North stayed in Nevada long enough to vindicate his name. He sued William Stewart and the *Territorial Enterprise* for defamation. The case was referred to a panel of referees who concluded that North had made some errors of judgment but exonerated him of the corruption the defendants had alleged. During the time he remained in Nevada he was counsel in six appeals to the newly created Nevada Supreme Court.

He continued to be moved by social justice issues. In 1865, he left Nevada for Tennessee and founded a colony promoting industry and education—with the intention of supporting Reconstruction and emancipated slaves. His ideas were too progressive for the time and location, and the project was unsuccessful. He also sought without success an appointment from President Grant as commissioner of Indian affairs—the same appointment he had sought from President Lincoln.

As his colony in Tennessee was boycotted and failure was in sight, North and a partner envisioned a city of ten thousand settlers who would each invest $1,000 for one hundred acres in a temperance community with schools, churches, a lyceum, and public library. They widely marketed their proposal, but only to limited success. In 1870, he moved to California and founded an area in San Bernardino County now known as Riverside. He had the pleasure of reconnecting with Judge Jones when he was in Riverside. Despite his energy and vision, he "was too busy helping others and directing municipal affairs to become a money-maker." He was removed from his management role in Riverside but remained president until 1876.

Yet again, North would be one of the founders of a city, now known as Oleander, in Fresno County. He also practiced law with his son, frequently lectured on education and water rights, and was involved in Republican politics. In 1879 he lost a nomination for justice of the California Supreme Court at the Republican state convention in Sacramento. In 1883, he returned to visit St. Anthony and the University of Minnesota that he had supported as a legislator and partially funded so many years earlier. He also went to New York for a reunion with old abolitionist friends.

In 1889, just months before his death, he delivered a lecture to the newly founded Unity Society of Fresno on the subject of "Science and Some Incidents in Its History." He died at his daughter's home in Fresno in 1890, at the age of eighty-four. Despite having earned substantial money throughout his life, he died with property worth $5,300 and debts of $8,000. He is buried in Riverside, the city he founded.

NEVADA SUPREME COURT

James F. Lewis

1864–1873

When the first three Nevada Supreme Court justices took office in 1864, their first act of business was selecting by lot the length of their terms. Justice James F. Lewis drew the shortest term of two years, but was also designated as the court's first chief justice. For a state just days old, with a hope of great success, Justice Lewis was the perfect choice. He was young—twenty-eight—and also showed promise for a great future. Justice Lewis met that promise through an exemplary career until his life tragically ended when he was just fifty.

James F. Lewis was born in Wales in 1836 and immigrated to Utica, New York, with his family when he was two. After some education at Whitesboro Academy near Utica, he moved with his family to Racine, Wisconsin, where he began studying law in 1855, while also working as a telegraph operator. He was admitted to the Wisconsin Bar in 1860.

Like many others, he heard the call of mineral wealth and traveled to California in 1862, but soon moved to the Nevada Territory and settled in Washoe City. He formed a partnership with John North, who would later be appointed territorial judge. As a single man, he boarded with the Norths (for $10 per week) and threw himself into his career. Although described as "exceedingly shy, melancholy, and home-loving," he was quickly recognized for his "able and incorruptible" character and legal ability. He "was so timid" that he once slept in his law office for two nights rather than tell the Norths he was sick. He suffered from severe asthma throughout his life.

Left to right: Henry O. Beatty, James F. Lewis, and Cornelius M. Brosnan

Lewis developed a successful law practice and was also elected prosecuting attorney for Washoe County in September 1863. He participated in four appeals to the territorial supreme court. He was active in party politics and elected to the supreme court on the Union Party ticket in 1864. The same month he traveled to San Francisco to marry Lizzie Raymond, whom he had met while still in Wisconsin.

A courageous jurist who authored many decisions, Justice Lewis embodied the judicial imperative of *doing right without the necessity of being right*. In one of his early decisions, he ruled against a supreme court colleague by denying a request that judicial salaries be paid in gold coin and not paper money. He began his written decision:

> Upon the first argument of this case, I confess, I was fully of the opinion that the writ ought to issue, but after further and more mature consideration, I am satisfied my first conclusion was incorrect. Nor do I hesitate to say that I entered upon the examination of the case with a desire to grant the peremptory writ, if it could be done upon correct legal principles; but we all know it was the general understanding, not only among the first State officers, but among the people at large, that the salaries of such officers would be payable in gold and silver coin; and I deeply regret that the law will not afford the learned relator [his colleague] the relief to which, in my judgment, he is justly entitled. But the members of the profession well know that the law, though embodying the wisdom of centuries, though adorned by the learning, and improved by the genius of proud jurists and great statesmen, has not yet attended to such perfection as to afford a remedy where justice gives a right.

Another brief excerpt reveals the depth of Lewis's intellect and commitment to justice. The court was faced with the question of whether African American children could be admitted in public school, despite a statute prescribing that "Negroes, Mongolians, and Indians shall not be admitted into the public schools, but the board of trustees may establish a separate school for their education." Lewis wrote an impassioned decision referring to Cicero, Rousseau, Locke, and others for immutable principles of justice:

> One of the great fundamental principles underlying our government, as indeed it must be an indispensable element of all truly republican governments, is, that every citizen is equal before the law, being entitled to all the protection which it grants to life and property, and all the immunities and advantages which it may afford for culture or the amelioration of the condition of any individual or class.

Justice Lewis authored several other statements of law that reveal his intellect and practical approach to the law:

It is for the public good that there be an end to litigation. . . .

The imperfection of human language renders the complete and exact expression of thought in all cases utterly impossible. To give expression at all times to exactly what is intended, to employ words which are neither too comprehensive nor too limited, is a power which, no proficiency in philology can bestow upon man. . . .

We have, however, no option but to follow the clear rules of law; for to declare, not to make, the law is the province of the courts. . . .

[C]onsequences should never influence a court in its construction of a law which is not ambiguous in its phraseology.

Justice Lewis was reelected in 1866, without campaigning for himself and "almost without a dissenting voice." A newspaper reported that "we feel, in common with others, that he is both honest and capable, and, as such, an ornament to the bench, we hope to see him retained." However, believing judges should not actively campaign for office, he only passively sought renomination to the Republic Party slate in 1872 and was ultimately not nominated for a third term. He returned to private practice and eventually practiced in both Nevada and California—sometimes with his old friend and partner Judge John North. He enjoyed significant success, which he parlayed into other business endeavors. In 1876, a newspaper wrote that "his practice is large, and much more lucrative, than when he was Chief Justice. We don't believe he would relinquish it for any office in the gift of the people. It is a deplorable state of affairs, but nevertheless is the rule, that good men can not be prevailed upon to accept public office." Lewis may have been an exception to the rule when he expressed interest in an appointment to the US District Court in 1882.

Always physically frail, Lewis opened a law practice in Arizona where he hoped the climate would improve his health. In August of 1886, while working on a mining case in Arizona, he died after being stuck on a broken-down train for more than thirty hours. He was only fifty. The presumed cause of death was heatstroke. His funeral was held in San Francisco, and he was buried in Carson City.

The Nevada Supreme Court published a memorial to Justice Lewis on September 6, 1886, noting his "high character and professional ability." It referred to his published opinions as "clear, concise, and learned." His former colleagues ascribed his success more to preparation and industry than "readiness of thought or language at the argument." He sought to mentor younger members of the bar, and his kindness and instructions "will long be borne in affectionate remembrance." Privately, he possessed a "purity of character" and was known for "many acts of unostentatious charity." He was an "able and upright judge, an honest lawyer, a good citizen, he commanded and retained the confidence and respect of his fellow men." Although randomly selected by lot, he appears to have been the perfect choice to be the first chief justice of the Nevada Supreme Court.

Henry O. Beatty

1864–1868

LITTLE IS KNOWN ABOUT JUSTICE Beatty's early life or legal education. Born in Kentucky in 1812, Henry O. Beatty was married in Ohio in 1836 and was the father of three daughters and one son. (His son William H. Beatty would also serve as a justice on the Nevada Supreme Court.) He practiced law in Ohio before relocating to California in 1851. The trip to California was difficult and long—he made his way through the Isthmus of Panama before sailing to San Francisco.

Beatty was interested in the appellate bench early on, having sought a position on the California Supreme Court in three separate elections on behalf of three different political parties: the temperance People's Party of California (1855), the Democratic Anti-Lecompton Party (1858), and the Union Party (1863).

Despite his successful practice in Sacramento and seasoned age, Beatty moved to the Nevada Territory in 1863. A historian explained that Beatty "had for a number of years been a prominent member of the Sacramento Bar before the lure of the Comstock brought him to Nevada. Past fifty years of age, he brought to the bench a mind trained from years of experience upon the Pacific Coast. Like his associates, the purity of his character, together with his legal ability, commanded the respect and confidence of the bar."

On his arrival in the territory he immediately became involved in litigation and politics. In August 1864, he was mentioned as "a good man, amply qualified, for the position of district judge after Nevada became a state." However, Beatty yearned for the studious work of an appellate court. He increased his public profile by giving many speeches supporting statehood and the Union Party, and on October 13, 1864, he was placed on the Union ticket for one of the three positions for the Supreme Court. After one campaign speech a few weeks later, a local newspaper provided insight into how he was perceived by the public:

> Beatty made a courteous, dignified argument, convincing every one that his ideas of what constitutes true patriotism are the result of a pure mind, carefully cultivated by study and rich in experience. [His] remarks ... were of a character far beyond any political haberdash, and we could not avoid the thought that such minds, and such patriotism as was his, were of the kind that in past years had made our country great and glorious.

He was elected to the Nevada Supreme Court the following month at the age of fifty-two. On transitioning to the bench, he sold his extensive legal library to the court for $1,790.

Justice Beatty was a prolific scholar who published more opinions than his two colleagues. However, he may be better known for filing a petition for writ of mandamus compelling the state treasurer to pay him in gold coin and not "greenback" paper currency. After he prevailed in the district court, the treasurer appealed to the supreme court. Beatty stepped down from the bench and personally argued his position before his two colleagues, though he did recuse himself from deciding the case. His colleagues ruled against him.

Beatty served as a trustee of the Carson City School District while also serving on the supreme court. During this time he also supervised the printing of the first volume of *Nevada Reports,* an annual publication that collates decisions of the Nevada Supreme Court. The work was difficult and required lengthy time in Sacramento, yet published volumes continue to the present and provide a detailed record of Nevada law.

An unsuccessful renomination bid led Justice Beatty to resign two months before the end of his term in 1868. He auctioned his goods and returned to California five years after arriving in Nevada. He left Nevada with a well-earned reputation, described as an example of "splendid, rugged and sterling American manhood." A newspaper reported about him on his retirement:

We have every reason for holding the opinion that no more pure, patriotic and upright man exists than H. O. Beatty. A Southern man by birth, he warmly espoused the cause of the Union in the earliest days of the war; and he has kept true to his principles and advanced with their cause ever since. We say it in no manner of disparagement to any other man, but we honestly believe that the state sustained a great and almost irreparable loss when Judge Beatty was defeated by our party for a renomination. No Judge makes infallible judgments, and Beatty may have sometimes been in error in his decisions; but while he wrought with rare industry, he decided fearlessly and promptly and in accordance with a conscientious understanding of the law. He has gone with his estimable wife and youngest daughter to reside in Sacramento.

In 1872, he lost a campaign for mayor in Sacramento. He died in 1892 at seventy-nine. The *Morning Appeal* newspaper in Carson City wrote of him on his death:

He was a most able jurist and progressive in his ideas. Although a man of firm convictions and most positive characteristics, he was always courteous and kindly in his manner, and faithful in his friendships. He was thoroughly temperate in all things and led a pure and upright life. Unassuming in his virtues he deserves a record of spotless integrity seldom equaled in this age of sharp practice and conviction.

Senator Cornelius Cole described Justice Beatty as "a quiet and genial gentleman and sound lawyer, [who] was in a large practice in Sacramento. He was of a most gentle nature and I can hardly believe he ever had an enemy in the world. He was a man of sterling integrity."

Cornelius M. Brosnan

1864–1867

BORN IN IRELAND IN 1814, Cornelius M. Brosnan was a superior student at Maynooth College in County Kildare. "Enraged by the despotism that crushed Ireland," and drawn to the American promise, he immigrated to the United States in 1831 and settled in Burlington, Vermont. He immediately entered Plattsburg College where he was both a student and a teacher of general sciences. He also read for the law and was admitted to the New York Bar in 1841. He married in 1844, but, tragically, his only child died at the age of one. His grief is reflected in a poem he wrote, "The Lament."

After his 1846 election as treasurer of Onondaga County, he loaned public funds to a gentleman who soon died in a railway accident. The practice of treasurers loaning money to private borrowers was widespread, but Brosnan was greatly troubled when the loan went into default, creating a deficit in the public funds he managed. He resigned from office in 1850, and sailed from New York City to San Francisco, which required overland passage through the Isthmus of Panama. Along the way, he wrote a series of letters about his travels, which were printed in the *Syracuse Daily Standard*.

He arrived in San Francisco in 1850 and was unimpressed with the "hurry and bustle" of the city, which included gambling, drinking, and other debauchery. He was also dismayed to discover a city overstocked with lawyers. Nonetheless, he committed himself to the law and enjoyed success for the next decade. One newspaper wrote about him: "His genial manners, his eloquence, learning and position, second to none of his brothers in the profession." Although he privately held the California Supreme Court in low regard, he appeared before the court eleven times between 1855 and 1862.

Like many San Francisco lawyers, he was seduced by the mining-related legal work in the Nevada Territory. He moved to Virginia City in 1863 but did not realize the success he sought, later inspiring Robert M. Clarke, the second Nevada attorney general, to say of Brosnan's Nevada career:

> That he did not succeed in amassing a fortune or establishing an extensive and lucrative practice reflects nothing to his discredit. He reached Virginia when the tide was receding. Reaction had punctured the balloon and the inflation was rapidly subsiding. The legitimate ground of the profession was preoccupied. Besides, at that day, the practice of the law was to some extent degenerated into the practice of villainy. Chicanery won more suits than eloquence and learning, and bribery and corruption more than solid merit. Judge Brosnan honored his profession and scorned these practices. He would have perished a beggar in the street rather than dishonor his calling.

Though undistinguished as a Nevada lawyer, Brosnan made significant contributions to statehood and the Nevada constitution. He was in Virginia City less than seven months before being nominated to serve as a Storey County delegate to the first constitutional convention. The *Territorial Enterprise* wrote of him: "He is one of your calm, considerate, unostentatious men, who always considers well what he is about to say, and a thorough-bred lawyer, who will do credit to himself and justice to our community in the Constitutional Convention."

Brosnan focused much of his attention on the judiciary and was one of a few delegates from the first convention selected to serve in the second constitutional convention. There, he chaired the judiciary committee and was an articulate advocate for the structure of the judiciary upon statehood being granted.

His work did not go unrecognized. Mark Twain, then writing for the *Enterprise* as Samuel Clemens, referred to his "stately eloquence, adorned with beautiful imagery and embellished with classic quotations." A fellow delegate later described his many contributions to the constitutional convention:

He assisted in planning and completing our political edifice; he was master mechanic; laid the foundation and erected the superstructure. As a member of the convention that framed the Constitution of Nevada, he rendered the people invaluable service, and won for himself an enviable distinction. As chairman of the Judiciary Committee he first originated and then enforced our present system of judiciary. His learning and judgment were promptly recognized, and his opinions were to a great extent adopted by the convention. His genius engrafted itself upon our fundamental law, which will forever stand a monument to his memory.

J. Giles McClinton, editor of the *Esmeralda Union* and a member of the second constitutional convention, described Brosnan as

a co-laborer with us in the convention which framed the Constitution of the State and we can therefore speak from personal knowledge of his character, abilities and qualifications. He is an old man, but still possesses all the faculties of a powerful mind in the full freshness, acuteness and vigor of youth. . . . [He] is one of the ablest lawyers on the Pacific Coast, is the very soul of honor and has a great heart, whose every pulsation beats for the cause of freedom and the salvation of his adopted country.

After the second convention in July 1864, Brosnan traveled throughout the territory speaking in support of statehood. The *Gold Hill Daily News* commented on September 3 that "Brosnan gave a good speech, a patriotic and a loyal speech, and one that did honor to his head and his heart." The *News* reported after another speech that Brosnan "made a fervent and eloquent little address that was enthusiastically applauded throughout."

After statehood was approved Brosnan immediately became a candidate for the supreme court. The *Virginia Daily Union* reported that "most prominent among the names mentioned for justices is that of C. M. Brosnan, an eloquent, talented, learned and popular Irish Lawyer of this city, of most ardent loyalty." The *Reese River Reveille* reported on his candidacy by noting "his nomination [is] certain. He is an able lawyer, a man of fine character, and his genial nature and natural dignity of character, coupled with his good habits, have made him a favorite with the bar and the people."

Brosnan was elected with slightly more votes than Justices Beatty and Lewis. Unfortunately, he was beset by illness during his brief tenure on the court and did not produce the number of decisions expected of him. Of the 190 appeals considered during his tenure, Justice Brosnan wrote only 11 majority decisions, 4 concurring opinions, 2 dissenting opinions, and he did not participate in 34 appeals. He did write a controversial decision examining the relationship between the federal Legal Tender Act, which allowed "greenbacks" as legal tender in all commercial transactions, and a state law that the first Nevada legislature enacted that required parties to adhere to the currency identified in their individual contracts. He wrote in favor of federal supremacy over state contract. The *Eastern Slope* reported on January 27, 1866:

> It is reported, and we believe on good authority, that the "money changers" offered Judge Brosnan seventy-five thousand dollars to resign his position on the Supreme Bench. The Judge, with an honesty of purpose, as rare as it is commendable in these latter days in which bribery and corruption is made the highway to wealth and political honors, rejected the humiliating offer with scorn. We are proud of the Judge that has elevated the standard of judicial morals and demonstrated the fact that there are men, whose price is above the price of gold. All honors to Nevada's incorruptible Judge.

Soon afterward, Judge Brosnan became increasingly feeble, probably with tuberculosis, and moved to San Jose, California, in late 1866. He hoped the milder climate would improve his health, but he died on April 20, 1867, at fifty-three. Despite several decades as a lawyer, he died an impoverished debtor.

The *Carson Daily Appeal* wrote of Justice Brosnan:

> There are no larger hearted, more genial men than Judge Brosnan was. There was so much of a "gentleman of the old school" in his demeanor that all recognized it, at a glance. He wrote law, as he wrote whatever else became his subject, with the ease, elegance and polished diction of a thoroughly trained scholar.

Nevada attorney general Robert Clarke eulogized Justice Brosnan:

> He loved the country of his adoption second only to his honor, which he loved more dearly than life. . . . His voice was ever raised against oppression and wrong, and ever gave forth its eloquent utterances, for

liberty and right. He was a Radical—that is to say he was earnestly, entirely and unhesitatingly for the right—never willing to compromise principles for the sale of temporary, doubtful expediency. . . . His career is above criticism. A man of strong prejudices and ardent friendships, the one nor the other have ever swerved him from the line of absolute justice. Upon the bench he knew nothing but the law, which he grasped with wonderful faculty, comprehended with almost intuition, and enforced with the precision of demonstration.

Finally, Nevada Supreme Court chief justice Beatty wrote of his former colleague:

Possessed of a fine taste, a classical education, ardent in his feeling and naturally fluent, he made himself known to the public as an eloquent and gifted speaker. His learning and acquaintance with the principles of his profession were all well known to the bar of the State. His firmness and decision, and the stoical resolution with which he resisted all the temptations which were attempted to be brought to bear upon his judicial decision are best known to his associates. It is with no small degree of pleasure that I bear witness to his unswerving integrity, and that firmness of character which enables him to pursue the straightforward course of an upright Judge, seeking only to ascertain the law and decide the right regardless of personal consequences to himself. In his judicial course he never stopped to enquire whether a decision might be popular or unpopular, whether it would result beneficially or injuriously to himself.

J. Neely Johnson

1867–1871

ALTHOUGH ONLY FORTY-ONE YEARS OLD when appointed to the Nevada Supreme Court, J. Neely Johnson had already enjoyed remarkable professional success. He was the former Sacramento city attorney, had been appointed by President Millard Fillmore as a special census agent, served in the California Assembly, was colonel in the California State Militia, and served as California governor between 1856 and 1858. His successes in California carried over to Nevada when he was selected as president of the 1864 constitutional convention. In addition to his public service, Justice Johnson was a successful mining lawyer who wrote the 1866 Nevada Civil Practice Act.

The Johnsons were a prominent family in Indiana who lost their fortune during the Panic of 1837; as a result, Johnson apprenticed as a printer in lieu of attending university. He later moved to Iowa, where he studied law and was admitted to the bar in 1845. Like so many others, Johnson heard the call of the gold and rushed overland to California in 1849.

Johnson mined for gold, drove a six-mule team between Sacramento and Stockton, and finally settled into a legal practice. During this time, he also served as a state agent for the Sacramento Relief Association and even joined an expedition providing relief to immigrants traversing the Sierra Nevada mountain range. He appeared as counsel in seven appeals before the California Supreme Court.

At the time, political parties in California were in flux. In 1854, the Democratic Party was split over the Kansas-Nebraska Act and the Whig party was in decline. Johnson, then serving in the assembly, made the fortuitous decision to join the Native American Party (known as the Know Nothings). At only age thirty, he was nominated candidate for governor of California in 1855 and ran against incumbent John Bigler. He won and described himself "the most startled man in the state." His opponents agreed, writing that his "chief political assets included an attractive wife 'who did a good deal for him,' pro southern inclinations, and the fact that he was not clearly identified with established political groups." He remains the youngest governor ever elected in California. His Sacramento home is listed on the National Register of Historic Places, and the J. Neely Johnson Park is located at 516 Eleventh Street in Sacramento.

While Johnson may have been lucky in ascending through California politics, he quickly became mired in unlucky circumstances after becoming governor. Unregulated crime and corruption led to unrest between citizens and government officials in San Francisco, which led to the creation of a vigilance committee that privately and unlawfully policed the streets. This private policing erupted into citizens' arrests (including the arrest of a justice of the California Supreme Court), barricades, assaults on government buildings, and lynchings.

To negotiate peace with the vigilance committee, Johnson traveled to San Francisco with General William Tecumseh Sherman (later of Civil War fame), who was then chief of the California Militia. Negotiations failed, and Johnson watched as vigilantes hung alleged criminals without due process or government protection. Johnson declared martial law and directed General Sherman to muster the state militia, but the militia did not respond and Johnson was forced to rescind his order. He later defended himself by saying, "In all that I have done or sought to do, I heeded not the plaudits of the populace, nor feared their threats. I know no higher law than the constitution of my country."

The problems in San Francisco overshadowed Johnson's gubernatorial term, and he lost his party's nomination for reelection. He was even targeted for assassination and was shot at while traveling from Shasta to Weaverville. (He was unharmed, the ball only passing through his clothing.) Frustrated, he moved to Virginia City when it was still part of the Utah Territory and served as a delegate to the 1863 and 1864 constitutional conventions.

The accusation that Johnson was sympathetic to the South is belied by his strong support of the Union Army. While in the Nevada Territory,

J. Neely Johnson

he spoke often about the Union and solicited men to join the Civil War as Union soldiers. And in his last address as governor, he expressly criticized laws that prohibited "nonwhites" from testifying in court, a rule that he described as "indiscriminate prohibition" and "at variance with the spirit of our constitution."

Johnson was immediately successful in the Nevada Territory as a lawyer and owner of mining interests. He was sued several times, and he appeared as a party or lawyer in the territorial and state supreme courts in fourteen cases.

He is best understood through his own words. After being unanimously elected president of the second constitutional convention in 1864, Johnson said:

For this evidence of your partiality and confidence in selecting me by the unanimous voice of the Convention to preside over its deliberations, you have my sincere thanks, and it shall be my constant endeavor to execute the duties of the position with strict impartiality, and with a just sense of their great responsibility and importance. But, gentlemen, whatever of rules you may adopt for our government, or however earnest and faithful may be your presiding officer in their enforcement, yet are we chiefly dependent upon the action of each individual member that our deliberations may be harmonious, and efficiency characterize the labors of the Convention, and with confidence I shall rely upon your aid and assistance, so that our proceedings may be marked with all the dignity and decorum befitting an assemblage of men convened for such a noble purpose as the present.

Then, just twenty-six days later when adjourning the convention, Johnson said:

The time has arrived when, having concluded the important labors for which we were convened, we are about to separate, and return to our several homes. Anxiously as we have desired this moment, it nevertheless brings with it feelings of sadness, for we are about to part, probably never, all of us, again to meet together on earth.

When I entered upon the duties of your presiding officer, gentlemen, I promised you that I would endeavor to discharge the duties of that trust with impartiality, and I can conscientiously say, that during the sessions of our body I have earnestly sought to discharge those duties. And I feel that I can receive the very flattering resolution of thanks which you have adopted, as at least an earnest and sincere expression of your judgment as to the manner in which I have fulfilled your expectations, and my promise....

[W]e have prepared with exceeding great care a Constitution to be submitted to the people of this Territory, for their approval or rejection—a constitution which, in my opinion, in all its essential features, will commend itself to the favorable judgment of the people. And even should their judgment be adverse at this time to its adoption, we shall have this upon which to congratulate ourselves, that although the result of our labors be not now adopted, it will nevertheless serve as a basis for the action of some future Convention, as the labors of our predecessors have served as the basis of our action.

Gentlemen, in bidding you good-bye, allow me to say that you carry with you, each and every one, my cordial sympathies in your future welfare, my sincere wishes for your continued prosperity. And I join with you, gentlemen, in the ardent hope that the labors which have brought us together, and which are now happily ended, may culminate in the advantage of the people of the new State of Nevada, for the government of which we have laid the foundation.

Johnson received high praise for his work as convention president. One newspaper described him as "a gentleman of fine legal attainments, untiring energy, and sound discretion.... The Governor is a warm and earnest supporter of the Union Party, and a man who commands the respect and confidence of the entire community."

He was nominated for the state senate at the Ormsby County Union convention, which he declined "on account of the pressure of business." On Justice Cornelius Brosnan's death in 1867, the Douglas County Bar petitioned Governor Blasdel to appoint Johnson to the Nevada Supreme Court. The Ormsby County Bar immediately joined in the petition. In May 1867, Blasdel appointed Johnson to the court. He was elected in 1868 to complete Justice Brosnan's term but did not run to succeed himself, leaving the court in 1871. His reasons for leaving judicial service are unknown, but the death of his fifteen-year-old daughter Elizabeth may have weighed heavily on him. During his short time as a justice he wrote 12 majority opinions, 11 dissenting opinions, and concurred in 130 opinions. He also recused himself in 49 appeals. On his departure from the court, the *Carson Daily Appeal* reported that Justice Johnson was "a man of singular integrity and first rate standing at the bar."

After traveling in Europe with Senator William Stewart in 1871, Johnson relocated to Salt Lake City to practice law. That year he was also appointed by President Ulysses S. Grant to the Board of Visitors of the US Military Academy. In 1872, he was in Salt Lake City "during the hottest portion of the day showing tourist friends around" and suffered sunstroke and was "mostly unconscious and sometimes delirious" before dying three days later on August 31, 1872. He was forty-seven. He is buried at Camp Douglas in Salt Lake City.

Bernard Crosby Whitman

1868–1875

BERNARD CROSBY WHITMAN WAS BORN in 1827 in Waltham, Massachusetts. His father was a clergyman. He attended Phillips Exeter Academy and graduated from Harvard College in 1846. After studying law for two years in Portland, Maine, he was admitted to the bar in 1849. Like so many others, he was captured by the promise of California gold and sailed from Boston to San Francisco in 1850. He settled into the practice of law and politics, yet he yearned for public service. He was elected to the California Assembly in 1854 and unsuccessfully sought a nomination to be the Know-Nothing Party's candidate for governor in 1855. The next year he was nominated to be a candidate for Congress but was defeated in the election.

Whitman married Mary Elizabeth Church of Grass Valley in 1858. Returning to public service, he was nominated as a candidate for the California Supreme Court in 1861 but was unsuccessful in the election. Finally, he moved to Virginia City in 1864 and immediately sought a nomination for candidacy for the US Senate. His efforts so soon after arriving in Nevada, avoiding many of the territorial conflicts, resulted in conflicting opinions. One newspaper wrote:

> This morning we present the name of B. C. Whitman as our first choice for United States Senator from Nevada. We are in favor of Mr. Whitman because we believe him to be better qualified for the station than any other whose name we had mentioned. He is the

Bernard Crosby Whitman

candidate of no clique or faction, and has been identified with none, nor participated in the struggles which have engendered so much ill-feeling in our midst during the past two years.

In contrast, another newspaper wrote:

It seems to us that all these reasons given . . . are so many reasons why Mr. Whitman should not be elected. A man who has not participated in our political struggles may be better entitled to the position of Senator than those who have labored to build up the Union party, but we don't see it.

Whitman was a potential nominee through several ballots but ultimately withdrew his name, which led to gracious remarks in response: "We like Whitman for this noble action, standing as it does, noble and grand amid political chicanery, and we have heard many people here express their admiration for the man. There is a future."

In 1868, at thirty-seven, he was appointed to the Nevada Supreme Court to complete the term of Justice Henry Beatty. He was elected to his own term in 1869 and served until 1875, including a term as chief justice from 1873 to 1874. He was a productive jurist, authoring 108 opinions, 3 concurring opinions, and 4 dissents. He was widely admired for his vocabulary and brevity.

After retiring from the court, Justice Whitman divided his time between Nevada and San Francisco. He was director of the Virginia & Truckee and Carson & Colorado Railroads. He was also suggested as governor in 1882, when one newspaper wrote:

> He is one of the very few of those lawyers and politicians of 20 years ago who gave to Nevada a reputation second to no other state for ability, and who now remains among us. There is no controlling reason why Judge Whitman should not be put in the line of political promotion. He is a man of mature years and wide experience. His record as one of the Judges of our Supreme Court is not contaminated by any undue leanings toward corporations. He is a man who has that self respect which in any high office would insure something more than mere subserviences to the exactions of the money power. He would think more of making an honorable record than all other things put together if he were once entrusted with the Chief Magistracy of this state.

Whitman did not pursue the governorship and died in 1885 at the age of fifty-seven. The Nevada Supreme Court opened a special session on September 14, 1885, to honor him. Chief Justice Charles Belknap reflected that "some associated with him upon the bench, and all enjoyed his personal friendship." Justice Belknap expressed high regard for Justice Whitman's public and private character, noting that he "attained the highest position in his profession because of industry, learning, and unsullied integrity." He further said:

> As a lawyer he presented legal propositions with precision, clearness and candor. His arguments and briefs were prepared with learning and ability, and greatly aided the court in the examination of the questions to be adjudicated.
>
> Upon his accession to the bench, he brought to this court the qualities that distinguished him at the bar. Of broad experience, great quickness in the apprehension of the material facts of a case, learned

in the legal principles and decided cases, and of ready and accurate judgment, he made a most valuable member of the court. To his associates he was uniformly kind and courteous, and in consultations his ready knowledge greatly lightened their labors. He was an able, learned and upright judge, and his opinions, to be found in our published reports, were the result of his honest convictions of right.

In private life he was an example worthy of imitation. His refined taste and attractive manners, united with a pure character and a generous manly nature, made him admired and loved. His considerate tenderness as a husband, his kindness as a father, his devotion to those to whom he was bound by the endearing relations of domestic life, were charming traits of his character. Without intruding upon their grief, we tender them our deep sympathy in this affliction, and commend them to the consolation to be found in the honorable life and exalted character of the husband and father they mourn.

John Garber

1870–1872

Justice Garber was a student of the law, and his short service on the Nevada Supreme Court is a brief snapshot of his long and preeminent legal career. John Garber was born in Virginia in 1833; tragically, his mother died when he was eleven, shortly after giving birth to her fourth child. Garber studied mathematics, Latin, chemistry, natural philosophy, and modern languages at the University of Virginia. He briefly taught school, then worked for two years as a civil engineer during construction of the Virginia Central Railroad before shifting careers to study law. He was admitted to the Virginia State Bar in 1853.

Garber moved to San Francisco in 1857 and began practicing law with his uncle, Joseph G. Baldwin. He soon became a part-time justice of the peace in Santa Cruz and ran for district attorney but was defeated "owing largely to his southern sympathies."

In 1858, Garber moved to Nevada City in Northern California, where he developed a successful law practice. He argued twenty-four appeals in the California Supreme Court between 1860 and 1863. Despite success in California, he moved to the Nevada Territory in 1863 presumably because of the unbounded opportunities for mineral wealth and associated litigation. In Austin, he created a successful mining and property law practice and became a vocal supporter of statehood. The *Reese River Reveille* reported that one of his public speeches for statehood was "forcible, eloquent and exhaustive. No report that we are able to give it could do it justice."

John Garber

He relocated to San Francisco in 1867, only to return to Nevada in 1870. The reasons for his moves are unknown now, but his move to California could have been influenced by the mining depression, and his return to Nevada was likely influenced by his desire to run for the Nevada Supreme Court. He was elected on the Democratic ticket in November 1870. While he was recognized for his abilities and character, his opponents emphasized his politics. One newspaper wrote: "Mr. Garber is a Southern man by birth, a Democrat now; and during the war of the rebellion, a most bitter and uncompromising secessionist." Whether Garber's Southern sympathies were accurate or exaggerated, he was elected and served twenty-two months before resigning in 1872, reportedly to earn more money in private practice.

A prolific author during his short time on the court (writing thirty-eight opinions), he examined a broad range of substantive topics; but his passion for the law is most evident when he wrote about the integrity of the trial process—whether it be the judge's legal instructions, sanctity of the jury, role of circumstantial evidence, or power of cross examination.

Justice Garber did not inject his personality or personal sentiments into the opinions he wrote; his neutral writing style reflected research, logic, and reasoning. In one appeal, the issue was whether a new trial was warranted because, "during the time the action was on trial, and before the jury retired to deliberate, the jurors, while under charge of an officer for the purpose of viewing the ground, went into a saloon and there drank liquors at the expense of the defendant." Garber wrote at length about the ideal jury and the necessity of preventing "improper intercourse or undue influence. . . . The honor of the bar and the perfect purity of a jury alike demand of their entire separation in their personal and social intercourse whilst trials are progressing." After examining common law rules protecting the jury, through various concepts of sequestration, he continued, "and there is no hardship or undue severity in [these rules]. If the prevailing party is put to the expense and vexation of a second trial, he can blame no one but himself. It is simply enjoined upon him to refrain from intermeddling with the jury; to keep aloof from them during the progress of the trial, and to see that his attorneys and agents do the same." He then wrote: "Of course, we impute no want of fairness or impartiality to the learned judge before whom the case was tried. Such inadvertence as this evidently will sometimes occur in the hurry of a trial, with whatever purity and ability justice is administered."

After his brief service on the Nevada Supreme Court, Garber returned to California, founded a successful law firm, and was involved in significant cases for more than forty years. He also continued to practice law periodically in Nevada. He presented thirty-nine appeals in the California and Nevada Supreme Courts. In 1899, a private organization conducted a statewide survey to identify the "twelve ablest members" of the San Francisco Bar then living. It concluded: "Judge Garber's vote exceeded the combined strength of all the other gentlemen named, and was nearly one-half of the total returned. . . . The qualities of mind displayed by Judge Garber in forensic discussion are pre-eminently those of strength and clearness. He seeks to convince by his learning and logic—not to dazzle by rhetorical pyrotechnics. His legal learning is extensive and accurate."

A California Supreme Court justice described Justice Garber in the survey report: "He has been and is now a great general reader of literature, history, poetry and the leading works of fiction. His conversation is bright, interesting and instructive.... He seems to have explored the fountains of the law, as well as its streams and rivulets. Such is his knowledge of the law, that to solve the intricacies of a case is to him no difficult matter."

His reputation extended to Washington, DC. Garber was friendly with President Roosevelt, who appointed him in 1904 to the Panama Canal Commission. But at seventy-one, he declined the appointment. Shortly before his death at seventy-five, a San Francisco newspaper published an article about him under the headline: "Former Justice of Supreme Court and Noted Lawyer Declared to Be Dying: Associated in Every Important Case in California Courts in Last Forty Years." He died on December 3, 1908, and was buried at the Mountain View Cemetery in Oakland. A portion of his residential property (thirteen acres), now known as the John Garber Park, remains available for public use.

The Nevada Supreme Court published a memorial to Justice Garber, writing in part:

> The opinions rendered by Judge GARBER ... show a perfect understanding of the issues made by the pleadings, the evidence to sustain them shown by the records, and the alleged errors brought to this court for adjudication.... They are the results of a thorough legal education, improved by practice and experience, and a perusal of them will convince the reader that Judge GARBER decided no case without diligent study, and with the sole purpose of doing justice between the parties and upholding those legal principles which make the law respected as a science, and which gives this court the high standing it holds as a guide to the people in their business relations.
>
> Judge GARBER's reputation as a lawyer will rest safely upon his preeminence as a practitioner of his profession.... Blessed by nature with a superb physique, capable of intense prolonged labor without apparent fatigue, he brought to the service of his clients and to the courts ... a well-trained mind and such industry in performing his duties as has never been surpassed.
>
> He seemed in the preparation of his cases to challenge every proposition and to submit them to a logical analysis, which was never

satisfied short of demonstration. His arguments were addressed to the reason and not to the passions or prejudices of his hearers, and, from the beginning of his professional career to the end, his modesty, until overcome by the heat of debate, was such as to amount almost to timidity. . . .

Socially he was easy of approach, a delightful companion, and a steadfast friend. In his youth he was the hope of his elders in the profession, and this hope was not disappointed, as in later years he was justly considered as an ornament to his profession, and an example worthy to be followed.

It is difficult to discern his personality through his written record on the Nevada Supreme Court. However, the court's memorial provides a glimpse into his style and passion: he was modest, *"until overcome by the heat of the debate."* One must wonder about the occasional events underlying this assertion. In total, however, it appears that Justice Garber was able to rise above his occasional heated debates to earn his well-deserved reputation as an exemplary lawyer and judge.

Charles Henry Belknap

1872–1874; 1881–1905

JUSTICE BELKNAP'S CAREER ILLUSTRATES THE importance of substantive merit and personal relationships. Charles Henry Belknap was born in 1841 in New York, and his immediate ancestors were described as "pioneer American stock" from which "he inherited sterling virtues and love of country." He attended both public and private schools and graduated from the Polytechnic Institute in Brooklyn. At age twenty-four he moved to Nevada, where he practiced mining law in Austin and Virginia City. He was law partners with constitutional convention champion Charles DeLong and served as mayor of Virginia City until he moved to Carson City to work as Governor L. R. Bradley's personal secretary.

Belknap's association with Governor Bradley was fortuitous and life-changing. In 1872, Bradley appointed Belknap, then only thirty-one, to the Nevada Supreme Court to fill the vacancy created by Justice Garber's resignation. The next year, Justice Belknap married Bradley's daughter at the governor's mansion.

Justice Belknap campaigned to retain his seat in 1874 but was defeated by Justice Warner Earll. Undeterred, he successfully sought election 1881 and served until January 1, 1905. He was a justice of the Nevada Supreme Court for twenty-six years.

In 1881, the Belknaps purchased a home in Carson City at 1206 N. Nevada Street, which is listed on the National Register of Historic Places as the Belknap House. An 1897 photograph of Justice and Mrs. Belknap in front of their home was displayed in the second-floor hall gallery of the state capitol for decades and now reposes at the Nevada Historical Society.

Justice Belknap died in San Francisco on October 6, 1926, at eighty-five. The Nevada Supreme Court memorial reads, in part:

> A review of the many decisions written by Judge Belknap reveals a conciseness of expression and a lucidity of thought that challenges the admiration of all lovers of unadorned truth. In no instance did he attempt to embellish either statements of fact or declarations of juridical principles with flights of rhetoric. While his opinions were almost laconic in brevity, yet they clearly and correctly applied all of the necessary legal principles essential for a proper solution of the controverted issues. His integrity was spotless and his courage was unwavering. He did not hesitate on several occasions to write opinions running counter to popular currents of public sentiment. On the bench he knew no friends and off the bench he knew no enemies. In private life he was always an urbane, courteous, and sympathetic gentleman and friend, and in domestic life he was an ideal husband and father.

The themes of courage, courtesy, and brevity were repeated by others who memorialized Justice Belknap. US Attorney Sardis Summerfield wrote that Belknap was a mentor to many newly admitted lawyers and ever cheerful, with a "happy faculty of condensation." Belknap "could write more law in one sentence than most judges could in a page," and his decisions demonstrate his ability to "present in concise, brief language the law which was virtually decisive of the case." Further, he went "against the current popular belief" in several cases and "other cases in which he rose to that high degree of judicial fairness, disregarding what might be the evanescent reasons of popular sentiment and adhering to the well-determined principles of the law."

His daughter Caroline Belknap Brown submitted a letter to the Nevada Supreme Court after her father's death introducing a personal element of her father's character:

> Despite father's long service upon the bench, it was his family life rather than his public life that really counted. There never was a truer gentlemen[sic]. In all his life I never knew of his saying, doing, or

thinking an unfair or unkind thing of anybody. Always gentle and always kind, during the last years of his life father was very feeble, and at times seemed to know very little, but there never was a time when he was not showing kindness in abundance.

Left to right: Charles Henry Belknap, Michael Augustus Murphy, and Adolphus Leigh Fitzgerald

Thomas Porter Hawley

1872–1890

THOMAS PORTER HAWLEY WAS BORN in 1830 in Indiana, where he remained throughout childhood. In 1852, he crossed the plains to California and lived in Placerville before moving to Grass Valley in 1853. He was a miner between 1852 and 1855, served as Nevada County (Grass Valley) clerk from 1855 to 1866, and began the practice of law in 1857. He married in 1858, and all three of his children were born in Nevada City. After serving two years as district attorney in Nevada County (elected on the Union Republican ticket), he first moved to Hamilton, Nevada, in 1868, then relocated to Eureka in 1870. There, "by his industry and close attention to business, he secured a first-class practice." A historian described him:

> As a lawyer he . . . went into Court fully prepared to try his causes intelligently, never trusting, as is too often the case to what someone has neatly phrased "the sublimity of luck." He was always clear-headed, quick at discovering the weak points of an opponent, and with tact to present his own strong points in the most favorable light. As an advocate, his manner was earnest and impressive. He always made his client's cause his own.

Hawley was elected to the Nevada Supreme Court when Justice Lewis retired in 1872. After eighteen years, President Benjamin Harrison appointed him to the US District Court. His nomination was preceded by a joint resolution of the Nevada Senate, urging his appointment

Thomas Porter Hawley

and describing him as a judge with "high integrity, eminent ability and undoubted honesty." Beginning in 1895, he was assigned to sit with the federal Circuit Court of Appeals in San Francisco.

Justice Hawley considered resigning from the federal bench in 1902 to run for the US Senate. His possible candidacy received a mixed response, as one newspaper wrote:

> His entire manhood days have been devoted to law and he has never, we understand it, held a legislative position in his life. . . . His judicial career has been an honorable and successful one, and when he chooses to retire to private life he would leave as enviable a record as was ever achieved by any retiring Judge on the Pacific or Atlantic coast.
>
> We are confident that Judge Hawley's best and most sincere friends of whatever political party, will regret, if, in the autumn of his days, he should conclude to abandon the channel in which his life's current has run, to enter a contest for a position which if attained would not add to the honor of his former career, nor afford him such pleasure in his remaining years as he has experienced from the performance of the duties for which he was, and still is, so eminently fitted, and which he cannot expect to enjoy at his age in an entirely different and unfamiliar branch of public service.

He elected not to run for the Senate and retired from the federal bench on June 30, 1906, having served more than thirty-four years as a judge. He died on October 17, 1907, at age seventy-three.

The Nevada Supreme Court memorialized Justice Hawley on December 2, 1907. After hearing several oral tributes, Chief Justice Coleman said, "As with loved ones in our immediate families, we are never ready to lose our eminent citizens who must go as inevitably as all others. It seems but yet yesterday they were with us in the strength of manhood and mental vigor. In the course of nature we are here this brief day, to-morrow we will be gone, and others will have taken our places." He continued:

> Their greatest fame and most enduring monument remains from what they did in furtherance of justice, and for the general good in fitting to the jurisprudence of this developing State the common law, which, although it is based on the wisdom and experience of ages in other countries before it was transplanted here, yet is progressive and elastic enough to meet and cover the new conditions and necessities which arise in the affairs of men. Their exemplary and industrious careers and self-acquired success remind us forcibly of what may be accomplished by right living, close application, and honest endeavor, and of the opportunities afforded under this great government and a beneficent Creator. . . .
>
> *Be It Resolved,* That we most deeply deplore the death of one who was not only our professional brother, but a just, upright, and able judge, worthy in every way of our honor, respect, and esteem.
>
> *Resolved,* That while keenly sensible of the loss we have sustained, we nevertheless feel a mournful pleasure in knowing that our deceased brother and friend had more than lived out the allotted age of man, and that, although he had personally gone from our midst, both his private life and his public career will be a source of inspiration and a beacon star of hope for untold generations to come.

Warner Earll

1875–1876

WARNER EARLL WAS BORN IN New York on January 18, 1816, and moved to Wisconsin as a young man. He was elected justice of the peace and served in the Wisconsin legislature. In 1849, he "followed the tide of immigration" to California. He lived in Red Bluff for ten years and was elected district attorney and judge in Tehama County. He later moved to Elko, Nevada, and was one of two lawyers admitted to practice in the newly created Eleventh Judicial District in 1869. Little is known about his practice in Elko, but he appeared as counsel in two appeals before the Nevada Supreme Court.

In 1874, the Republican Party selected Earll to run for the Nevada Supreme Court against the newly appointed Democrat Charles Belknap. Against Belknap's youth and familial connections, Earll, who was supported by the railroads and other commercial interests, won by a mere 580 votes. During his tenure, Justice Earll wrote thirteen opinions on the subjects of mining, corporate, constitutional, criminal, and divorce law. His opinions are direct and free of personal style; they follow a common format that reveals his thorough research and dispassionate analysis. His statement of statutory interpretation is still applicable in modern times: "It is a settled rule that several statutes relating to the same subject-matter are to be taken together and comprised in the construction of them, and, if possible, they are to be so construed as to give to each a reasonable effect, agreeable to the intention of the legislature which passed them."

After a single term on the Nevada Supreme Court, he briefly practiced law in San Francisco before moving to Arizona to represent the Southern Pacific Railroad. Ten years later he returned to California and formed a law partnership with his son.

One historian described him:

> He was simple in his tastes, quiet and unassuming in his demeanor. His character as a man and as a judge was above reproach. He was absolutely free from any pretension of superiority over his fellow-men, and was ever ready to consult with his associates and to discuss, with great candor and fairness, all questions upon which any difference of opinion might be expressed. He readily grasped the main points of a case and his general knowledge of the principles of the law enable him to give a clear, comprehensive, and convincing statement of the controlling questions which, in his judgment, ought to govern the decision in the case at hand.
>
> Without any pride of opinion his desire was to reach a conclusion founded on the settled principles of the law, and based upon the equity and justice of a particular case. When convinced of the correctness of his position he was positive and unchangeable.

Earll died unexpectedly on January 10, 1888, at the age of seventy-one. The *San Luis Obispo Tribune* reported about his death:

> The community was greatly shocked . . . by the report of the sudden death from heart disease, of Judge Warner Earll. Seated in his office in consultation with his client . . . apparently in his usual health, without premonition death called him. He leaned back in his chair and became insensible. Kind hands supported him, friends and physicians were hastily summoned but the end had come and in a few moments the last flickering evidences of life ceased. It was the close of a long career of usefulness, of the record of a blameless life. A man of profound learning, eminent in his profession, distinguished in public life, and greatly loved and esteemed in every social and private relation, full of years and honors, our friend has entered a new life, meeting the great change, just as he himself had in fact indicated he would have desired it, instantly and painlessly, "in the twinkling of an eye." With his hand upon the plow, he sank down in the furrow.

The Nevada Supreme Court memorialized Justice Earll six days after his death: "Although his term of judicial service was brief, and the number of opinions written by him limited, he remained long enough and wrote enough to impress the judiciary and bar of this state very favorably, both as to his legal learning and judicial ability, as well as to his high personal and moral integrity, and secured for himself a permanent abiding place in the regard and esteem of his associates." After other accolades, the court concluded: "Whether as an attorney, judge or citizen he conscientiously sought to do that which he believed to be right, and around his memory there will ever remain, to those who knew him well, a fame that no amount of financial success, so eagerly sought by most men, can give."

WILLIAM H. BEATTY

1875–1880 (Nevada Supreme Court); 1888–1914 (California Supreme Court)

JUSTICE BEATTY HAS THE RARE distinction of being the son of a Nevada Supreme Court justice and serving as chief justice of both the Nevada and California Supreme Courts. His place among jurists is legendary.

Born in 1838, William H. Beatty spent his formative years in public schools in Ohio, before moving to California in 1853. When not in school, Beatty nurtured his love for the outdoors: "When I was a boy I lived in the country and liked hunting and fishing better than anything else. To do one or the other was by long odds my first choice whenever I had a whole day, or even a part of a day to myself. If for any reason fishing and hunting were both out of the question (on account of bad weather or a crippled gun, or exhausted ammunition), I cannot remember any other sport or occupation that was a second choice. It was anything to get through the day, and generally it was a dull day at best."

For two years starting in 1855, Beatty put away his fishing pole and gun to pursue his university education in Virginia. He soon returned to California to study law in his father's office. Under the guidance of his father, H. O. Beatty (who served as one of the first three Nevada Supreme Court justices), Beatty was admitted to the California Bar in 1861. Father and son practiced together in Sacramento until 1863, when they both moved to Nevada. Beatty explained, "Nevada was then in the height of the fame of its marvelous mining discoveries, and drew men from all parts of the world," and "in those days the legal profession had fewer representative practitioners in that state than at present, and the people were not slow to recognize the caliber of the young lawyer in their midst."

Beatty served as city attorney in Austin, and in 1864 was elected to the district court bench in the same election his father was elected to the supreme court. A newspaper reported a few weeks before the election:

> One of the most important of the offices to be filled . . . is that of District Judge. . . . It is, therefore, seen that it is of great importance, and its occupant should be a man of experience, a man above suspicion or reproach, who has made the law his study, not only for a livelihood, but for the eminent position it may bring him. Such is W. H. Beatty; a young man of superior talent, improved by a rare education, deep study and devotion to his profession. He is, at present, City Attorney of Austin, and in that capacity has acquired a reputation for ability and energy of which he may well be proud.

Beatty was elected, and he presided in the district court during a time of transition from territory to state. One case before him reveals how emotionally difficult judicial work can be. A twenty-one-year-old man named Rufus Anderson was convicted of murder and sentenced to die. He sought retrial by arguing he did not commit the murder with premeditation. As Judge Beatty announced his decision denying retrial, Anderson's mother made an "emotional outburst" in court. After pausing for a moment, Beatty remarked that Anderson "enjoyed to the amplest extent all of the rights which the humane laws of the State guarantee to those who are charged with criminal offenses." He then encouraged Anderson to "devote himself to the preparation he must make for the death which was so soon to overtake him." Anderson was hanged, but only with difficulty in the process that must have been personally agonizing to Beatty:

> On October 30, 1868, Rufe was led to the gallows in Austin. . . . The condemned man said a few words to the crowd, had the noose tightened around his neck, and was dropped through the trap. But the rope was not secured to the gallows and Anderson landed on his feet with the noose flopping down his back. Rufe again was led up the 13 steps to the gallows floor. The rope was again secured to the wooden arm, and Rufe dropped through the trap. Amazingly, the noose slipped and Anderson landed on the ground. Stunned,

almost insensible, Anderson was strapped to the chair, and on the third try was finally hanged as prescribed by law.

Beatty was elected to the Nevada Supreme Court in 1874. He enjoyed wide support from the press during his campaign, with one newspaper reporting, "We have had a long and intimate acquaintance with Judge Beatty, and can bear testimony that he is a man of marked ability, incorruptible integrity, and whose judicial rulings were always dictated by an evident desire to deal out impartial justice to all who had business in his court."

Justice Beatty served one term, being defeated for reelection in 1880. The campaign was bruising, and his decision to reverse a murder conviction in a high-profile case involving the death of a police officer may have determined the outcome. He then returned to private practice in California and enjoyed a successful career in Sacramento. He was counsel in thirty-three appeals to the California Supreme Court during the 1880s. He was described as "reserved yet pleasant, kind but not demonstrative, learned, studious and temperate, his opinions always challenge contradiction. . . . [He is a] convivial, interesting conversationalist . . . [who] is plain and neat in his dress and always obliging."

In 1887 he was elected to the California Supreme Court and served until 1914, including twenty-five years as the chief justice, producing an immense catalog of work: "His opinions . . . are to be found in ninety volumes . . . covering a period of distinguished service unequaled in judicial history." Aware of his failing health, he died of a heart attack on August 4, 1915, at age seventy-seven.

One event from 1899 reveals a side of Justice Beatty that cannot be gleaned from his judicial decisions. At age sixty-one, while serving as chief justice of the California Supreme Court, he returned to Austin, Nevada, to join in Fourth of July festivities. As reported, "In the early days of Austin a number of fun-loving citizens of that then flourishing camp inaugurated the custom of holding burlesque Fourth of July celebrations after the regular exercises of the day were over. Upon this occasion Judge W. H. Beatty, now Chief Justice in California, arrayed in female apparel and representing Miss Susan B. Anthony, acted as President of the day." Beatty's lighthearted appearance reveals an affable personality under the formal robes of a distinguished career.

The Nevada and California Supreme Courts both memorialized Justice Beatty. The California memorial begins: "The death of no other man in the State of California could have moved its legal profession so profoundly as it was moved by the recent death of the revered Chief Justice, William H. Beatty." After reciting the highlights of his life and career, the court wrote: "He feared no man, and he never failed to meet unflinchingly every danger. Throughout his long life he knew but one fear, and that was the fear of doing an injustice to his fellow man. His judgments sprang from his convictions alone, unswayed by popular clamor, uninfluenced by thought of consequences."

The California court continued: "His opinions are the works of a master, not only in their logic and in their evidences of profound learning, but also in the literary quality which marks the cultured scholar." Justice Beatty "put honor before opportunity; he revered the law and strove to make it always the instrument of justice; he loved his friends; he feared not his foes, and he dedicated his life to the highest service of the Commonwealth."

The California State Bar joined in the memorial:

> The opinions of Chief Justice Beatty are in general characterized by clear statement and cogent reasoning from legal rules and adjudicated cases. They command the respect of those who are compelled, sometimes, to dissent from the conclusions drawn.... His description of mining processes is a delight to the reader, who has a general knowledge of the subject, but who is yet not an "expert" in that line; while his statement and application of the law have been questioned only by those whose misfortune it has been to be on the losing side.

Despite his prolific career, Justice Beatty did not live to contribute to his memoirs, a fact the California Supreme Court lamented: "It was the hope of those who knew him best that years and health might be vouchsafed him, after the close of his judicial career, in which he might be induced to put his recollections into permanent form. That hope has failed, but his genial tones, his anecdotes of the brave days of old, and his attractive personality are abiding treasures to those who will continue to count amongst their most cherished memories the fact that he was their friend."

The Nevada Supreme Court noted its "pride in the fact that this State first recognized and honored his high abilities both as a lawyer and a judge." Chief Justice Talbot wrote: "His industry kept pace with his capacity, and his integrity was never questioned. Possessed in a high degree of the judicial temperament and that impartiality which holds the scales of justice in equal poise, his decisions were always rendered with a view to the right and to the advancement of the welfare and happiness of his fellow men."

The Nevada Supreme Court's assessment of Justice Beatty may be inspirational for all: "After the years of honor, he went to rest, leaving behind him a record which should be an example and an inspiration to men of his profession and a guide to good citizenship."

Orville Rinaldo Leonard

1877–1889

ORVILLE RINALDO LEONARD WAS BORN in Gaysville, Vermont, in 1834, and reared on a farm. After attending college for three years (sources put him at both Randolph Academy and Dartmouth College), he left for California in 1860 before completing his degree. On arrival in Marysville, he began studying law and was admitted to the California Bar in 1863. A local newspaper wrote, "He is a young man of studious habits, and has made good use of his time and talents." He relocated to Humboldt County, Nevada, and was elected district attorney in 1866. Two years later, the politically minded Republican Leonard traveled to the 1868 Chicago convention at which President Grant was nominated, and during the same trip went to Vermont to be married. He and his wife did not have children.

He returned to the private practice of law in 1869 and was elected to the district court bench in 1872. He was elected to the Nevada Supreme Court in 1876 to succeed Justice Warner Earll, and reelected in 1882. While Justice Leonard was a prolific author during his twelve years on the court, little is recorded about his personal life. For unknown reasons, the Nevada Supreme Court did not publish a memorial after his death. He was described by one historian:

> He is a married man and is happy and contented when in the bustle of his own family. A desire to do right and the strictest impartiality, based upon a thorough knowledge of every subject upon which he renders a decision, are the leading characteristics of the man. He

looks quite young and has a temperate, mild disposition but a determination and will that eminently becomes one in so high a place. Very neat and tasty in dress, born of educated and pleasant society, he adds much to the attractions of the state capital.

Justice Leonard appears to have been religiously moderate for the time: "In religious faith he believes in the Overruling Providence, and that we cannot escape punishment for wrong doing, but in no other sense [did] he believe in eternal punishment."

A newspaper report during his successful 1882 reelection campaign provides some insight into his judicial character:

> [Justice Leonard is] winning golden opinions everywhere by his urbanity of manner and the excellent record he has made while occupying the bench. His name adds a dignity and power to the Republican ticket that is excelled by no other candidate. As to his race against Col. M. N. Stone there will be no unkindness. Each candidate respects the many personal and professional good qualities of the other, and the appeal to the voters will be upon merit. The judicial campaign will be of that nature which ought to characterize such a contest. The office for which they contend is the most honorable within the gift of the people.

Leonard and his wife lived in Elko after his public service ended, but he left Nevada after his wife's death on March 4, 1890. He spent time in Utah, Florida, New York, and Vermont. He married again in 1882 but died within a month while still on an extended wedding trip. He was fifty-nine.

Michael Augustus Murphy

1889–1895

BORN IN NEW YORK IN 1837, Michael Augustus Murphy grew accustomed to hard work in difficult conditions. The son of an influential farmer and county commissioner who was "a man in whom the most implicit trust was placed," he moved to Illinois with his family when he was young. He attended school during the harsh Illinois winters and worked on the family farm during the summers. At age sixteen, he joined his brother in California to engage in farming, freighting, and placer mining in Trinity County. Like so many others pursuing mineral wealth, he moved to the Nevada Territory in 1863, settling in Aurora, to work in the mines. He also began studying law.

Five years later, he was elected Esmeralda County assessor, beginning a public career bolstered by his reputation: "His ability and sterling character marked him for prominence in his adopted state." He was elected district attorney shortly after his admission to the Nevada Bar, and in 1878 he defeated the incumbent to become Nevada's fifth attorney general.

In 1882, Murphy was elected to the district court bench in Esmeralda County, where he served four years. He then turned to private practice for two years before winning election to the Nevada Supreme Court. After a single term, Justice Murphy ran for reelection as a Republican but was defeated by M. S. Bonnifield, who was the nominee of the Silver Party, "which was then all-powerful" in Nevada. (The justices still campaigned with party affiliation, and several were swept out of office when political parties rose and fell with shifting public sentiments.)

Justice Murphy's judicial career is unique because he returned to the trial bench after his service on the appellate court. Instead of retiring or returning to private practice, he was elected to the First Judicial District Court, then comprising Douglas, Esmerelda, Lyon, Ormsby, and Storey Counties. "The fact that in this last election he was the only one of his ticket to be elected demonstrates his personal popularity and that the people of his district have unlimited confidence in his ability, judgment and fairness of action." He retired from public service in 1907 and resumed the private practice of law in Carson City. He died two years later on October 26, 1909.

The Nevada Supreme Court memorialized Justice Murphy on April 30, 1910, noting his long career of "almost 50 years was to bring to him among the highest professional and public honors that the friendship and devotion of a people could confer." While he was "not an orator, and neither did he possess what may be termed a scintillating mind," he "owned a firm and steady intellect, unfailing industry, and a confidence that loyal service has its reward, and with these attributes he won success and died honored and loved by thousands." Justice Murphy was "characterized by a sincere devotion to the cause of charity," and "it [was] doubtful whether the State ever afforded a more striking example of kindly benevolence." He focused his thoughts "on those he loved, and his countless acts of comforting kindness, sometimes at great personal sacrifice, [came] as a sweet and noble heritage to those he left behind."

Murphy survived his wife by seventeen years. Perhaps his greatest tribute is the observation that, "blessed with success in his profession and with domestic happiness, he died looking back upon the successful years that devotion to duty had won."

Rensselaer R. Bigelow

1890–1897

Justice Rensselaer Bigelow's imprint on Nevada law is mostly known through his involvement in a high-profile murder case tried before him as a district judge. On January 1, 1888, Miles Faucett entered the home of Josiah and Elizabeth Potts in Carlin, seeking payment on a debt before the Potts moved to Wyoming. Faucett never left the home alive. Eleven months later, his partially mutilated body was found in the cellar of the Potts residence, and the Potts were charged with murder. Denying the accusation, Josiah Potts argued Faucett had committed suicide because of his salacious misbehavior with the Potts's young daughter. The case would prove historic for the state and solidify the reputation of Bigelow, who imposed a sentence that the Potts were "to be hanged by the neck until dead."

The death sentence was controversial because many "violently opposed hanging a woman, especially one convicted on circumstantial evidence." Perhaps most poignantly, the opposition to the death sentence included Bigelow himself. Evidently, he had issued the sentence because the law compelled him to do so, despite his personal reservations about hanging a woman.

Nonetheless, the convictions and punishment were affirmed by the Nevada Supreme Court. Thereafter, Justice Bigelow, the Elko County sheriff, and three hundred Elko citizens unsuccessfully petitioned the Board of Pardons to commute Elizabeth Potts's sentence to life imprisonment. She was the second and last person to be legally executed in Elko County, and the only woman executed in Nevada. She was also the first woman to be legally executed in the entire Pacific Coast region.

Aside from the Potts case, little is known about Justice Bigelow's personal life or professional service. He was born in 1848 in Essex County, New York, and admitted to the Nevada Bar in 1872. He practiced law in Elko until his appointment to the district court in 1882. In November 1890, he was elected to the Nevada Supreme Court and appointed to the court a month later (before his elected term began) to fill the vacancy created by Justice Hawley's resignation.

Bigelow remained engaged in Republican Party politics during his judicial service and was interested in bimetallism. When serving as chief justice, he wrote a letter to the editor of the *Reno Gazette* arguing against the free coinage of silver. His letter was republished by the Home Market Club of Boston and received considerable national attention.

He retired from the Nevada Supreme Court after one term and moved to San Francisco to practice law. He left his law practice because of failing health in 1906; he died in 1907 at the age of fifty-nine. The Nevada Supreme Court memorialized Justice Bigelow by writing that "in his professional and private life [he] exemplified the highest type of patriotic citizenship, of the skilled and honest lawyer; in his official life, of the able and upright judge; and his domestic life, of the loving husband and father."

McKaskia Stearns Bonnifield

1895–1901

In 1875, before emerging as an author and advocate for Native Americans, Sarah Winnemucca was charged with assault with intent to do great bodily harm. The "knife by which the cutting was alleged to have been done" was a penknife. Winnemucca explained that she reacted defensively when the victim attempted to touch her without permission. She turned to her friend, M. S. Bonnifield, a well-known lawyer and friend to Native Americans, who would be elected twenty years later to the Nevada Supreme Court. Bonnifield submitted the small knife to an expert for examination and subpoenaed more than six possible witnesses, including medical doctors and "prominent church members." On reviewing the defense case, the district attorney dismissed the charge. Bonnifield's vigorous defense demonstrated his commitment to a rule of law available to all.

One of fifteen children in his family, McKaskia Stearns Bonnifield was born in 1832. At the age of three, his family moved from West Virginia to Iowa; within three months of the move, both his father and mother died. Always known by his initials, M. S. returned east to attend Allegheny College in Pennsylvania, and served as president of Richards College for one year following his graduation.

After marrying in Pennsylvania in 1855, he moved to Kansas and was admitted to the Kansas Bar by 1856. An active member of the Free-Soil Party, he was soon elected to the Kansas State Senate. In 1861 he traveled to Red Bluff, California, and was instrumental in establishing a high school at which he was the teacher. In 1862, he moved to Unionville, the seat of Humboldt County, Nevada Territory. He opened a law office and enjoyed what was called a "large and lucrative practice," though Mark Twain, who lived in Unionville briefly, described the town as "eleven cabins and a liberty-pole." He was counsel in forty-four appeals to the Nevada Supreme Court. Fittingly, when the interstate railroad was completed, he moved to Winnemucca, the city named after his famous client's family.

He returned to legislative service in the Nevada State Senate between 1868 and 1872, "and by energy, wisdom, and ability made himself a leading factor in that body, in all occasions displaying a patriotic interest, not only on behalf of his constituents and locality, but for the entire State." He was described as careless in his dress and "was fair game for newspaper political comment and cartoonists," but was respected for his political views—including supporting women's suffrage.

In 1884, he was appointed district attorney to complete the term of J. H. Windle, who had died in office. He magnanimously paid half his salary to Windle's widow.

Always active in politics, he was a presidential elector in 1892. He and his two elector colleagues traveled to Washington, DC, to cast their electoral votes. In a gesture demonstrating the importance of their mission, they engraved their ballots on silver plates. Two years later, he was elected to the Nevada Supreme Court, where he served a single term. A newspaper reported after his election that Justice Bonnifield "has practiced law in this State for thirty-two years, and is recognized by the profession as one of the ablest members of the bar in the State. He knows the law and will administer justice impartially."

Justice Bonnifield was a prolific author, writing more than eighty opinions during his six years on the court. When he retired in 1900 a newspaper reported that "Carson suffers a loss when we lose such citizens and Winnemucca is ahead by a long margin."

Justice Bonnifield's wife died in 1887, and he later remarried Nellie Lovelock, whose father founded the town of Lovelock. In 1912 he was the July 4th orator in Unionville, where he had been the July 4th orator fifty years earlier in 1862. He died on July 14, 1913, at the age of seventy-nine. He was memorialized by the Nevada Supreme Court on October 6, 1913. The court described Justice Bonnifield's "entire life [as] one of industrious and unusual activity, not confined to his legal business alone, but identified with every industry of our State. He was an able writer, and contributed greatly to literature touching the subjects of paramount interest to our State."

Nevada Supreme Court justice William Massey added his own reflections to the court's memorial, writing there was no other lawyer in the state who knew Justice Bonnifield "as intimately and as well" as he did because they occupied adjoining chambers. He described three traits of character that "younger members of the profession and the people who did not know him could well emulate." These traits were "unbounded charity—not from the purse, but the broader Christian charity spoken of in the New Testament." He recollected that "no matter what was said; no matter how bitter the saying was . . . Judge Bonnifield never complained, and when his attention was called to unkind criticisms and unkind things that were said and done, with a smile he stated that life was too short to be annoyed or to suffer annoyance with matters of so little importance as those things were." The second character trait worthy of emulation was "discharge of duty." Justice Bonnifield was "early to his office; he was late to leave his office . . . and, there being nothing but a door between his chambers and my chambers, I saw him nearly every hour of the day; and I have tried . . . to remember an occasion when [he] was idle . . . and I am unable at this time to recall a single instance when I have entered those chambers, either on business or in a social way, and did not find [him] bringing to the discharge of his duties of the office of a Justice of this Court his constant time and his constant energy." Finally, Justice Bonnifield had a "clear, clean, analytical mind." He brought to his "judicial functions a profound knowledge of the law, a clear, calm, and analyzing intellect, unbiased by fear or favor."

WILLIAM A. MASSEY

1896–1902

BORN IN OHIO IN 1856, William A. Massey and his family moved to Illinois when he was nine. During these early years, Massey's father earned his reputation as a distinguished Civil War veteran. Fighting for the Union Army, he served as both a frontline soldier and rear-echelon physician.

After studying at the "common schools" of Union Christian College and Indiana Asbury (now DePauw University), Massey was admitted to practice law in Indiana in 1877 before moving to San Diego in 1879. After one year he relocated to the mining town of Tuscarora in Elko County where he mined and practiced law. His time in Elko County was a proving ground for the characteristics that would be important for the remainder of his career: "These years were trying ones, and called for the exercise of tenacity of purpose, resourcefulness in adversity, fidelity and fortitude, such as Judge Massey possessed in marked measure. For these were hard years, involving personal privations and discomforts; loss of fortune through the vicissitudes of the mining business; and long periods of the closest economy, devoted to grinding manual toil in the depths of the earth." Yet, "out of it emerged the man whom the citizens of the State never ceased thereafter to honor."

His service to the state began when he was elected to the Nevada Assembly in 1892, continued when he was appointed Elko County district attorney in 1894, and culminated with his election to the Nevada Supreme Court in 1896. He returned to private practice in Reno after serving only one term.

In 1910, Massey was one of the Republican Party's possible candidates for governor. Despite the support of mining magnates George Nixon (then serving in the US Senate) and George Wingfield, he lost in the primary election to Tonopah miner Tasker Oddie, who attacked Massey for his mining and railroad connections. Nonetheless, when Senator Nixon died two years later in July 1912, Governor Oddie appointed Justice Massey to the US Senate—a tribute from a former political opponent that transcended partisan politics.

After six months in the Senate, during which he chaired the Committee on Mines and Mining, Justice Massey was defeated by Democrat Key Pittman in the November election. On his return to Reno in January 1913, he formed the law firm Cheney, Massey & Smith, "which [had] a very large and distinctively representative clientage, embracing connection with much of the most important litigation tried in the courts of the state."

In 1914, at the age of fifty-seven, Massey died of natural causes "in the midst of his activities, while on his way [to Susanville] to engage in the trial of a case." In the years before his death he and his wife lived in "delightful apartments at the Riverside Hotel, and they enjoy[ed] the hospitality of the best homes of Reno." He is buried in the Mountain View Cemetery in Reno.

The Nevada Supreme Court memorialized Justice Massey on April 6, 1914, noting:

> Judge Massey's was a well-rounded life. He lived well the roles of a good citizen, a capable legislator, an able lawyer, an upright judge, a staunch friend, a dutiful husband and father, and an honest man; a splendid example of the Western type of manhood. But above all ... he will be best and most tenderly remembered for his courtesy, geniality and the never-failing sympathy, helpfulness and kindliness with which he was so generous, when the struggles and impetuousness of the forum were laid aside.

Adolphus Leigh Fitzgerald

1901–1907

THE YOUNGEST OF TEN CHILDREN, Adolphus Leigh Fitzgerald was born in North Carolina in 1840. He completed his undergraduate degree at the University of North Carolina in 1861, and then completed a master's degree a year later. The ink still drying on his degrees, he enlisted in the Confederate army and served in a cavalry regiment during the "sanguinary battles of the Wilderness, Petersburg, and the Siege of Richmond." After General Lee admitted defeat at Appomattox Court House in April 1865, Fitzgerald quickly reunited with the country "to which his devotion and loyalty was unbounded."

He moved to California to teach Latin and Greek at Pacific Methodist College at Vacaville. After a brief interlude as deputy superintendent of public instruction of the state of California, he returned as president of Pacific Methodist. During his five-year presidency, he read law and was admitted to practice in California in 1878. Later that same year he moved to Eureka, Nevada—then a prosperous mining town—and practiced law until his election as district judge in 1887. "His service on the district bench covered the time of greatest [economic] depression in the State of his adoption."

In 1900, Justice Fitzgerald began his sole term on the Nevada Supreme Court. "His entry of service on the supreme bench was coincident with the revival of the mining industry of Nevada and the beginning of its rapid growth in agricultural and kindred pursuits." His opinions were "couched in the language of one versed in the classics, his opinions will stand as monuments to his ability and integrity more lasting than chiseled marble."

Fitzgerald's wife died after only thirteen years of marriage, and his second wife died while he was serving on the Supreme Court. His two sons both attended Harvard Law School and enjoyed prominent careers. He died in Boston at his son's home on August 31, 1921, age eighty-one.

The Nevada Supreme Court memorialized Justice Fitzgerald on September 9, 1921, recognizing him as a "genial and lovable man, and the finest type of the southern gentleman[;] he was, nevertheless a man of strong and unyielding convictions as was evidenced by the fact that he declined a renomination to this Court which was equivalent to an election, rather than to endorse a political policy with which he was not in entire accord."

Thomas Van Camp Julien

1902–1903

THOMAS VAN CAMP JULIEN SERVED on the Nevada Supreme Court only four months and did not write any opinions. Nonetheless, he lived a remarkable life that credits the Nevada judiciary. He was born in Ohio in 1838 and moved to Indiana when he was young. At age eighteen he moved to Iowa and began studying law. Three years later, in 1859, he went west to make a name for himself.

He began in the mining camps of Shasta County, California, working as both a miner and accountant while studying the law. He moved to the Nevada Territory in 1862 and lived in Winnemucca for the next fourteen years. During that time, he worked as a railroad agent, deputy sheriff, lawyer, and journalist. He was elected to the Nevada Assembly in 1866 and elected speaker pro tem in 1867. While in office, he supported antigaming efforts and chaired a controversial select committee examining relations with Native Americans. He traveled to Washington, DC, in 1868 and observed the impeachment proceedings of President Andrew Johnson, which he described satirically in the *Carson Daily Appeal* as "capital theatre." His correspondence about the event revealed his keen mind and political persuasions.

Julien was an early and consistent advocate for women's suffrage. He attended a convention of "Friends of Female Suffrage" in 1870 and was described by the newspaper as a "brilliant genius" who "being the champion of women's rights in this State, is a bosom friend of the fair sex throughout this land of milk and honey." He was later named to a state committee created to organize the "Friends of the Enfranchisement of Women in Nevada." He continued developing his public reputation and was considered by others a strong candidate for Congress in 1872. Instead, he was elected Humboldt County district attorney in 1874.

During the next twenty-five years, he focused on his career and family. He was married in 1875 to Mary Brewer in Washington, DC. He and Mary moved to Reno and had six children. One died in infancy and another tragically died young after suffering a heart attack while visiting with Julien in his law office in 1902.

Julien was counsel in twenty-one appeals to the Nevada Supreme Court; he owned several mining interests and remained involved in partisan journalism. He was often noted for his character and eloquence, described in several newspaper articles as industrious, kind, and deeply devoted to family. However, in 1877, one partisan newspaper wrote of him in editorial language unique to the time: "Oh! mother of Moses, what shall we say of Thomas? What shall we compare him to for smoothness? Oil, honey, glass, soft-soap—no; all smooth things fade into insignificance when compared with that exceedingly smooth-tongued individual, Tom Julien."

After moving to Reno, he ran for Washoe County district attorney in 1880 and received an endorsement from the *Reno Evening Gazette*, which described him as "poor, but honest." The *Gazette* continued:

> He is an easy and interesting speaker, always ready and full of anecdotes and illustrations. As a friend and companion "Tom" is most agreeable. He is always cheerful and good natured, always ready for a joke. He has any number of friends and admirers.... Tom is always at work, always sober, always in earnest in what he undertakes. He never trifles about matters of business. If he becomes District Attorney he will have no foolishness. He will neglect nothing. He wants the salary and he wants to work for it and earn it honestly and fairly.

While Julien lost that election, his 1884 bid for Washoe County clerk was successful. During the campaign the *Gazette* reported him to be "an open-hearted, generous fellow, whom nobody could dislike if they tried. He has a pleasant wit and a cheerfulness that has kept him young and buoyant where thousands of men would have broken down. No man has tried harder or lost more in the endeavor to develop Washoe County and build up Reno."

Julien recognized the importance of codifying professional standards for lawyers and was influential in the creation of the Nevada State Bar. He was also rumored to be a candidate for state controller in 1890. He publicly declined to run, revealing his authenticity and commitment to family: "I have a large and growing family of six, and all my aims in life are centered in them; I have a very comfortable home in Reno, in fact as nice a cottage family residence, with good garden and out-premises, as anyone, and my family are happy. Although my means are not at all large, I make a good living as I am, but should I be elected to a State office I should have to remove to the Capital and as it is a well accepted fact that but few State officers ever come out with a dollar, it would be a great sacrifice on my part and injurious to the best interest of my family to accept the nomination if tendered me."

Julien's commitment to family is best illustrated by a poem his fourteen-year-old daughter wrote for him on his fifty-second birthday:

On the fourteenth of November,
Let us ever remember,
Our father came into this world.
He was young and fair,
With long flaxen hair,
Which might have looked better if curled.
While that may be so,
This much we do know:
For fifty-two years, if no more,
He's got on quite well,
And how can we tell
What future there may be in store?
Whether health, joy and gladness,
Or misery, sorrow and sadness,
Or whether it be betwixt and between,
This much we can say,
Be that as it may,
We know he married a Queen.
A lady by birth,

If there's one on this earth,
Her equal--there can be no other.
And, throughout all our days
Let heaven be praised,
We rejoice to call her our mother.

Despite his previous decision against statewide office, his desire for local public service continued. He lost his second bid for Washoe County district attorney in 1894 by thirty-five votes to Frank Norcross, who later served on the Nevada Supreme Court. Undeterred, he ran again in 1896 and was elected. In 1898, he set his sights on district judge but once again lost. In addition to his business and family, he remained engaged in political and civic affairs, advocating for water rights, tax reform, religious freedom, and public education.

In 1901, at age sixty-three, he began experiencing kidney problems and diminished health. At one point, the local newspaper reported he was "quite ill" and could possibly be placed in a sanitarium in California. Instead, he went to San Francisco and underwent surgery. While the surgery prolonged his life, his physical health continued to degrade and some considered him an "invalid." Despite his poor health, Governor Sadler appointed him to the Nevada Supreme Court on September 15, 1902, to fill the vacancy created by Justice Massey's resignation. Justice Julien served on the court four months, leaving office at the end of the term on January 5, 1903.

At the time of his appointment, the *Reno Evening Gazette* was again effusive: "Hon. T. V. Julien is one of the best known men in the State. For years he was identified with the interests of Humboldt County and has a record there that we may well be proud of. He came to Reno when the town was a village, reared a family that is a credit not only to the town but the State and is here today an honest man, a true friend and a generous neighbor."

Fifty years after he came West to make a name for himself, he had created a career marked by persistence and commitment to principle, even in the face of repeated defeats. He tragically lost his twenty-two-year-old son in 1902. His wife died at their home in 1903, and three years later, in 1906, he died in the same home at age sixty-eight.

The bar met in the Washoe County district courtroom two days after Justice Julien's death to reminisce about his long service to the legal profession. A report indicates that "[a] number of attorneys, members of the Washoe county bar, including the court, dwelt upon the life of the dead jurist and at the close of the session it was ordered that court be adjourned out of respect to his memory." The following resolutions were adopted:

> Whereas, the Supreme Judge of All has, by his unappealable decree, taken from us our friend and brother, the Hon. Thomas V. Julien, and
>
> Whereas, our deceased brother was a man upright and honorable, genial and courteous to all, loyal to his friends, true to his professional obligations and frank and manly with the court, and
>
> Whereas, for many years he was closely identified with this court, as one of its officers and as a practitioner at the bar, and in all the walks of life, personally and professionally, bore himself with courage and fidelity:
>
> Therefore, be it resolved, that the bar of Washoe county, recognizing that our brother's protracted and hopeless suffering has been mercifully ended, yet deplore his loss and desire to express their friendship for their deceased brother and their appreciation of his character and extend to his children their hearty sympathy, move the court that it adjourn out of respect for the memory of the late Thomas V. Julien, that this preamble and resolution be spread upon its record, and that a certified copy thereof, be forwarded to the relatives of the deceased.

George Frederick Talbot

1903–1915

An only child, George Frederick Talbot was born April 16, 1859, in Connecticut. In 1868, he sailed with his mother to California to join his father who had traveled overland. The Talbots lived in Grass Valley for a year and moved to Elko County in 1869, where they farmed barley and potatoes. Talbot attended public school in Nevada between 1869 and 1871 before returning to Connecticut in 1872 to live with his grandfather while continuing his education. He later attended Dickinson Seminary in Williamsport, Pennsylvania, where he studied mathematics, physics, Latin, political economy, and science of government. He began reading the law in Pennsylvania and completed his legal studies in the chambers of Elko County district judge Rensselaer R. Bigelow, who later became a justice of the supreme court.

Talbot was admitted to the state bar in 1881 and then began a string of successful campaigns. In 1884 and again in 1886, he was elected Elko County district attorney. After declining to run for a third term in 1888, he was elected as a district judge in 1890. After two reelections to the district court, he successfully sought election to the Nevada Supreme Court in 1902 to fill the office vacated by Justice Massey and temporarily occupied by Justice Julien. He was reelected in 1908. Through his steady climb and unflagging service, Justice Talbot earned a stellar reputation. One account of him reads, "Few lawyers in the country are as well read and highly educated as Judge Talbot, and his decisions are marked by their clearness, justice and impartiality."

Talbot was a prolific author during his time on the Nevada Supreme Court, and two of his decisions were affirmed by the US Supreme Court. In 1914, after twelve years of service, he retired from the court and commenced the private practice of law in Reno. He was also "a large stockholder in several very valuable mines" and owned several thousand acres of land for sheep and cattle livestock. In his later years he was president of the State Historical Society and a regent of the University of Nevada.

Justice Talbot died in Los Angeles in 1938 at age seventy-nine. The Nevada Supreme Court published a memorial on January 18, 1938, noting that he "was known as a Judge of outstanding ability, and particularly rose to his greatest heights in mining cases."

Frank H. Norcross

1905–1916

When Frank H. Norcross was elected to the Nevada Supreme Court in 1904, his connections and deep roots in Nevada were without peer. Born in 1869, he was the first Nevada-born member of the court. He grew up on a farm near Reno, attended the University of Nevada, and became a member of its first graduating class in 1891. While attending UNR, he was elected Washoe County surveyor and served as an officer in the Nevada National Guard. Following graduation, he taught school for one year and was acting principal of Reno Public School for a short time. Norcross eventually left Nevada to study law at Georgetown University. After he graduated in 1894, the *Nevada State Journal* reported that he had

> come back to his native State where his eyes first saw the light of day, the scenes of his happy boyhood; where he first trudged to the little county school; in sight of the high school building where reminiscences of his boyhood woes and loves will be recalled, the University of Nevada where he studiously earned the honors of a graduate and the mountain district where he taught his first school. To these scenes of his youth he comes with distinguished honors as a graduate of the Law Department of the Georgetown University, and here he will launch and be master of the ship that will bear him on the sea of his professional career. He will occupy offices with Messrs. Summerfield and Torreyson, and the Journal hereby wished him the success he justly deserves, and that his future may be as bright as the skies under which he was born and grew to manhood.

Norcross was admitted to the Nevada Bar in 1894 and elected Washoe County district attorney a year later. In 1897, he was elected to the Nevada Assembly. During his sole term, he chaired the judiciary and education committees; he publicly supported women's suffrage. During this same time, he began practicing law with John Orr (who later became a district judge in Washoe County). After losing a district court race by eighty-one votes in 1903, Norcross was elected to the Nevada Supreme Court in 1904 and reelected in 1910 without opposition.

After twelve years on the Nevada Supreme Court, Justice Norcross returned to private practice in 1916. But he again heard the call to public service twelve years later when President Coolidge appointed him to the US District Court for the District of Nevada. In 1933, he declined President Roosevelt's recess appointment to the Ninth Circuit Court of Appeals, and his nomination to the same court in 1934 was never voted on by the US. Senate. He assumed senior status in 1945.

Throughout his career, Justice Norcross was deeply involved in legal scholarship and civic matters. Ever the proponent of education, he supported public libraries and was chairman of the board for the first public library in Reno. He also chaired the Nevada State Council of the National Civic Federation and was a commissioner on Uniform State Laws. He lectured and wrote frequently, and his 1909 presentation on criminal law reform to the San Francisco Bar Association led to his work as associate editor of the *Journal of American Institute of Criminal Law and Criminology*. He later served as vice president of the institute.

Norcross died in San Francisco in 1952 at age eighty-three. On his passing, the *Nevada State Journal* wrote:

> When a keen sense of humor and human understanding are combined with an equally keen sense of justice and an understanding of the legal principles which guide and protect us, we have a rare combination of attributes in a judge that redound to the benefit of all. Judge Frank H. Norcross, an illustrious Nevadan, possessed those qualifications and he used them. Generous to a fault, surprisingly aware at all times of the ills, the ambitious and the pitfalls that are common to the average man, Judge Norcross, on and off the bench, never lost sight of the human equation and he tempered his decisions accordingly. He was a man among men, a sincere and generous friend, a civic leader of notable attainments and a man who left a lasting imprint on the state. His memory will be revered.

The Nevada Supreme Court published a memorial on November 6, 1952, writing: "Besides rendering excellent service as a public official in our State he took an active interest in its civic and economic affairs and represented the State at many conferences and sessions dealing with crime problems, uniform State law, patriotic gatherings, and was a power in political activities for the good of his native State. He also contributed articles to various publications dealing with the various subjects in which he took a deep interest." The court continued:

> Besides being a kindly person he had an exceptionally fine personality and a mind that fitted him admirably for the many official positions held by him as well as in his capacity as a practicing attorney. He was a pioneer and builder of the State of Nevada as well as our Nation. The United States and his native State are deeply indebted to him for his valuable contributions as a builder of their civic, economic, legal and political history during his brilliant career.

James G. Sweeney

1907–1913

Justice James Sweeney was described by his Supreme Court colleagues as a "unique character" who was "brilliant to the point of being spectacular." His career was remarkable given his premature death at the age of forty-one; one can only imagine what would have been possible had he lived longer.

Sweeney was born in Carson City in 1877 with "no unusual advantages." His parents were miners, and he "had no wealthy and influential relatives to aid him in his onward and upward march." He attended public schools in Carson City and graduated from high school at age sixteen. He then attended St. Mary's College in Oakland, graduating as the youngest member of his class, "accomplishing four years' work in two, and receiving high class honors."

He returned to Nevada to work as a miner in Virginia City while studying law in the evenings. After passing the bar he made the unusual decision to continue studying law at Columbia Law School, "establishing for himself a name as one of the institution's most brilliant students."

After returning to Nevada, he helped organize the Democratic Party in Carson City and was elected to the Nevada Assembly at age twenty-three. He chaired the Judiciary Committee but left the legislature after one term when he was elected Nevada attorney general. In 1906, when he was just twenty-eight, he was elected to the Nevada Supreme Court. Justice Sweeney authored several notable opinions while on the court. *American and English Leading Cases,* a "law encyclopedia of international standing," quoted ten of his opinions. Then, at age thirty-six, "an age at which most men are just beginning their official careers, he voluntarily retired to private life."

The records are sparse, but Justice Sweeney was defeated in a 1910 election for the US Senate while still serving on the supreme court. His marriage of ten years ended in divorce. Some speculate that he was ill when he retired from the court; others believe he retired to pursue a more profitable livelihood in the law. He opened a practice in Carson City, but within a few years was living with his sister in California with "pernicious anemia." Although many knew he was unwell, his death in 1917 was a surprise. Shortly after his death, his former wife sued his estate for alimony and child support, which the supreme court ultimately denied, concluding his obligations did not extend beyond death. The court's decision is analytical and without personal reference to its former member.

Justice McCarran said after hearing of Justice Sweeney's death: "Your court of last resort is steeped in sorrow at this time. The name of James G. Sweeney has been written indelibly in the records that speak for the law of this state. His name will stand with the history of this state as long as this state endures; his name will stand with the history of this court as long as this court endures. Today his memory is written in letters of love on the records of this tribunal."

His swift ascent to the highest levels of the judiciary and his staggering industry inspired one memorial to speculate on what he could have accomplished if he were given more time: "With his ability, his temperament, and his segregation from judicial environment, his reappearance in some public way was about as certain as anything in human affairs can be. Judging from what he had accomplished in the past, it is hard to place a limit upon what his achievements might have been had he lived the allotted years of man."

The Nevada Supreme Court published a memorial on October 1, 1917, describing Justice Sweeney as "ambitious for himself," but "at the same time absolutely true to his friends and was ever ready to go to all honorable lengths" for those people and issues dear to him. His "open-hearted and open-handed generosity to those who deserved it—and even to some who, perhaps, did not—was almost without limit." He was "a natural politician. Always active, always aggressive, and, until the later years of his life, intense in his partisan feeling."

Patrick A. McCarran

1913–1919

BETTER KNOWN AS US SENATOR McCarran, after whom the McCarran airport (later Harry Reid International Airport) in Las Vegas and McCarran Boulevard in Reno were named, Patrick A. McCarran was born in Reno in 1876. While his career would take him to Washington, DC, McCarran's personal and professional lives were tethered to Reno and his family's sheep ranch adjacent to the Truckee River, fourteen miles east of town. His formal education commenced when he was ten and able to ride his horse to public school in Reno. At twenty-one, he began his academic career at the University of Nevada, Reno, but withdrew during his last semester in 1901 to work on his family's ranch. As one of the last "saddleback scholars," he finished his education where it started: reading the law while in the fields tending to sheep and other livestock. When he was admitted to the bar in 1905, his first case brought him home to defend his father against charges he had illegally cut down telephone poles on the family property.

McCarran was called to public service throughout his life. Between 1902 and 1932 he ran for eight political offices—winning three and losing five. He was elected to the Nevada Assembly in 1902 but defeated in his campaign for the Nevada Senate in 1904. After his admission to the bar, he practiced in Tonopah and Goldfield and was elected Nye County district attorney in 1907. In 1909 he returned to Reno to practice law and mounted a successful campaign for Nevada Supreme Court in 1913, where he served until 1919. After authoring 123 decisions, he was defeated in his reelection bid and once more returned to private practice in Reno.

His brief judicial service undoubtedly influenced his subsequent public life—most notably in the US Senate. The Nevada Supreme Court recognized this influence when it wrote of him: "his great individualism, which even his enemies respected, was forged in the courts of our own State of Nevada." Described as "bullheaded and uncooperative" by his political enemies, he was also known as a generous public official who attended to his constituents. He remained involved in many public endeavors, including sitting on the Board of Library Commissioners and the Board of Pardons, and he served as president of the Nevada Bar (1920–21) and vice president of the American Bar Association (1922–23).

On September 28, 1954, he died of a heart attack immediately after addressing a political rally in Hawthorne. He was seventy-eight. The Nevada Supreme Court published a memorial noting, "It is our purpose to raise high his magnificent example for all to view, so that we may in life be guided by it and approach our grave as he did, 'with an unfaltering trust,' when that time comes."

Benjamin W. Coleman

1915–1939

Justice Coleman's character and personality jump from the historical records, and he is as endearing in death as he was in life. The supreme court's memorial to him is the longest of all memorials to Nevada's deceased jurists. In total, a committee of seven lawyers and judges, the Young Lawyers Club of Reno, four individual lawyers, a former supreme court colleague, the president of the Nevada State Bar, the Nevada attorney general, two supreme court colleagues, and the chief justice contributed their reminiscences and remarks. The common threads woven throughout the tributes are Justice Coleman's exemplary judicial service, collegiality and industry, mentorship to young lawyers, and personal affability.

Benjamin W. Coleman was born in 1869 in Ballsville, Virginia. Forty miles west of Richmond, Ballsville consisted of six families, two small stores, and one blacksmith shop. By the time he was twenty-three, Coleman had graduated from Richmond College (now the University of Richmond) and was admitted to the Virginia Bar. Western wanderlust called him to Colorado the next year, where he practiced in Denver-area mining camps between 1892 and 1906. After being married in Boston in 1906, he moved to Ely, Nevada, and practiced law until his election as district judge in 1910. After successful campaigns for the Nevada Supreme Court in 1914 and 1920, he was unopposed in the 1926, 1932, and 1938 elections. In his twenty-four years of service, Justice Coleman authored 415 opinions.

During his fifth term, in the winter of 1939, his career came to a tragic end. On his return to Nevada after driving his wife to Colorado,

Benjamin W. Coleman

he was in a weather-related accident. He survived the accident but suffered persistent neck pain. As part of his rehabilitation, he began using a "neck-stretching" harness. On February 25, at age sixty-nine, he died "due to strangulation while trying to render treatment for stiff neck."

The Nevada Supreme Court published its memorial on March 28, 1939. The lengthy excerpts reveal the depth of Coleman's imprint on Nevada jurisprudence and the legal community. Former colleague Justice Jon Sanders noted how pleased he was the memorial would be "in whatever volume of the *Nevada Report* it may be published, for the edification of the young members of the Bar, that they may read it and be careful to thereby measure their course in the practice of the law." The following excerpts summarize the lengthy tributes to Justice Coleman.

Exemplary Judicial Service

It is given to few men to be endowed with those qualities of personality, character, and mind which make them eminently fitted for judicial service. The ideal judge possesses a personal dignity and poise which commands respect for the court; an intensive knowledge of the law which inspires ready acceptance of and respect for his rulings; that perfect sense of justice that enables him to do equal and exact justice between litigants; that degree of humanity which makes him temper justice with mercy; and finally, that combination of characteristics that we attempt to express by the words "judicial temperament."

To you who occupied this bench with him, and likewise to us who appeared before him as advocates, it is equally well known to what a remarkable degree Justice Coleman possessed these essential qualities of the ideal judge. We know that the Creator gave him these qualities which he developed by his own untiring efforts, and we realize how unsparingly he drew upon them in the service of the Bar and State.

Collegiality and Industry

He was always ready to bear his share of the duties of the court, and more than his share if the necessity arose. He was helpful to the highest degree. His great store of learning and background of experience made him a wonderful helper indeed. His discussion of cases submitted to the Court was always intelligent and direct, and carried on with the utmost candor. In these discussions he committed his opinions to his associates without reserve and paid the utmost deference to theirs. His mind was an open forum in which suggestion, argument, and authority received candid consideration. Withal, he was kindly, considerate and courteous. . . .

He was an ideal associate, not only on account of his bountiful store of legal knowledge and aptitude for juristic work, but because of that fine personality which made contact with him in the solution of mutual problems a pleasure indeed. His uniform willingness and anxiety to be helpful in this respect made less arduous the labors of the Court. His experience and learning, his keen discriminating mind and diligent methods equipped him to cope with legal questions with great facility. The opinions of the Court which fell to his lot to write were always promptly submitted for the consideration of his associates. He died in the fullness of his fame, leaving no unfinished work for others to do. . . .

The years we spent together in this Court were happy years of congenial employment—happy years of striving and cooperating towards the objectives of this Supreme Tribunal. They brought us into the closest friendship. I shall miss him in the daily round of life as one familiar and beloved. His figure in the moving crowd before my memory will always speak of that rare fellowship which I had the precious privilege to enjoy. Nothing low or mean ever came near the mind or heart of Justice Coleman. He lived well. He laughed freely. He thought deeply, and he worked hard. He died poor in worldly goods but rich in the golden opinions of those he served.

Mentorship to Young Lawyers

I had both the privilege and the honor of knowing Judge Coleman when I was a young man living in Ely, Nevada. He passed my house on his way home and stopped to chat with me almost every evening. I was a frequent visitor at his Chambers at his invitation, where he encouraged and helped me in my aspiration to become a lawyer....

His passing is of a particular loss to the younger members of the bar. His sympathetic understanding, his always extended hand of help and encouragement to the young man, have left indelible impressions that molded character and integrity in the young lawyer—impressions that will be manifest . . . even when his name has been lost from memory by the inexorable passing of time.

Affability

In social gatherings his vivacity and wit and quick repartee added charm to the occasion....

In company with a group of congenial spirits he was jolly, companionable, sometimes satirical and always the best of story tellers—was prone to be reticent, exclusive, and shy, but the few who were made happy by his confidence were held in the bonds of the strongest manly friendship....

At meetings . . . his geniality infused itself through the group. He added greatly to the charm of the meetings which I had the privilege of attending with him. He was thoughtful, and . . . interested in the other fellow and in his successes and his failures. He had that broad point of view that so comparatively few persons have....

He had that geniality of manner, that charm and magnetism which added to the enjoyment of every gathering in which he was present.... He was a man easy to make friends with because his character invited friendship.

John Adams Sanders

1917–1935

JOHN ADAMS SANDERS WAS BORN in Wythe County, Virginia, in 1866. Little is known of his family, except that his father was a captain in the Confederate army. He was educated in public schools and graduated at age eighteen from Emory and Henry College (where he competed in debate). He then attended the University of Virginia Law School before his admission to practice law in Virginia in 1890. In addition to the private practice of law, he worked for a short time as a deputy clerk and librarian for the Virginia Supreme Court. He was married in 1897, but tragically, his wife died in 1908.

Sanders's narrative is closely tied to mining, one of the major industries of the time. In 1900, he relocated to Spokane, Washington, to represent shareholders in corporate mining disputes. Four years later he moved to Nevada to work as a mining lawyer in Goldfield and Tonopah. He was "one of the colorful group of mining men, lawyers, businessmen and promoters who made the camps of Goldfield, Tonopah, Manhattan, Silver Peak, and Rhyolite hum in 1904 and a few years thereafter." He was elected Nye County district attorney in 1910 and reelected in 1912 and 1914.

Deemed an "orator of more than average ability," Sanders was active in Democratic Party politics and, before becoming a judge, was "always in demand in the political campaigns." Elected to the Nevada Supreme Court in November 1916, and reelected in 1922, Justice Sanders studiously reviewed the records on appeal and legal authorities from other states. Although he occasionally dissented from the majority opinions of the court, the tone of his dissents was cordial. Nonetheless, he revealed his apparent frustration with his colleagues in one dissent when he wrote that his "earnest study of this voluminous record . . . and [his] 'tentative' drafts of several 'preliminary' opinions for approval by the judges in conference, is labor lost."

In 1923, while chief justice, Sanders visited his home state of Virginia where he was hosted by his cousin, who was then serving as governor. On his arrival, a Virginia newspaper editorial drew on Nevada's notoriety as a divorce state by saying that "Judge Sanders has, in all probability, handed down more decisions in divorce cases than any other supreme court justice in the United States." The newspaper later published that "commenting upon the unfavorable reputation Nevada has won as a mecca for persons seeking divorce, Judge Sanders said the divorce laws of Nevada are not a failure and whatever abuse may be attributed to the state because of the six months residence clause lies in the court and not the law. Reno, the haven for persons wishing to free themselves from the bonds of matrimony, was described by Justice Sanders as being a church and university city, with a social and industrial life of the highest order."

After Sanders won a difficult reelection in 1928, he announced he would not be a candidate in 1934, not because it would again be difficult, but because he wanted to "devote all his enthusiasm and energy to mining." He continued, "As I see it, it will be through mining development that the prosperity of the state will be restored and hereafter I mean to perform my part in that direction. I cannot do this and continue my place on the Nevada supreme bench." At the time, Nevada and the rest of the country were mired in the Great Depression.

In 1945, Sanders contracted a "tropical ailment" while in Bermuda and spent the last three years of his life at Washoe General Hospital in Reno. At one point early in his convalescence, he reported to the press that he was improving and his only complaint was "lonesomeness." He was a widower, and his only child lived in Michigan. He died in August 1948 at age eighty-three.

The Nevada Supreme Court's brief memorial was respectful, but not effusive. The court noted that Justice Sanders "had a personality and mind that fitted him for judicial service. While on the Bench he rendered many opinions that for sound reasoning evidence special ability as well as exhaustive legal research, and stamped him as an able lawyer and judge. The State is indebted to him for his valuable contributions to its legal history."

Edward Augustus Ducker

1919–1946

EDWARD AUGUSTUS DUCKER WAS BORN in Visalia, California, on February 26, 1870. He was educated in public schools in Modesto and moved to Nevada when he was seventeen. During his childhood and early adult years, he worked with cattle and other livestock. He was an avid outdoorsman and fly fisherman throughout his life and "a familiar figure to every rancher and ranch hand of those ranches that border the trout streams of western Nevada. He enjoyed to the fullest extent these frequent fishing excursions and the companionable chats that he had with those he met upon these excursions."

Ducker studied law in Winnemucca with M. S. Bonnifield (who later served on the Nevada Supreme Court). He was admitted to the Nevada Bar in 1902, and two years later was elected district attorney in Humboldt County. In 1910 he was elected to the Sixth Judicial District Court, but "Judge Ducker was seemingly not one given to publicity as to his life story," so he was only briefly profiled in the 1913 *History of the Bench and Bar of Nevada*.

Ducker began a campaign for the supreme court in 1916, and "he would have received the nomination without opposition and his election was an absolute certainty," if he had not withdrawn from the campaign because of the death of his thirteen-year-old daughter. In 1918, he renewed his campaign and defeated incumbent Patrick McCarran. He was subsequently unopposed in the 1924, 1930, 1936, and 1942 elections. Apparently perceiving some difficulty in his 1942 election, he announced his intention to run early, issuing the following press release:

> I desire to say to the public that I will be a candidate for re-election to the supreme court of this state, of which I have been a justice for now going on 24 years. I make this rather early announcement to still certain rumors that have gained some circulation, that I intended retiring from the supreme court. Such rumors are baseless. I have never contemplated doing so, stated or intimated that I would take such action, and will not voluntarily retire so long as I am able physically and mentally to render services by doing my share of the work of the supreme court. I thank the people of this state for the confidence so long reposed in me, and assure them that I will always work to merit a continuance of that confidence.

Throughout his career, he demonstrated great respect for the legal profession and for the role of the judiciary. On receiving the symbolic keys to the supreme court's first courthouse across the street from its first courtroom in the original capitol in 1937, he said of the relationship between the judiciary and bar:

> It has been truly said that men cannot act with effect unless they act in concert; they cannot act in concert unless they act with confidence; they cannot act with confidence unless they are bound together by common opinions, common affections and common interests. . . .
>
> The judiciary, out of respect for the dignity of its character and station, does not enter the political forum in defense of its judgments and decrees. It rests silently on its conscious rectitude of purpose and to that defense of its contributions to government and justice made vocal and potent by the clear voice of a great bar.

As a sign of his esteemed reputation, the Nevada Senate unanimously issued a joint resolution upon Justice Ducker's seventy-third birthday. It reads, in part:

> Believing that the record of this outstanding jurist is unparalleled in the Nation, we do now take this means of inscribing these words upon the pages of legislative history to the end that future generations of Nevadans may learn that greatness is but a happy blending of rugged honesty, industry and human understanding. . . . [Justice Ducker as] a man, a lawyer, and a judge stands as a monument to the freedom of opportunity open to all under democratic

government. . . . The achievements of Judge Ducker are the more outstanding when one appreciates that his alma mater was the buckaroo camp and cattle trail, his desk a creaking saddle, and his campus the limitless stretch of sage and pine.

Justice Ducker died while still in office on August 14, 1946. He was seventy-six. The supreme court's memorial was lengthy and personal, revealing the great fondness the bench and bar had for him. The common themes from the various contributors were courage, integrity, devotion, mentorship, scholarship, simplicity, kindness, and an enthusiasm for life. His four unopposed reelections were "not by accident" and were "a glowing tribute" of the confidence he enjoyed. He was a judge "who never lost the human touch, who was sincerely friendly and whose judicial dignity was enhanced by a smile and a cheerful greeting."

His frequent mentorship of lawyers was appreciated: "He was a man in whom you could place implicit trust and faith. He was a man to whom you could go for counsel and advice with the assurance that you were welcome and that he had the time and the patience to listen to you. He was a person of sound judgment and one who had the courage to tell you and warn you if he believed you were wrong or that you were making a mistake."

The supreme court noted that by "his passing the judiciary of this State has lost its dean; the Bar has lost an able advocate; the people of this State have suffered the loss of one of its loyal and outstanding citizens; his family, a loving and devoted husband and father. His spirit will always remain with us. He leaves behind an everlasting monument recorded in the pages of the judicial records of this Court that will serve to guide the coming generation in the sound principles of justice and equity. To his family he leaves the rich inheritance of a spotless name." The tribute concluded with words that remain inspirational in our contemporary times:

> We are reminded on occasions such as this that the span of life is of brief duration. Quietly we come, tarry but a moment, then quietly depart. The greatness of men is not arrived at from the richness and grandeur of their possessions, but rather on the basis of what they may have contributed to their fellows by way of courage, loyalty, sincerity, and an adherence to that way of life so simply expressed in the Golden Rule.

Erroll James Livingston "E. J. L." Taber

1935–1947

ERROLL JAMES LIVINGSTON "E. J. L." Taber was born in Austin, on November 29, 1877, to pioneering residents of Nevada. His mother was born in Quebec, raised in Chicago, and later moved to Evanston, Illinois, before coming to Nevada in 1869 as a passenger on the first Central Pacific train to arrive in Nevada. She married Joseph M. Taber shortly after her arrival, and in 1886 the Tabers moved to Elko, where Joseph was a deputy sheriff. Two years later, his father died of unknown causes. His mother married local attorney E. S. Farrington, who would be appointed to the US District Court by President Roosevelt in 1907. Taber enjoyed a close personal and professional relationship with his stepfather.

After attending public schools in Elko, Taber matriculated at Lowell High School in San Francisco, California. (Other distinguished graduates of Lowell are California governor Edmund G. "Pat" Brown Sr., Hewlett-Packard cofounder William Hewlett, Nevada Supreme Court justice Milton Badt, and US Supreme Court justice Stephen Breyer.) Taber received his undergraduate degree from Santa Clara University and attended seminary in St. Paul, Minnesota, for two years before enrolling at Columbia Law School. On graduating in 1904, Justice Taber returned to Nevada, where he lived the rest of his life. He was admitted to the Nevada Bar and began practicing in Elko with his stepfather.

A lifelong Republican, "interested in politics and possessing a flare for political activities," he was elected district attorney of Elko County in 1908 and served two years before his election to the district court. He was a popular and effective trial judge.

Despite his success on the bench, and for reasons unknown but probably financial, he returned to private practice in Elko in 1922. He constructed the Taber Building on Railroad Street and worked in its second-floor offices, renting the ground level space to a drugstore.

He enjoyed a varied and successful practice until he was called back to public service with his election to the Nevada Supreme Court in 1934 to fill the position vacated upon Justice Sanders's retirement. He was reelected in 1940 and 1946 without opposition.

After arriving at the supreme court, he withdrew from general political affairs and devoted himself to the administration of justice. He was president of the Western States Probation and Parole Conference and a member of the American Law Institute and American Judicature Society. With an impressive industry, he fulfilled his duties with such dedication that one friend lamented Justice Taber "seldom had time to do the things he wanted to do; he was too busy with his work and doing things for others."

In the personal time afforded him, he was a lifelong sports enthusiast. In high school, he excelled in basketball, and as a sprinter he was said to have run 100 yards in "ten seconds flat." But it was baseball that captured Justice Taber's heart. He enjoyed meeting professional players, tracking box scores, and talking baseball at every opportunity.

In his early adulthood in Elko, he devoted time to the athleticism of "the younger people of his community," which made him "very influential in the development of character of those young associates." Even when the heat of Elko's summer days inspired him to take a dip, he used the occasion to teach others to enjoy the salutary effects of crisp river water. One friend recalled: "Many, many times in Elko I have seen him going to the old swimming hole in the Humboldt River surrounded by a coterie of little fellows, whom he was teaching to swim, and there is many a man in Elko today who learned to swim under Justice Taber's tutelage." Another friend added: "It was his practice in the summer time to take the Elko boys to the old Eshelman Dam in the Humboldt River, almost daily, and he taught virtually a generation of Elko boys how to swim. Nor did their parents have any concern for their safety. They knew that the boys would be brought safely home."

Unfortunately, his ability to enjoy athletics diminished with time. A few press reports and professional references describe his corpulence in later adulthood—one newspaper estimated his weight to be more than three hundred pounds. A colleague reflected that one of Justice Taber's regrets as he aged was his inability to enjoy outdoor activities: "His great love, outside of that for his family and friends, was the Ruby Mountain range. There, year after year, he traversed those dizzy heights that reached into the clouds. When his growing weight made this a great physical stress and a strain on his great heart, he persevered in walking the trails of the Rubies."

A "devoted husband and father," many observed that his "family life was ideal." But his personal friend Attorney General Alan Bible knew of his "sorrows and troubles." In addition to losing his father when he was only eleven, his twenty-eight-year-old daughter was killed in an automobile accident in 1939.

Though increasingly unwell and afflicted by grief, Justice Taber diligently continued his professional duties to the end of his life. One of his supreme court colleagues recounted seeing him a mere three days before his death: "[On] seeing me approaching, [he] stopped his car, waited, and, in his kindly way, invited me to ride. Observing that he did not look so well, I asked concerning his health, and he said, 'I am not so well today—I worked several hours yesterday, and came back and worked last night, and I am tired.' He stated that he had read more than two hundred cases pertaining to the particular case upon which he was then engaged, in order to make sure the Court was right in an order previously made in that case." This image made a deep impression on the jurist, who said:

> Here was a man slowly, but surely, dying, who must have realized the end was near, working far into the night, on a holiday, to make certain that the decision served the cause of justice and of right. He had no other motive. This was an example of devotion to duty, in spite of illness, seldom paralleled, I believe, in civil office. It was not prompted by the glamour, excitement or necessity of war, but occurred in the calm of peaceful surroundings, and was the fine response of a worthy soul to the still, small voice of conscience calling to duty a willing servant, in order that, through him, justice and right might prevail in the particular case.

Justice Taber fell seriously ill at his chambers in Carson City on February 6, 1947. He was transported by ambulance to Washoe General Hospital in Reno, where he died. He was sixty-nine. In respect, the supreme court draped his chair and the bench and ordered the drape not be removed until his successor was appointed.

The Nevada Supreme Court's memorial contains lengthy and varied tributes from his friends and colleagues. The newspapers also favorably reported on his life. Together, excerpts from the memorial and news stories illustrate Justice Taber's character and can inspire the highest standards of professionalism:

> As a trial judge he was patient, humane, and possessed a remarkable ability to reach exact justice in the matters submitted to him. As an appellate judge he was hard working, conscientious, studious, and at all times influenced by that same sense of justice. . . . His kindliness and courtesy endeared him to all members of the Bar. . . .
>
> [H]is unfailing courtesy, his high integrity, his great ability and his untiring patience and loyalty have been continuously and increasingly manifested to all with whom he has come in contact. He was "able, efficient and possessing a sense of humor that kept his touch human." . . .
>
> Fitted by temperament and experience to serve on the bench of the state's highest court, Justice Taber established a reputation for tincturing justice with common sense. A native Nevadan, his intimate knowledge of the people of this state and their problems enhanced his ability to serve them well as a jurist. . . . Each time Nevada voters evinced their faith in Judge Taber, they wittingly or unwittingly took cognizance of the counsel of that English judge who advised: "Fill the seats of justice with good men, not so absolute in goodness as to forget what human frailty is." . . .
>
> There can be no question . . . of his profound learning in the law and his ability to interpret it. As a lawyer and as a Judge, he had the happy faculty of winnowing the chaff from the wheat and thus analyzing the cases brought before him, and he exercised that fine faculty as Justice of this Court. . . .
>
> In spite of physical infirmity, Justice Taber's strong devotion to duty impelled him to perform prodigious labor, involving not only the sacrifice of his convenience, but the further impairment of his health. . . .
>
> If in doubt about the correct result, he would pursue his studies and research until every uncertainty insofar as humanly possible,

had been removed. He was not satisfied until assured by his inner consciousness that he had then discerned the light of truth, and by its rays could see the pathway of justice and of right. . . .

Justice Taber embodied in a large measure all that a judge should be. His example did much to implant in me love for the law as a great profession, and instill in me respect for the courts. He was a profound legal scholar; however, he would have been the last to claim any such distinction. He excelled in dealing with facts, and brought to that work a remarkable knowledge of human nature, and a lively imagination. . . .

He possessed the confidence and respect of the Bar, and its affection as well. I never heard a lawyer complain that he was deprived of a full, fair and patient hearing in his Court. Neither did I ever hear one of his decisions criticized as affected by political bias or inspired by religious prejudice, nor condemned as influenced by friendship for lawyer or partiality toward litigant. . . .

[He] presided over this Court with modest dignity and calm content. He was, at all times, a gentleman of the robe, which is to say he was patient, courteous and considerate with whomsoever he had to deal. His kindly nature showed itself to strong advantage in his treatment of young practitioners, with whose difficulties he was always sympathetic, and with whose faults he was always indulgent. . . .

May the dear ones, whom he has left for a little while, take comfort in the fact that he has left to them the priceless heritage of a splendid record of service to his State, and to his fellow men and women, of which they may always feel justly proud. They may also cherish the thought that he possessed the love and affection of all who knew him well. . . .

[W]hat is the test of an individual's personal and social worth? That he shall be sincerely missed by those among whom he lived and worked, has seemed, to me, at least one good answer—"Though lost to sight, to memory dear."

WILLIAM E. ORR

1939–1945

HIS PUBLIC SERVICE SPANNED SIXTY-THREE years, from justice of the peace in Pioche, Nevada, to the US Court of Appeals for the Ninth Circuit. Though his judicial career engendered great public acclaim, evidence suggests Justice Orr would want to be best remembered as a husband, father, and Nevadan. Nonetheless, his conduct as judge is a model for his successors on the bench and a standard all lawyers and litigants should expect from their judges.

William E. Orr was born in 1881 in Frisco, Utah, as one of nine children. His father was a blacksmith. At age six he moved with his family to the small mining community of Pioche, Nevada. After attending a local grammar school, he enrolled in a college preparatory self-study program because there was no high school in Lincoln County. He quickly completed his high school education and matriculated at the University of Nevada, but after only one year his university education was permanently interrupted because of a serious hip disease that affected him for life. Orr lamented that he never completed a university degree or attended law school, and he was deeply honored when awarded an honorary degree from the University of Nevada, Reno, in 1952.

Orr did not allow his physical limitations to affect his ambition for public service, and his first public offices in Lincoln County belie the maxim that "no prophet is accepted in his own country." Beloved in his hometown of Pioche, he continued to be well regarded wherever he later lived. After his university education abruptly ended, he was elected justice

William E. Orr

of the peace in Pioche. He read the law for the next several years while serving as the elected clerk and then treasurer in Lincoln County. After years of toil, the largely self-taught Orr realized his career goal when he was admitted to the Nevada State Bar in 1912. The next year, he was elected district attorney of Lincoln County.

Orr was elected to the district court in 1918, with responsibilities in the Eighth and Tenth Judicial Districts, then comprising Lincoln and Clark Counties. For twenty-one years he served on the trial court bench, never facing an opponent during reelection. His service on the trial bench ended when Governor Carville asked him to fill the vacancy on the Nevada Supreme Court created by Justice Coleman's death. The choice was evidently so clear that the appointment was made the very week of Coleman's death. A newspaper reported at the time, "Only 58 years old, he has gained a reputation of one of the state's leading judicial experts."

During his term on the court, many Nevada lawyers thought Orr would next be appointed to the US District Court to replace Judge Norcross. However, Senator McCarran thought otherwise. As chairman of the Senate Judiciary Committee, Senator McCarran knew a vacancy on the Ninth Circuit Court of Appeals would soon arise and made it known that he wanted Justice Orr to fill it. In a 1945 memo to President Truman, US Attorney General Tom Clark supported the plan: "As you know, the Judiciary Committee of the Senate can be most helpful to us in the administration of our duties in the Department and I believe the nomination of Judge Orr would be of great benefit in this regard. Senator McCarran is most anxious that the nomination come up before the planned recess of the Senate." President Truman accepted the recommendation and appointed Justice Orr to the position, making him the first Nevadan to serve on the Ninth Circuit Court of Appeals. He was sixty-three.

To fulfill his new role, Orr moved to California, but he never lost touch with his Nevada heritage. In 1950, he spoke to the Nevada State Bar and expressed how it felt to "come home" to Nevada, and the "only greater pleasure that I could have, I think, would be to come into the State permanently. I hope that will occur someday." He retired from active service in 1955 but was recalled periodically to hear cases as a senior judge for an additional ten years.

Justice Orr was invested in his law clerks' careers, though he had a strict policy of allowing clerks to serve only one year. He believed longer service would have a negligible benefit while depriving another young lawyer the rare opportunity to work in chambers. The law clerks did more than research and write memoranda; they participated in all phases of Orr's work. They read briefs, attended oral arguments, and assisted in opinion writing. He "invited criticism and attack on his own analysis and that of his fellow judges. He listened patiently to [his law clerks'] arguments and respected [their] judgment. When he disagreed, he did so only after first demonstrating the fallacy of [their] reasoning—and then always with the utmost kindness and tact."

Although deeply interested in the success of his federal law clerks, he personally only selected one: Harvard Law graduate and recently returned military veteran Caspar Weinberger. (Weinberger later served as chairman of the Federal Trade Commission, director of the Office of Management and Budget, secretary of health, education, and welfare, and secretary of defense.) Orr was so pleased with Weinberger that he decided all of his law clerks would come from Harvard. He delegated selection of his clerks to the dean of Harvard Law School and accepted the annual selection without question or interview. He maintained close relationships with his former law clerks and took pride in their accomplishments. He met with his law clerks semiannually: once to introduce his newest clerk to the former clerks and again on his birthday. One of his cherished possessions was an album containing a photograph and personal note from each of his former clerks.

In 1961, recognizing Judge Orr would soon turn eighty, the Nevada State Bar celebrated him at its annual conference. Unfortunately, he was unable to attend because he was "not feeling well and was indisposed." Judge Roger Foley offered reminiscences in Orr's absence: "I think that he is one of the quickest men to grasp the real meaning of a legal proposition of anyone I ever knew, either on the bench or in the practice of the profession, and he was always courteous and kind and considerate, his [c]ourtroom was a dignified [c]ourtroom, not through any exercise of authority on his part but his mere appearance on the bench commanded and received respect." The bar then approved a resolution, including among other things:

> We send our congratulations and felicitations to you, Judge William E. Orr, upon your eightieth birthday.
>
> We wish you to know how much we have appreciated your wisdom, your knowledge of the law, your understanding, your courteousness, and the respect in which you have held the members of this Bar in the various courts in which you have served over a period of almost forty-two years.
>
> We further wish you to know of the deep affection and great warmth of feeling that this Bar has for you. We have taken great pride in your career and we regard you as a great American and as one of America's great jurists.

Upon Justice Orr's death in 1965, the Ninth Circuit convened a memorial session at which former colleagues and clerks spoke. Excerpts include the following:

> [Judge Orr was one of the] best loved judges. [Whether] "in good health or in failing health he did not lean on others; he was leaned upon."
>
> No matter how long he had known any particular lawyer or how close he was to him socially, Judge Orr catered to no favorites. Possessed of a strong sense of humor, pleasant to talk with in his chambers, and courteous and patient on the bench, the young lawyer, the older lawyer, and the newly arrived lawyer, all were treated equally by him.
>
> [He] was forthright and sincere. He had courage and used firmness when firmness was required. It was not of his nature to shirk obligations or responsibility, and his energy never lagged. It can be said of him that he sought justice, with the law as a means to justice.

When he was on the bench he was attentive, considerate and polite to counsel and respectful of the views of his fellow judges. [There is not] a single instance when he had harsh words with counsel or any of his colleagues. All of the judges who served with him on this Court . . . had the greatest respect for his legal ability, his integrity and his sound judgment. More than that, they had a genuine affection for him as a close personal friend and associate. By his patience and skill, he helped to harmonize and unify the sometimes divergent views of his colleagues.

In spite of his high position and the honors and recognition which he enjoyed during his lifetime, Judge Orr remained a man of great modesty. He disliked ceremony and unnecessary formality. He possessed that rare ability to make one feel completely comfortable and at ease, while at the same time preserving dignity and respect.

In addition to the qualities which made him an outstanding judge, William Orr was the kindest and gentlest person. . . . He was a gentleman in the truest sense of the word. His keen sense of humor was ever present and always enlivened our conversations.

Charles Lee Horsey

1945–1950

Charles Lee Horsey was born in Delaware in 1880 and, despite professional success and familial happiness, died in California in 1958 as a "rather tragic figure." At age five he moved to Philadelphia, where he attended public school and worked in his grandfather's mercantile store. Early life was difficult for him, "being compelled by circumstances to remain out of school for several years, working in order to assist his invalid, widowed mother and aged grandparents." He returned to Delaware as a teenager and graduated from high school in 1898.

Immediately after high school, Horsey left for the West, stopping in Denver to work in a department store and study for a teaching license. He taught during the 1899–1900 academic year at a "country school in a log schoolhouse in northeastern Wyoming. Often, when the thermometer was far below zero and cowboys who were supposed to furnish the wood for the school were too busy or had forgotten, Horsey was compelled to saw and cut the wood for the school house. This was real pioneering."

Teaching school during the Wyoming winter persuaded Horsey that he wanted to do something different, so he returned East and began law studies at the University of Virginia. He married in 1903 and graduated from law school in 1904. With his wife and young daughter he returned to the West, stopping briefly in Spokane before settling in 1905 at Pioche, Nevada, "then a bustling Lincoln County mining community."

Although drawn to Pioche because of his interest in mining, Horsey immediately entered the "Nevada political scene" and remained a "lifelong Democrat." In 1906, one year after his arrival in Nevada, he was elected district attorney, and he served as president of the Pioche School Board. As part of his 1910 bid for the district court, he appears to have softened his partisan language. A letter to the editor of the *Pioche Record* about the young thirty-year-old who had been in Nevada only five years reveals the political hyperbole of the time. The "author" (possibly a campaign operator) listed five reasons to vote for Horsey:

> 1. Mr. Horsey is a gentleman whose character is above reproach and who is conceded by both republicans and democrats alike to be one of the ablest attorneys in the state.
>
> 2. He is competent to fill any position in the state of Nevada from district judge to the governor of this great state.
>
> 3. While district attorney of Lincoln [C]ounty he made a record for himself and party for his untiring efforts to punish crime and save the county thousands of dollars. His cases were handled in a straightforward manner.
>
> 4. Through his untiring efforts to do justice, he not only gained the respect and esteem of his fellow-townsmen, but gained the respect and confidence of every resident of Lincoln [C]ounty by convincing them beyond doubt that he proposed to do his duty without fear or favor.
>
> 5. Today Mr. Horsey stands practically alone in his profession in Lincoln [C]ounty and there is not a man in the state more competent to fill the position of district judge. Gentlemen of both political parties, "tis a duty at this time we owe to ourselves and our fellow-men to lay aside politics and unite hand in hand and elect Mr. Horsey judge of the Fourth judicial district with the largest majority ever given a candidate for this position."

Despite this appeal to "lay aside politics," Horsey lost the 1910 election and turned his attention to mining. In 1911, he and friends incorporated the Virginia Louise Mining Co., which ultimately produced 300,000 tons of ore containing lead, zinc, and silver. Bolstered by financial success, in 1913 he was elected to the Nevada Senate. He chaired the judiciary committee and "was closely identified with the writing of many statutes . . .

which liberalized benefits for workers and tightened safety laws affecting the mining industry." After one legislative term, he again set his sights on the judiciary and was elected to the district court in 1915.

Horsey balanced his continued work for the mining company he founded with his duties as a district judge. Ultimately, though, he resigned his judgeship in 1919 to devote his full-time efforts to mining and the private practice of law. Sensing a decline in Pioche, he moved his law practice to Las Vegas in 1922 and was involved in many important legal matters for more than twenty years, including serving as president of the Las Vegas Bar Association in 1929. However, he was never far from the politics of his heart. He was the unsuccessful Democratic nominee for Congress in 1928, and he accepted an appointment to return to the Nevada Senate in 1939.

An article in the *Reno Gazette-Journal* that same year reveals Horsey's rhetorical flourish and style. When most of his peers in the legislature supported repealing the state constitutional prohibition against gaming, he made lengthy floor arguments in opposition that included references to Louisiana's gaming problems and to the "gamblers [who] got into control with the result that the state bore the burden of their dishonesty." Observing world events where "we see dictators growing in power and the progress of nations in the past few years hampered," he "assailed the persecution of Jews and Catholics in Germany, the blood purges in Russia and the violation by Japan of international law to satisfy its lust for power." He argued that Nevada has "more or less compromised with evil" and insisted "it is not a question whether wide open gambling is right or wrong" but the "pendulum has swung along so-called liberal lines and the country has forgotten the teachings of its forefathers." He asserted, "it would be better for the people of Nevada if they would encourage thrift and production rather than to appeal to the love of easy money," and finally concluded that "we may have compromised with vice and immorality, but I don't think we should compromise with dishonor."

Horsey actively supported Vail Pittman in his successful 1944 primary campaign against Senator McCarran for governor. In turn, Governor Pittman appointed Horsey to the Eighth Judicial District Court, thirty years after he was elected judge while living in Pioche. Just months later, in October 1945, Pittman appointed Horsey to the Nevada Supreme Court to fill the vacancy created when Justice Orr resigned to accept a position on the federal bench. Pittman announced: "It was a difficult decision because of the fact that each applicant for the post is eminently qualified."

Justice Horsey was elected in 1946 to complete the term to which he was appointed. One of his campaign flyers touted his legislative accomplishments, including "retirement annuities for teachers," "books, equipment and materials free to students of public school," creating the "State Board of Health," adopting a measure "to provide for care and education of 'feebleminded children'" and a "measure known as Workmen's Compensation Act," women's suffrage, and a "constitutional amendment for the election of United States Senators by direct vote of the people."

In 1950, Justice Horsey was defeated by Justice Charles Merrill in his reelection bid. He blamed his defeat on a newspaper advertisement run two days before the election reporting that he was biased in favor of organized labor. In 1952, after moving to Santa Barbara, California, in the wake of his loss, he sued the *Las Vegas Review Journal* and the Southern Nevada Chapter of the Nevada Citizens Committee. Represented by his own son, he alleged the untrue advertisement was published "maliciously, wickedly, with hatred, evil design and ill will." As a result of the slander and defamation, he was defeated in election, "crushed in body and spirit," and "disabled and incapacitated from further pursuit of his work as an attorney." He requested damages of $328,171.05, which represented lost judicial earnings, lost judicial retirement, lost earnings from private practice, and punitive damages.

The defendants responded that Horsey was more disturbed about losing the election than anything that was published about him during the campaign. He prevailed on his substantive claims at trial but was awarded only $2.00 in damages. US District Judge Roger Foley granted retrial because the damages were incommensurate with a finding of malicious libel. Horsey again prevailed at retrial and was awarded $10,000 in compensatory damages and $15,000 in punitive damages. One juror later stated that the jury reached an "early agreement" that Horsey had been libeled, but spent the remaining seven hours of deliberations discussing the amount of damages to award.

However, the litigation continued, and Horsey suffered another defeat when the Ninth Circuit reversed the jury's award. The court acknowledged Horsey "has become a rather tragic figure, suffering from great mental depression since his defeat" but concluded that evidence of the election loss was improperly admitted as relevant to questions of loss of esteem, as it was "too speculative and conjectural."

Justice Horsey died two years later in Santa Barbara at age seventy-eight. The Nevada Supreme Court memorial was brief but gracious: "Besides being a kindly person he had an exceptionally fine personality and a mind that fitted him admirably for the many official positions held by him as well as for his profession as a practicing attorney."

Edgar Eather

1946–1958

EDGAR EATHER WAS BORN IN Eureka, Nevada, in 1886, and educated in local public schools. He worked in the mines and in a "mercantile establishment" until elected auditor/recorder of Eureka County in 1911. He studied law through correspondence courses in the evenings and was admitted to practice in 1916. The following year, he married Rose Tognoni, with whom he had four daughters.

Eureka was then a vibrant community, and Eather formed a law partnership with W. R. Reynolds, who also served as Eureka County district attorney. In 1922, Reynolds was elected to the district court bench and Eather was elected to replace him as district attorney.

At the time, alcohol prohibition was controversial and enforced differently throughout the state. The *Reno Gazette-Journal* reported in 1923 that enforcement of the Eighteenth Amendment "now looms as a potential primary consideration in future political campaigns," and in Eureka County the "authorities . . . have taken the bull by the horns, so to speak, and have served formal notice that 'defiance of the law in whatever form it may exist must stop.'"

With a reputation as a tough-on-crime prosecutor, Eather was offered the job of prohibition prosecutor (second assistant to the US attorney). While the details of his federal service are unknown, he did cause the following notice to be published in the *Eureka Sentinel:*

To whom it may concern: District Attorney Edgar Eather and Sheriff James Rattazzi have requested the Sentinel to state that in the light of recent occurrences in Eureka county they will make a complete clean-up of all undesirables; liquor law violations will not be tolerated and all men picked up in an intoxicated condition will be severely dealt with and a close investigation made of where they secured the liquor. Defiance of the law in whatever form it may exist must stop and to this end every effort will be directed.

A member of the Brotherhood of Elks, Eather was also active in Republican Party politics for several years. In January 1926, the *Reno Gazette-Journal* reported that he had met with Senator Oddie to seek appointment as US attorney, but he failed to receive the appointment. In 1929, though, when Judge Reynolds retired due to "ill health," Governor Frederick Balzar appointed Eather to Reynolds's position on the district court. Reynolds's ill health must not have been debilitating, because he immediately applied to the Eureka County Commission for appointment as district attorney, the position he held earlier and which was most recently occupied by Eather, his former law partner. The media described this shift of jobs under the headline "Eureka Officials Trade Jobs and Judge Is Now Prosecutor."

Judge Eather served on the trial court for seventeen years, though the last few years he lived in Reno and commuted to Eureka to conduct judicial business. He owned "considerable property" in Reno, including a hotel. In 1942, while still a trial judge, he created some public controversy when he ruled that George Whittell (the Lake Tahoe sybaritic heir of a fortune that would be valued at more than $700 million today) was not obligated to pay a $70,000 gambling debt to a Reno casino because collection of gambling debt violated public policy.

In 1945, Eather declined a draft movement to name him a candidate for the Nevada Supreme Court against incumbent Justice Lee Horsey. A year later, on April 4, 1946, he announced he would not be a candidate for reelection to the district court. Although there were whispers he would seek a position on the Nevada Supreme Court, he did not indicate his future plans when he made his announcement.

In September 1946, Governor Vail Pittman appointed Eather to the Nevada Supreme Court to replace Justice Edward Ducker, who had died while in office. Governor Pittman received recommendations for potential replacement jurists "from every section of Nevada," including endorsements from "the state's various bar associations." (Interestingly, W. R. Reynolds was later appointed to fill the district court vacancy created by Justice Eather's appointment to the Supreme Court—the very office he resigned in 1929 to allow Eather to begin his judicial career.) Justice Eather immediately announced his candidacy to complete the unexpired term to which he had been appointed. Given the late date of his appointment, he was required to submit a petition bearing 5 percent of the votes cast in the previous general election. He was elected in November 1946, to the term ending in 1948.

At age sixty-one, Justice Eather sought reelection in 1948, despite having been ill for several months. The *Reno Gazette-Journal* reported in June that he was convalescing in Reno but would return to his duties in July. He was elected in 1948 and again in 1954, but he retired in 1958, having served as a Nevada judge for twenty-five years. In recognition of his service, the University of Nevada, Reno, awarded him an honorary Doctor of Laws degree in 1959.

While serving on the Nevada Supreme Court, Justice Eather authored 127 opinions. He died in Reno on September 1, 1968, at age eighty-one, and is buried in the Mountain View Cemetery. His honorary pallbearers were distinguished Nevada citizens whose names are recognizable to many: Gordon Thompson, Cameron Batjer, Jon Collins, John Mowbray, David Zenoff, R. C. Davenport, William K. Woodburn, Russell McDonald, Joe DeRosa, Frank Bacigalupi Sr., H. B. Chessher, district judges Grant Bowen, John Barrett, John Gabrielli, and Emile Gazelin, US Representative Walter S. Baring, and US Senators Howard Cannon and Alan Bible.

The Nevada Supreme Court published a memorial to Justice Eather on March 24, 1970. In addition to noting his lifelong passion for mining, the court observed he "was a devoted family man and respected by all who knew him. He had a wide circle of friends who enjoyed his keen sense of humor and amusing stories about old timers that had resided in Eureka County and the surrounding area."

Justice Merrill expressed the court's "warm association" and "respect for [Justice Eather's] integrity and legal abilities." He said:

> The contributions that our brother has made to the cause of justice through his many years on the bench are not to be found simply in the cold pages of the Nevada Reports or the decisions of the District

Court, but they are to be found in the hearts and consciences of his fellow men. I have never known a man who had such an instinctive sense of justice and a conscience which could manifest itself so unerringly. A measure of his quality of justice, I think, is to be found in everyone who has come in contact with him either as lawyer or as judge.

Milton B. Badt

1947–1966

A LARGE PORTRAIT OF JUSTICE Milton Badt hangs prominently in the public foyer of the Supreme Court Clerk's Office. Next to the portrait is a bronze plaque—a gift to Nevada from Justice Badt's lifelong friend Sidney Schwartz. Among other accolades is the tribute: "Whose life and character embodied all that one could ever wish for in a man or judge. Eager and frequent visitor into the world of books and poetry."

Badt was born on July 8, 1884. His father worked as a merchant and cattle rancher in Elko. While Badt lived in San Francisco with his mother and seven siblings, his father lived a difficult life after moving to Elko in 1868 when it was still a tent city, and he suffered long absences from his wife and children. Because travel between Elko and San Francisco was difficult, he made the journey only two or three times each year.

In 1897, Badt moved to Nevada and attended a two-room school for students who were between the first and ninth grades. He later remembered that he "had some wonderful teachers there, and I will be eternally grateful for what they taught me." He was introduced to poetry and classical literature in that small schoolhouse and remained intrigued by these subjects throughout his life. He was particularly moved by Browning, Milton, Tennyson, and Wordsworth, and he believed the most beautiful poetry ever written were the last four lines in the final stanza of Wordsworth's "Ode: Intimations of Immortality": "Thanks to the human heart by which we live, / Thanks to its tenderness, its joys and fears, / To me the meanest flower that blows can give / thoughts that do often lie too deep for tears."

Milton B. Badt

Badt spent two years in Nevada before his father died in 1899. Although he returned to San Francisco to attend Lowell High School, he described his time in Elko with fondness. As his was one of three Jewish families in Elko, he was delighted he never experienced anti-Semitism in Nevada; instead, he maintained warm memories of friends, teachers, cowboys, miners, and Native Americans. He remained an ally, advocate, and admirer of Native Americans his entire life.

While a student at the University of California, Berkeley, Badt was in San Francisco during the 1906 earthquake, after which he joined his fellow residents fighting the fires that raged throughout the city. Despite the resolute effort of countless citizens, hundreds died and many more were threatened as the buildings in the storied city fell to rubble. Southern Pacific was "issuing tickets to anyone to get out of San Francisco," so Badt and several siblings took the train to Wells, Nevada. Upon their safe arrival, the depth of the Badt family character was revealed. Unprompted, he and his brother sent a check to Southern Pacific to pay for the travel, and the *San Francisco Chronicle* published an article highlighting the Badt brothers' honesty. Badt denied there was anything newsworthy, saying: "We thought it was very kind of them to advance the fares" because "nobody had any money."

Badt graduated from Hastings College of Law and was admitted to practice in 1908. Like his father before him, he attempted a life divided between Elko and San Francisco, with practices in each city. After five years, he chose to return to Nevada full time:

I had cases pending in San Francisco and cases pending in Elko, and I was running back and forth, I just had to make up my mind to give up one of them, and I had always intended to come to Elko to practice. So I finished up my San Francisco business and went to Elko and opened up my offices there. That was in 1913. I had a very, very interesting and lucrative practice there in Elko.

Badt practiced law for thirty-one years, never once taking a criminal case. He focused instead on grazing, water and land rights, mining, Native American treaties and affairs, and sundry commercial matters. At various times he was the city attorney in Elko, Carlin, and Wells. He was privileged to argue a federal lands grazing case before the US Supreme Court in 1941.

Badt described himself as a bachelor who "led a typical bachelor's life" until he was married at age forty to a schoolteacher from Chicago. He and his wife raised two children, yet he still found time to serve as an elected member of the school board and remain involved with Rotary, the Chamber of Commerce, the Elks Lodge, the Masonic Lodge, and the Boy and Girl Scouts of America. He was a frequent guest speaker at social and civic clubs and was president of the state bar in 1933.

Governor Pittman appointed Badt to the district court in 1945, but the decision to leave private practice for the judiciary was not easy because of the reduced salary, which he described as a "financial beating." He was concerned about paying for his children's college because he had a "good practice and I [had] to cut my income in two."

Not long after he became a trial judge, he was solicited to apply for the Nevada Supreme Court vacancy created by Justice Taber's death. The decision to apply presented another challenge because the appointment would require him to relocate from Elko to Carson City just as his daughter was about to enter her senior year in high school. He described her as a flourishing student who was set to "get all kinds of honors in Elko, and we'll have to move her down [to Carson City]." He ultimately did apply, and was appointed to the court in 1947.

Justice Badt described the work of an appellate jurist as "wonderful," though he could not say he "enjoy[ed] the criminal appeals. We're compelled to reverse convictions . . . which I don't like at all. And I'm not too fond of those hundreds of personal injury cases that come up on appeal. But still the whole thing is very, very interesting to me." He described his relationships with judicial colleagues and the internal operations of the court with warmth. He was especially complimentary of attorneys:

> I think we have a fine bar in Nevada. There are a bunch of lawyers who can practice law in any company and I'm very proud of them. They come up here and they give beautiful arguments, they file wonderful briefs, exhaustive briefs. They make it easy on the court; they exhaust the authorities on any point.

Elsewhere, however, he lamented the grammatical errors "happening all the time in the briefs. I think it's sort of a disease with me. I don't think I'll ever get over it. It just hurts me to see one of these sentences badly 'gobbled.' I'm reconciled to the disappearance of the subjunctive mood," he said. "That's gone forever. But I'm not reconciled to abandon parts of speech or case or tense or things like that."

A child of the second industrial revolution—he watched in wonder the transition from horse to car, photograph to film, and telegraph to telephone—Justice Badt was involved in the evolution of Nevada law, including the rules of civil procedure, probation, pardons, and the commercial code. He also strengthened the administrative leadership of the Supreme Court over the entire state judiciary. While chief justice in 1951, he convened a conference of all eleven district judges to discuss the disparate application of various laws and procedures. The press described this as an "extraordinary" conference from which only one judge was absent.

He was never opposed in judicial election. As his career began slowing down, he was named the 1963 Hastings College of Law "Man of the Year." The University of Nevada Oral History Program was established in 1964 to develop primary sources about "significant events, people, places and activities in the twentieth and twenty-first century Nevada and the West." Justice Badt sat for two interviews in 1965. Unfortunately, he was unable to review or edit the transcript before his death. His oral reminiscences describe a fascinating journey into the past through first-person narration, divided into five sections: (1) "Early Days in Northern Nevada," (2) "Memories of My Education," (3) "The San Francisco Earthquake and Fire," (4) "My Years on the Bench and Bar in Nevada," and (5) "Observations."

In March 1966, a Las Vegas newspaper reported that Justice Badt would retire within three days. He had been ill for a month and his doctor predicted he would be unavailable for several more weeks. This was an election year and Badt responded by telegram to the press, writing: "I categorically deny that I presently entertain any plan for such resignation. Such report is without any foundation whatsoever." However, he died three weeks later on April 2, 1966, at age eighty-one. Interestingly, he had ended his oral history the previous year by saying: "The word retirement isn't in my vocabulary at all, unless its [sic] compulsory retirement. I've told my associates, 'If you ever find me mentally slipping, tell me, and I'll get off.' The tragedy is that the man himself is the last one to know it. My plans for the future are just to keep on working here. I'm eighty-one years old and I'm not ready to give up!"

Lieutenant Governor Paul Laxalt eulogized Justice Badt, saying among other things: "This indeed was the whole man—the full and complete development of all that we hold best in the qualities of the human spirit. This was the man who as judge had few peers. This was the attorney who counseled wisely. This was the community leader. This was the cultured man. This was the loyal Nevadan. This was the human being, the husband, father and friend. Integrity, honesty, graciousness, kindliness, humility—these were his marks." The Nevada Supreme Court's published memorial was equally honorific:

> He enjoyed an ideal family life. He was of a kindly disposition, yet firm in the matter of personal habits. He enjoyed his neighbors, and was modest and retiring. He was equally at home with the prince and the ordinary citizen. He was beloved by his fellow lawyers. . . .
>
> He enjoyed the confidence of the people of his community—confidence in his legal ability, his loyalty, his absolute integrity and trustworthiness. . . .
>
> Justice Badt, although a busy man, and eminent in his profession, was an outstanding citizen. He loved his country and his state. He was generous in his contribution of time and substance in all worthwhile community projects.

Finally, the court observed that Justice Badt was an avid scholar until the end of his life, pursuing a "vigorous study" not only of the law but of literature, music, art, and foreign languages. He was "flawless and effective" in his use of the spoken word. It was this "unquenchable thirst for knowledge and perfection" that made him "an inspiration to all who knew him."

Charles M. Merrill

1951–1959

Justice Merrill does not leap from the pages of history as a larger-than-life personality, yet the historical records demonstrate he was a judge of great depth and exemplary service.

Born in Hawaii in 1907, Charles M. Merrill moved to California in 1911, when his parents bought a ranch in Collinsville, on the banks of the Sacramento River. He began his education in a one-room, one-teacher school but later moved to Piedmont, California, where he graduated from high school.

As a student at UC Berkeley, Justice Merrill worked on the student newspaper, played the cello, sang with the glee club, and was a senior varsity yell leader. He graduated in 1928 with a degree in political science and immediately enrolled at Harvard Law School, from which he graduated in 1931.

He returned to San Francisco and was admitted to the California State Bar, but "given the economic conditions" at the time, he was unable to find employment. With a referral to Reno attorney Robert Price, who would soon serve as president of the Nevada State Bar, Merrill and his wife moved to Reno where he worked as an associate until becoming Price's partner in 1934. He continued the practice after Price died in 1940 and later formed a law partnership with John Robinson and Leslie Gray. Merrill's practice areas were water, mining, and corporate law.

He quickly rose to personal and professional prominence. Active in the Washoe County Bar Association, he was appointed chair of the Board of Bar Examiners and later served on the Board of Bar Governors. For many years, he was the attorney for the Washoe County Water Conservation District, and he served as a member of the Lake Tahoe Conference Committee on the Adjustment of Interstate Waters.

Meanwhile, he participated in many civic endeavors, particularly music and singing. He joined the Society for the Preservation and Encouragement of Barbershop Quartet Singing in America and became its youngest president in 1947. He founded and was the first president of the Reno Men's Chorus, which he also conducted. He was a member of the Associated Male Choruses of America and was a member (and music arranger) of the Bonanza Four Quartet, which made more than three hundred appearances for charitable and church organizations. But his interests were not limited to music: he was active in the Nevada Square Dance Association, Reno Exchange Club, Reno Chamber of Commerce, Nevada Area Council of the Boy Scouts of America, Washoe County Girl Scout Council, and the Kiwanis Club.

In 1950, at a meeting of the Reno Lawyers' Club, Merrill announced his candidacy for the Nevada Supreme Court seat held by Justice Charles Horsey. At the time, Justice Horsey had not indicated if he would retire or seek reelection. When Horsey did seek reelection, the two engaged in a spirited campaign. Merrill was a relentless candidate, making appearances throughout the state. The *Nevada State Journal* noted that he campaigned "just as strenuously as he does when he is endeavoring to draw harmony out of his barber-shop quartet." He carried a majority of the counties and won by almost ten points. After this hard-won initial victory, he was unopposed in his 1956 reelection campaign.

Through his service, Justice Merrill earned the confidence of US Senator Alan Bible, who was his political benefactor for appointment to the federal bench. Although unable to secure Merrill's appointment in 1956, Senator Bible and Senator Howard Cannon persuaded President Eisenhower to appoint Merrill to the Ninth Circuit Court of Appeals in 1959. He was the second Nevadan to serve on the federal appellate court. At the time of this appointment, Nevada Supreme Court justice Milton Badt said of his colleague: "I think I can say without any hesitation at all that I have never encountered and worked with a keener mind, a more analytical mind, a mind more attuned to not only the abstract justice of the case but to the logic of the arguments of counsel, cutting through many of the issues that have been raised and going unerringly to the meat of the case."

Justice Merrill participated in several high-profile appeals while on the Ninth Circuit Court of Appeals. In 1970, he authored a controversial opinion protecting freedom of the press. In that case, *New York Times* reporter Earl Caldwell challenged a subpoena ordering him to testify before a federal grand jury about his confidential interviews with members of the Black Panther Party. Writing for the majority, Merrill observed that "the need for an untrammeled press takes on special urgency in times of widespread protest and dissent. In such time the First Amendment protections exist to maintain communication with dissenting groups and to provide the public with a wide range of information about the nature of protest and heterodoxy." Although he acknowledged the competing interests of the grand jury, Merrill ultimately concluded that "the very concept of free press requires the news media to be accorded a measure of autonomy; that they should be free to pursue their own investigations to their own ends without fear of governmental inference; and that they should be able to protect their investigative process." Accordingly, the court held that Caldwell was entitled to refuse attendance at the grand jury altogether. Although the ruling was later overturned by the US Supreme Court, the case would engender debate about reporters' privilege for many years to come.

The case illustrates Justice Merrill's thoughtful approach to the law. In an academic speech at the University of Nevada, Reno, Center for Religion and Life (during a time of national civil unrest), he acknowledged specific laws must adapt to changing circumstances, but the "framework [of] the rule of law must be protected." Balancing competing interests, he concluded that "it is wrong to break the law and it is that assumption that must be preserved. If it is not preserved then the tremendous power of deterrence of the law is lost and law enforcement will fail." However, he acknowledged an exception for those whose consciences could not accept a law perceived as morally wrong. He further explained that "when a law is challenged on moral grounds, only that law should be challenged through violation only after all other channels for change have been exhausted. And if efforts to change the law fail, the violator should accept punishment."

In 1971, another of Justice Merrill's loyal friends attempted to advance his career. Twelve years after Senator Bible proposed him for the Ninth Circuit Court of Appeals, Merrill's former law partner Leslie Gray urged President Nixon to consider Merrill for appointment to the US Supreme

Court to fill one of the vacancies created by the resignations of Justices Hugo Black and John M. Harlan. Senator Bible supported the suggestion and wrote that Justice Merrill is "one of the soundest and ablest in the entire federal system. . . . He has served on many committees and commissions, notably the American Law Institute. He is a westerner and you'll find he has the high regard of the American Bar Association and leaders in the bar and bench throughout the country. He is a Republican and a conservative of the quality we need on the high court." Despite these glowing recommendations, President Nixon instead appointed Justices Lewis Powell and William Rehnquist to the positions.

After being passed over for the US Supreme Court, Justice Merrill continued serving on the Ninth Circuit until 1974, when he accepted senior status. His federal colleague Senior Justice Ben C. Duniway said upon Merrill's retirement: "He is a delightful associate, courteous to everyone, considerate, hardworking, and efficient. He gets his work done, and promptly. His opinions are models of clarity and conciseness. He is much more than an associate. He is in the eyes of his brothers and sisters, first and foremost a friend—one who is not only admired, but greatly beloved."

Merrill died in San Francisco in 1996 at age eighty-eight. He was the last living attorney who argued before the Nevada Supreme Court when it still met in the Capitol. Upon Merrill's death, Ninth Circuit Chief Judge Procter Hug, a fellow Nevadan, said: "We will miss our cherished colleague and his many years of devoted service to our court. He will be remembered as a true gentleman and an outstanding jurist. We in Nevada will particularly feel his loss as he made his home—and his mark—here for almost 30 years before joining the court of appeals."

The Nevada Supreme Court published a memorial to Justice Merrill on May 23, 2003. Among many tributes, Justice Cliff Young described Merrill as "a witty and very bright man. Everyone had a great deal of respect for him." Secretary of State Bill Swackhamer added, "He was a gentleman first, last and always. He was not a man who got much publicity. He didn't want it."

Frank McNamee

1958–1965

IN A TRAGIC EPISODE FOR the Nevada judiciary, Justice McNamee's career and life were ended by a violent crime that entered the public consciousness through local and national news coverage.

Frank McNamee was born in Pioche, Nevada, in 1905, to a prominent Lincoln County family. His mother was an early graduate of Eureka High School, and his father was a justice of the peace in the Eureka Township. In 1913, his family moved to Las Vegas so his father could practice law. After a public school education in Nevada, McNamee attended and graduated from Stanford Law School in 1930 and immediately became a municipal judge in Las Vegas before entering private practice in 1933. Among his notable clients was the wife of Clark Gable, whom he moved into his own home for six weeks so she could acquire Nevada residency for a divorce.

McNamee was politically ambitious. He made the following pledge as the Republican candidate for lieutenant governor in 1938: "As a young man still in my thirties, I have no theories as to what will bring about a Utopia for Nevadans. I only pledge myself to a progressive, sane attack upon the problems of our state. I shall at all times courageously guard the factors that will protect the investments of this state in mining, agriculture, and stock raising. I pledge a liberal and progressive attitude toward labor to insure better working conditions and liberal wages." His campaign was unsuccessful, and a 1940 bid for the state senate also failed.

He suspended his legal career and set aside his political ambitions to enlist in the US Army at the outset of World War II. He worked in the office of the Judge Advocate General in Washington, DC, and completed his military service as a lieutenant colonel. He later participated in several organizations supporting military veterans.

In 1946, Governor Vail Pittman appointed McNamee to the Eighth Judicial District Court. A successful and well-liked trial judge, he was also a courageous jurist unafraid of public criticism. For example, he opposed his judicial colleagues' request for an additional judge in the district, going so far as to lobby Governor Charles Russell by asserting that caseloads were manageable with increased diligence, and thus the expense of a new judge was unnecessary. According to Justice McNamee, if his colleagues needed help, they could obtain assistance from less-busy judges in other districts.

In one controversial case, he dismissed an indictment against a district judge in Ely who was accused of perjury for filing false affidavits of pending cases. At the time, judges were required to sign compliance affidavits to receive their salaries. The indicted judge apparently considered the requirement ministerial and delegated compliance to his staff. Justice McNamee concluded the affidavit could not be perjurious because the judge never took an oath and "the oath is the foundation of perjury. In order to perjure himself, a person must make a false statement after taking an oath." In yet another public case, he ordered a religious leader to show cause why his license to solemnize marriages should not be revoked because he did not have a congregation. Without a congregation supporting the religious leader, any marriage ceremony he performed was deemed to be nonreligious, and the performance of a nonreligious ceremony was, at that time, a privilege reserved only for judges. Each of these cases, and several more, were reported in the press during McNamee's public career.

While Justice McNamee was making a name for himself on the Eighth Judicial District Court, Nevada Supreme Court justice Edgar Eather announced his retirement in 1958. Even as he was leaving office himself, Governor Russell appointed McNamee to fill the vacancy and incoming governor Grant Sawyer confirmed the selection during the transition in governorship. The appointment was widely approved by lawyers and judges, including Justice Eather, who said of McNamee, "I have always had the highest regard for him as an attorney and as a judge, and I know that he will be a credit to this Court."

Justice McNamee soon thrived in the position and became an administrative leader of the courts and legal profession. He wrote 178 opinions, which "seldom departed from the high standard of excellence which the Justice imposed upon himself. All members of the bench and bar are familiar with the clarity of analysis and economy of words which marked his judicial work." According to colleagues, he read the complete record of almost every case and "promptly dictated a summary of material facts and noted his preliminary conclusion. The quality of his mind and the breadth of his learning were such that only rarely was he obliged to modify his first judgment."

The Las Vegas Chapter of the City of Hope named McNamee its Man of the Year in 1959 for his "outstanding civic and philanthropic contributions to the whole community." The honor was the culmination of a life of civic engagement that included leadership positions in organizations such as the Las Vegas Chamber of Commerce, US Junior Chamber of Commerce, Elks Lodge, Rotary Club, and American Cancer Society.

Despite his reputation and long career of service, Justice McNamee was opposed in his 1960 reelection. Supreme Court elections were rarely contested—the last contested election occurred in 1950 when Justice Charles Merrill defeated Justice Charles Lee Horsey—and McNamee's opponent, Ernest Brown, was a serious candidate. Brown had been the Washoe County district attorney and had served briefly in the US Senate in 1954 when appointed to fill the vacancy created by Senator McCarran's death. One of Brown's campaign positions was that the Supreme Court was too collaborative; it had issued 150 unanimous opinions in the two years preceding the election. In response, McNamee declared that he was "not afraid to stand alone." He won reelection and later served as chief justice, but through tragedy was unable to complete his full term.

On Friday, February 12, 1965, he told colleagues he was going to Sacramento for the weekend but would return for work on Tuesday. When he did not appear at work, a court employee drove to his apartment in Zephyr Cove to check on him. He was found wearing pajamas and wrapped in a blanket, lying comatose in a pool of blood. He lived alone and there were no signs of a struggle, forced entry, burglary, or accident. He had endured multiple lacerations and bruises, a skull fracture, concussion, and contusions of the brain. He never recovered from his injuries. A few days after the assault, a spokesman for the Washoe Medical Center said of McNamee: "He tries to make conversation. He will attempt to answer questions, but I don't think he knows where he is or what happened to him." He remained in intensive care for more than three months and then was flown to a convalescent home in Las Vegas. He was bedridden and brain damaged for the short remainder of his life.

Speaking for the Nevada judiciary, Justice Milton Badt described the attack as "a horrible thing, shocking and beyond comprehension." Governor Sawyer initially appointed a series of district judges to assist the Supreme Court on a case-by-case basis. However, doctors were skeptical Justice McNamee would ever resume a normal life, and Justice Gordon Thompson told legislators it was "reasonably certain Judge McNamee will never be back on the bench." A month after the attack, Sawyer met with Justice Thompson, Justice Badt, and six legislators to develop a succession plan. Sawyer appointed District Judge David Zenoff to serve until Justice McNamee returned to work or his term expired in 1966.

The search for McNamee's assailant started slowly in Nevada but quickened when McNamee's 1963 Corvair was found with a flat tire in a ditch in northwest Missouri two days after the assault. A farmer saw a young man hitchhiking near the car, presumably seeking a ride into nearby St. Joseph, Missouri. Police in St. Joseph learned a young man resembling the farmer's description had purchased a bus ticket for Miami. The local police and FBI were waiting for the bus when it made a scheduled stop in St. Louis. There, they arrested twenty-one-year-old Phillippe Denning. Although Denning denied knowledge of the crime, he possessed McNamee's gasoline credit card, business card, and cufflinks. Denning was charged with the federal crime of unlawful interstate transportation of a stolen motor vehicle and extradited to Nevada.

Denning was charged in Nevada with assault with intent to kill, theft of personal property, and auto theft. The prosecution alleged McNamee picked Denning up as a hitchhiker in Sacramento and took him to his home in Zephyr Cove, where Denning worked as a cook. Although only twenty-one, he already had a significant criminal history. At fifteen he dropped out of high school, began running away and finding trouble, and spent time at the California Youth Authority the following year. He was later convicted of burglary and carrying a weapon in Salt Lake City, automobile theft in Moab, Utah, and two burglary charges in Lake Tahoe, in addition to serving one year in the Placerville County jail for burglary.

The prosecution involved several irregular events, which the press described as a "political football to the detriment of the individual and to the best interests of the state of Nevada." Denning ultimately pled guilty to attempted manslaughter and was sentenced to a one- to five-year prison term. The federal charges were dismissed. Denning first appeared before the parole board on March 1, 1967. He said he was unable to express remorse for something he did not recall but expressed sorrow for what happened, "if it did." All he ever said about his participation in the crime was "there isn't much for me to say, except things happen that are hard for me to understand, much less explain. I feel I have to do something destructive, but yet I feel like I am doing something wrong—but then not wrong at all." Parole was denied. Justice McNamee died in a Las Vegas convalescent home on November 4, 1968, age sixty-three, and Denning was paroled on March 29, 1969.

The Nevada Supreme Court published a memorial in March 1970. Among other tributes, it concluded, "Justice McNamee's quick perceptions and sense of humor made him a delightful gentleman."

MILES N. "JACK" PIKE

1959–1961

JUSTICE PIKE HAD ONE OF the shorter tenures on the Nevada Supreme Court, but his contributions to Nevada justice are rich and inspiring.

Miles N. "Jack" Pike was born in Wadsworth on November 24, 1899, to a pioneering Nevada family. His maternal grandfather established a trading post for emigrant trains in 1849 and became a landowner and cattleman in Elko County. His mother was born in Ragtown, near Fallon, and was educated in a Virginia City convent. His father, W. H. A. Pike, was born and educated in Maine, where he studied law and became a lawyer. In 1874, W. H. A. Pike came to Nevada and taught school in Washoe County until he became Churchill County superintendent of schools in 1878. He represented Churchill County in the Nevada Assembly for three terms before returning to Washoe County, where he was elected to another legislative term in 1893.

In 1900, soon after Pike's birth, the family moved the short distance from Wadsworth to Reno when his father was elected district attorney of Washoe County. In 1907, W. H. A. was elected district judge and served on the Second Judicial District Court until 1910. During this time, Pike began his education in Reno public schools and later graduated from Reno High School. He began his university studies at the Naval Academy but was forced to withdraw after two years because of ill health. He continued his academic career at the University of Nevada, graduating in 1923, before obtaining his law degree from Hastings College of Law. He practiced briefly in San Francisco before returning to Reno. Meanwhile, his desire to serve his country led to his commission as an infantry officer in the US Army Reserve in 1928. He married in 1932, and he and his wife raised two sons: Russell and Roy Robert.

In 1934, Pike was appointed assistant US attorney. While serving under US Attorney Ted Carville, he developed a friendship with Thomas Craven, another attorney in the office and one whose career would eventually become entwined with Pike's.

Pike resigned as federal prosecutor in 1938 to run for district judge. In a crowded primary to fill the vacancy created by Judge Thomas Moran's resignation, Pike placed second and faced William McKnight in the general election. McKnight had the "advantage of a cohesive organization." Press reports and Pike's campaign materials depicted McKnight as the establishment candidate. Relying on "personal" outreach to voters, Pike pledged that "every person, poor as well as rich, will receive even-handed justice" because he "represents no special interest" and is not "supported by any political group." Promising voters that if elected his "obligation will be to all the people, and to them alone," he further pledged to "temper justice with mercy" and noted "nothing is more important to the people than their courts. Keep them clean. Keep them in the hands of upright, impartial, capable, and absolutely independent judges."

Pike was endorsed by the *Reno Gazette-Journal* as the better candidate "by far" because he "knows the law" and "is an experienced practitioner. He is familiar with both criminal and civil procedure. And his integrity and independence are above all question." The newspaper concluded its endorsement by asserting judges must be "free from political alliances and beyond every improper influence. His past record as a lawyer must be above reproach." Despite this strong endorsement, Pike lost the election.

In 1939, President Roosevelt nominated William Boyle to serve as US attorney for the District of Nevada, but Boyle was opposed by Senator Pat McCarran and failed to obtain senate approval. Both Pike and his former colleague and friend Thomas Craven sought the nomination. Senators Key Pittman and McCarran agreed on Pike, who was then nominated by President Roosevelt and quickly confirmed by the Senate. The *Nevada State Journal* reported that Pike "will not accept the position if there are any strings attached. He is scrupulously honest and sincere." Craven was magnanimous in defeat, saying, "Pike and I are old friends and I would not be a party to any movement to discredit him in any particular at any time. Naturally, I was hopeful of being appointed to the position, but Pike was given it and I know of no one better qualified or more deserving." Pike responded by appointing Craven to be his assistant.

Although a lifelong Democrat, Pike mostly avoided partisan activities. He was identified as a possible appointee to the US Senate when Senator Pittman died in 1940. Instead, Berkeley L. Bunker was appointed, leaving Pike to occasionally ruminate about running for governor.

Pike's political ambitions, however, paused when the rising tensions of World War II brought the opportunity to serve his country. Since receiving his commission as an Army officer in 1928, he had continued training in the reserves, ascending to the rank of major and commander of the Reserve Officer's Association. At age forty-three he was called to active-duty service for World War II. Traveling with Washoe County District Attorney Ernest Brown, who had also been called to active duty, he reported to Fort Benning, Georgia. He resigned his position as US attorney; his friend and assistant Thomas Craven was appointed in his place.

Pike served thirty-one months on active duty, with the primary assignment to train young soldiers preparing for combat. He returned to Nevada expecting to enter private practice but mostly managed his in-law family's extensive land holdings known as the Russell Land and Cattle Company in Elko, Lander, and Eureka Counties, with offices in Battle Mountain. However, in a second magnanimous act, Craven resigned as US attorney so Pike could be reappointed to the office he held before military duty. Craven said, "At the time I accepted the appointment I did so with the conviction that Miles N. Pike should be re-appointed upon his return from military service if he so desired. Mr. Pike has indicated a desire to have the office. My resignation follows his wishes." Pike was reappointed the US attorney in March 1945. (Craven later served as a district judge in Washoe County between 1961 and 1974.)

Pike "genuinely believed that a lawyer's role in society demanded something more than just practicing his profession; throughout his career he gave unselfishly of his time, energy and ability to civic and charitable activities." He was president of the Washoe County Bar, served on the Board of Governors, and was president of the Nevada State Bar. He was president of the University of Nevada Alumni Association, second vice president of the Sons of the American Revolution, district chairman of the Boy Scouts of America, and chairman of the Nevada Heart Fund Association. He was also a member of the Masonic Lodge, Kerak Temple of the Shrine, Knights of Pythias Lodge, Fraternal Order of Eagles, Reno Lodge of the Elks, Reno Lions Club, American Legion, and Boys' Clubs of America.

In December 1951 the press reported that Pike suffered a "heart ailment," which contributed to his decision to resign as US attorney in 1952. Following his resignation, he practiced law and enjoyed rifle and pistol shooting, fencing, handball, riding, golfing, skiing, and remained active in Reno social events.

In 1959, Governor Grant Sawyer appointed Pike to be the first chairman of the Nevada Gaming Commission "because of his talent, qualities of leadership and impeccable integrity." However, that same year Justice Charles M. Merrill resigned from the Nevada Supreme Court to accept appointment to the Ninth Circuit Court of Appeals, and Governor Sawyer appointed Pike to complete Merrill's term. He described Pike as "one of the top legal minds of the country" and "eminently qualified to maintain the high standards on the state supreme court set by previous jurists." A press report suggested Pike would perform his duties with impartiality because he had "never been involved in the partisan feuds that have beset Nevada politics for many years." Finally, outgoing Justice Merrill described Pike as an "outstanding lawyer and dedicated public servant" whose appointment was "most welcome news to the court."

Justice Pike was unopposed for reelection in 1960, but shortly after beginning his new term in 1961 rumors arose about his desire to leave the court. In addition to whispers about strained relationships with his two colleagues, some questioned whether Pike enjoyed the isolation of an appellate court. Unfortunately for him, his scrupulous honesty—an admirable characteristic in his personal life—made him a soft target for the press. When a reporter from the *Reno Gazette-Journal* asked about the rumors that he intended to resign, he first answered, "I don't feel free to comment on these reports. If I were to resign it would be to the governor and any announcement would be from him." When pressed, he equivocated and said, "I would assume something would materialize in the foreseeable future." When asked if his answer could be inferred as substance to the resignation rumor, he capitulated and said, "That's probably true."

He resigned from the Nevada Supreme Court in May 1961. He publicly denied any discord among the justices, writing "my resignation was not influenced in any way by personalities." He also denied rumors he would seek reappointment as US attorney. Instead, he accepted the presidency of the Nevada Historical Society, returned to private practice, and continued his high-level sociality. While he had a fair amount of self-deprecation in his repertoire, others described him as a "charismatic spellbinder." He regularly joined the Kind Words Club for coffee with other notable lawyers of the time. In these social circles, his affability shined. He would tell his fellow members, "When I stand, get my knees locked into joint and commence talking, who knows how far I'm going to go?"

He was hospitalized for heart problems in July 1968 and died in May 1969, at age sixty-nine. The Nevada Supreme Court acknowledged in its memorial the difficult task of putting "into words our profound sorrow and deep sense of loss." It wrote of Justice Pike:

> While serving on the court he was always and unfailingly courteous and helpful to others, with an easy and natural dignity. His manner was forthright and friendly. On the bench, he was fair and just, and invariably courteous. His conduct, both as a lawyer and as a judge was always characterized by his wisdom, ability and integrity. His warm genial nature coupled with a delightful sense of humor and keen interest in people and his concern for the problems of others brought him many friendships with people in all walks of life. . . . More than most, [he] lived by the Golden Rule. Generous and sympathetic, he was never too busy to give the aid of his services regardless of any monetary reward. His life was characterized by thoughtfulness of others. Nothing finer can be said of any man. . . .
>
> When William H. Seward made his great plea for justice in the trial of William Freeman, he expressed the hope that when he shall have paid the debt of nature and his remains were put to rest with those of his kindred and neighbors, that some wandering stranger might erect over them a humble stone and inscribe thereon the epitaph "He was faithful." Truly, these same words also described the life and public service of Miles N. "Jack" Pike of Nevada.

GORDON R. THOMPSON

1961–1980

JUSTICE THOMPSON EMERGES FROM THE historical records as a courageous scholar whose commitment to social justice, civil liberties, and individual rights foreshadowed our modern jurisprudence. His imprint remains deep and palpable. Upon retirement, he was described as the "old, liberal warrior of the court." And like most warriors, he was not immune from controversy or criticism.

Gordon R. Thompson was born in 1918 on the one-acre family property at 1101 Riverside Drive, along the banks of the Truckee River. His mother was born in Iowa and proud of her father's service in the Union army during the Civil War. His father was an ordained Baptist minister who was born in Wasco County, Oregon. After completing his degree at Harvard, Thompson's father was hired in 1908 as principal of the University Preparatory High School in Reno, which helped rural Nevadans supplement their public educations before beginning their formal studies at UNR. Thompson's father later taught at UNR, chaired the philosophy department, and was dean of students. UNR's Thompson Building, now home to the College of Liberal Arts Student Center, is named in his honor.

Thompson's oldest brother died of typhoid fever at the age of five. With another older brother, Bruce (later US district judge for the District of Nevada), and two sisters, he worked on the family farm: milking cows, chasing chickens, and maintaining a large vegetable garden. To earn extra money they grew raspberries on their neighbor's property, sometimes beginning work at 4:30 in the morning during harvest season. As a young boy, Thompson milked the family cow and sold milk throughout the neighborhood. He attended McKinley Park Grammar School, Northside Junior High, and Reno High School, and he was active in student government and athletics. He played on the UNR basketball team that won the Far-Western Conference Championship in 1938. Except for his time at Stanford Law School, Thompson lived his entire life in Nevada.

Thompson was admitted to the Nevada Bar in 1943. He was elected to the state assembly in 1944, where he served on the Education Committee and as chair of the Judiciary Committee. His colleagues also selected him as chair of the Washoe legislative delegation. After ending his legislative career, he turned his public service to education, serving eight years as a trustee in the Reno and Washoe County School Districts. He was involved in several other professional and civic efforts, such as county and state bar leadership, the American Judicature Society, the Institute of Judicial Administration, and the Elks and Masonic Lodges. He also sang well and enjoyed being in the Reno Men's Chorus and Silver State Barbershop Quartet.

In 1946, Thompson worked in the Washoe County District Attorney's Office with Grant Bowen and John Bartlett. He joined the law firm of Woodburn, Forman, and Woodburn in 1948 and became a named partner in 1956. Known for his "easy manner before a jury," he tried several high-profile cases and was later elected a fellow of the American College of Trial Lawyers.

Between 1957 and 1959, Thompson moved closer to the Nevada Supreme Court when he served as one of five members of the court's Advisory Committee on Rules of Civil Procedure. When Justice Miles Pike announced his retirement in 1961, Thompson expressed his interest in serving on the court to Governor Grant Sawyer. Several prominent lawyers lobbied the governor on his behalf. For example, Procter Hug Jr. wrote that Thompson possessed the perfect qualities for an appellate judge: "a keenness of mind to search out the law, comprehend it and apply it to the circumstances at hand, together with the conviction and courage necessary to establish new doctrines of law as they become warranted." Governor Sawyer appointed Thompson to the Nevada Supreme Court in 1961. He was then forty-three.

Upon his appointment, Robert Taylor Adams emphasized Justice Thompson's ability to focus on what is most relevant:

One very interesting thing to lawyers about Gordon is the quality which he has of relevant thinking. All of us, I am afraid, depart from that kind of thinking from time to time, and the one time it should not be departed from is in the practice of law and, above all, when sitting as a Judge. We know Gordon has a good mind. We know how likable he is. We know he has experience. But those of you who have not known him as a lawyer will perhaps not realize the really keen sense of relevance which he has. It is said that lawyers should be experts in relevance; Gordon is such an expert.

Thompson was reelected twice without opposition and defeated challenger Charles Springer during a third reelection in 1974. He authored hundreds of opinions and assisted the court in its expansion from three to five justices in 1967.

Well respected for his scholarship and compelling opinions, he became the social conscience for the court within the boundaries of law. He was courageous despite criticism, and his progressive positions were not well received by some lawyers, legislators, and the public. For example, he was part of the majority that granted a new penalty hearing in a high-profile death penalty case involving Thomas Lee Bean. Senator William Raggio, then serving as Washoe County district attorney, described the decision as the "most outrageous and shocking in the history of the court." The press summarized the numerous letters it received in opposition to the decision and editorialized: "The courts need the kind of public scrutiny that has been given during the last few days. There is a feeling the courts have gotten away from the people and become more of an intellectual ground for lawyers. This is not right. The courts . . . are the property of the people."

Though described as "soft on crime" and urged to stop "coddling the criminals," Justice Thompson persisted in writing decisions described as the "liberalization" of controversial criminal concepts. When defending a decision limiting police interrogation tactics, he said, "the causes of crime are not in the Supreme Court decisions. They're created in poverty, in the ghettos, that type of thing. Crime will never be eliminated until they are eliminated. I don't think you can trace the high crime rate to these rulings."

Thompson also engaged in public outreach through legislative testimony, civic club speeches, and debates, always promoting the law as

Gordon R. Thompson

the tool for social reform. His remarks reveal a keen interest in civil rights and the constitutional protections for the criminally accused. He once observed: "Our nation need not worry about a court that zealously protects individual liberty. When it ceases to do so, then we shall have deep concern." He accepted an invitation to debate the tension between a free press and fair trial with Warren Lerude, then news editor of the *Reno Evening Gazette* and later preeminent professor of journalism at UNR. During this same time of public outreach he engaged in legal scholarship, publishing an article in the *Notre Dame Law Review* examining "the myth of harmless error." There, he noted that a "perfect trial" rarely occurs and that the "fair trial" is "perhaps . . . the most difficult of appellate functions."

Because Justice Thompson occasionally commented publicly about colleagues, judicial candidates, and trial judges, he was criticized for extrajudicial activism. During Watergate, he spoke publicly about how justice can be available for the affluent while unavailable for the impoverished. At a Law Day speech before the Reno Rotary Club he urged caution for the "law and order" movement, which he believed threatened the individual liberties protected by the Bill of Rights. He referenced Nazi suppression of rebellious and rioting students as an example to avoid, thus subtly criticizing "contemporary thinking that puts law and order above individual rights. There should not be law and order for all, but liberty and justice for all."

While a few criticized Thompson because his "controversy has overshadowed contribution," he was, nonetheless, a justice beloved by many, including staff, former clerks, work associates, and judicial colleagues. "To Nevada's young lawyers, Thompson became something of a folk hero: A justice who wrote each word of his authored opinions, who worked quickly and well, and whose facile mind always seemed to find the most probing questions." Though his published opinions softened and shortened as his career progressed, they remain the aspirational standard for appellate analysis and writing. One lawyer said, "[Justice Thompson] was the liberal on the court. . . . Now, the rest of the court has come more around to what [he] argued in the first place. It's not that [he] is running down, but that the rest of the court is catching up."

Throughout his career, Justice Thompson maintained intellectual honesty even when he knew his position would be unpopular. During reelection he publicly urged merit selection over judicial election because it "seems incongruous . . . that a non-political office should be subjected to the political process." He added, "voting for a judge is like voting for the surgeon who is going to operate on your wife. It's the kind of situation where you try to get someone in whom you have confidence. You don't rely on popular votes." He maintained his position after retirement when he testified in 1981 in support of Senator Sue Wagner's merit selection legislation.

Thompson's remarkable career was not without its costs. He struggled personally, underwent open-heart surgery, and lamented the court's personality fractures as he approached the end of his third term. Although he wanted to be known as a "builder of stone walls and brick walks" during the last season of his life, the "long-simmering hostilities" between the justices influenced his decision to retire in 1980. Justice John Mowbray offered the first of many accolades: "Gordon has one of the finest legal minds in the United States." The *Reno Gazette-Journal* reported that "for nearly two decades Thompson has been a star—probably 'the star'—of the Nevada Supreme Court." The Nevada Legislature issued a joint resolution noting that Justice Thompson was "considered by all those who worked with him to be one of the most intellectual and highly respected members of the court." It further resolved that "Judge Thompson will long be remembered as one of Nevada's outstanding jurists who, along with being admired for his astute knowledge of Nevada law, was a man recognized for his integrity, honesty and fairness."

In retirement, Thompson retreated to the solitude of his property and animals. He built rock walls, pathway borders, and a shake-roofed barn for his horse. He spent time at the Ophir Mill and the old Bundy guest ranch in Washoe Valley. But he also helped form the faculty and taught at Old College School of Law in Reno. During his two years at Old College, he enjoyed his relationships with students and contributed to yet another generation of young lawyers.

Thompson died in Reno on February 4, 1995, at age seventy-six. Judge Brent Adams said of him: "He was a jurist of perfect integrity and exceptional scholarship. He was known as one of the most intellectual members of the court and a lucid and concise writer. He was a model of what a jurist should be and all those who worked with him in court and clerked for him loved him so much. He was a deeply human man. I heard him speak many times. He was very moving on those occasions. He was a very sweet, sensitive person." The Nevada Supreme Court published a memorial to Justice Thompson in 2003.

David Zenoff

1965–1977

Justice David Zenoff emerges from the public records as a principled and passionate public official who left a deep imprint on Nevada law. As a justice in the 1960s and 70s, he served during a difficult period of national and local civil unrest—a time when jurisprudence was racing toward expanded individual liberties. In this atmosphere, Justice Zenoff's work was scrutinized by competing interest groups and occasionally criticized by those who felt judges were "soft on crime." But even critics respected Zenoff's commitment to family, friends, faith, community, and the law.

The youngest of six children, Zenoff was born in Amherst, Wisconsin, in 1916 to parents who emigrated from Russia. He initially wanted to be a journalist, but while a student journalist at the University of Wisconsin he was persuaded by the football coach to become a lawyer. He graduated from the University of Wisconsin Law School and began his legal career in Milwaukee in 1940. He knew then that he wanted to be a judge or law professor, but he left the law in 1942 to join the fight as a marine in World War II. He rose to the rank of major and was awarded the Bronze Star for his actions in the Okinawa campaign.

Zenoff returned to the law when his military service ended in 1946. His mother-in-law, who had recently traveled through Las Vegas, suggested it was a city of growth and opportunity, so he moved to Nevada and was admitted to the bar in 1948.

He first worked with a law firm that later evolved into the statewide firm of Jones Vargas. He enjoyed quick and high-profile success, which allowed him to begin planning his transition to the judiciary by intermittently working as a magistrate judge in the municipal court. He also joined political efforts, began volunteering for the state bar, and contributed to many civic endeavors—all of which increased his public profile. Even though he found success during this time, he later reflected that private practice was "too profitable to be happy in it."

To some, Zenoff appeared partisan, but he explained he was simply grounded in principles and friendship. For example, he initially registered as a Democrat but changed his party registration to Republican because he was "very teed off at former President Harry Truman." He publicly supported Republican governor Charles Russell's unsuccessful campaign for reelection in 1958, but returned to the Democratic Party after concluding Senator Goldwater had pushed the Republicans too far to the right. Zenoff was admired by his political peers, who attempted to enlist him as a candidate for governor in the 1960s.

One of Governor Russell's last acts before leaving office in late December 1958 was to appoint Zenoff to the district court to fill the vacancy created by Justice McNamee's election to the supreme court. The timing of the appointment caused some controversy, partly because Zenoff had campaigned against incoming governor Grant Sawyer and many doubted Sawyer would have appointed him to the court. Whatever Governor Russell's motivation, Zenoff immediately vindicated his confidence by becoming a highly regarded trial judge.

Juvenile justice was the animating issue of Justice Zenoff's judicial career. He volunteered for the juvenile delinquency cases and used his judicial prestige to improve the lives of abandoned and neglected children outside of the courtroom. He advocated for a separate system of juvenile justice and led the effort to create the Spring Mountain Youth Camp. He was an executive leader of the National Council of Juvenile and Family Court Judges and was deeply moved when the Clark County juvenile detention facility was named in his honor. In recognition of his advocacy, he was named the 1960 Most Outstanding Adult in Youth Work in Southern Nevada by the Interdenominational Youth Council of Southern Nevada.

When Justice McNamee was seriously injured during a violent crime at his home, Governor Sawyer (against whom Zenoff had previously campaigned) commissioned Zenoff to participate on the supreme court as a district court judge, a decision that reflects highly upon both Governor

Sawyer and Justice Zenoff. The press reported Zenoff was "not shy" about his ambition to be a permanent member of the court when he announced his intention to run for the seat the following year. He was elected without opposition in 1966.

Justice Zenoff gave many speeches on a variety of social and legal subjects throughout his career. These include the death penalty, merit selection of judges, free speech, government ethics, and the creation of a Nevada law school. He occasionally shared his own partisan opinions, but with a little reflection realized he could never fully speak as a public citizen while also serving on the supreme court.

Nonetheless, he showed his personality, for instance, when he encouraged young 4H club members to exercise free speech rights despite conservative warnings against an "overabundance" of free speech. But, he cautioned, free speech is most effective when it is respectful, and some go too far and became militants who "demand, swear, and threaten." He also wanted to "draw [a] line at boys who . . . are unkempt, unwashed and who smell bad."

Zenoff's deepest passion remained juvenile justice—even after joining the supreme court. As an appellate justice he became a statewide and national advocate for children. He often repeated certain themes: "We are willing to help children who have colds but we don't seem willing to be able to help those who are mentally sick," and "young people need help to return to the right highway because they've gotten on the wrong road." His daughter reminisced after his death that he was more interested in rehabilitation than punishment, and his motto for those sent to youth camp was, "You got yourself in there, now work yourself out." His remarks at the 1969 annual conference of the National Council of Juvenile and Family Court Judges were often repeated:

> We have delinquency all right, adult delinquency. Father slobbers by the gallon at the corner bar about how his family doesn't appreciate him and perhaps mamma is lapping it up someplace, too, so she won't be home either. This is graphic, of course, but you experienced judges know as well or better than I that delinquency begins at home or the lack of one. If there is anything poignantly apparent today it is that our most serious problem is people pollution and it is no wonder that the children are behaving like they came from sewers judging from the conduct of the grownups.

Justice Zenoff authored many published decisions but is primarily known for his defense of individual liberties. His decisions reveal his courage to enforce the law as he understood it, despite criticism and public clamor, which ultimately led to him being targeted for impeachment and recall by various groups. In one interesting press conference, Governor Laxalt identified Zenoff as part of a "liberal coloration" on the court who was more interested "in the rights of the individual with insufficient regard to the rights of the public."

While facing external criticism, Justice Zenoff demonstrated an inspirational degree of self-scrutiny that revealed a greater interest in doing right than in being right. In one high-profile decision, he wrote an opinion reversing an earlier decision he had written. In admitting his mistake, he subordinated his personal interests to the rule of law and showed intellectual honesty and professional courage.

In addition to his stature in the judiciary, Zenoff was also known within popular culture. In 1967, he was the subject of national and international news when he presided over the wedding of Elvis and Priscilla Presley. This was not the first time he was involved with celebrity matrimony. In 1959, he presided over the divorce of Debbie Reynolds and Eddie Fisher, and later the same year he attended the marriage of Eddie Fisher and Elizabeth Taylor. He was good-natured about his notoriety, claiming "that one enjoyable benefit of being a judge in Nevada was meeting celebrities and presiding over their marriages."

In his free time, he was an athlete and involved with athletic organizations. Although he judged many boxing matches, he was particularly gifted in racquet sports. A charter member of Tahoe Racquet Club at Lake Tahoe, he was in high demand as a doubles partner and feared as a singles opponent. In one amusing event he organized a club match against an unnamed team in Carson City. His teammates were surprised when they were admitted into the Nevada State Prison to play a "club" team of prisoners. He joked that he had sentenced some of their opponents, so they should "stay close [to him] once we get inside." Always looking to help the youth, he founded the Annual Governor's Cup Tennis Tournament for "tennis aspirants" and formed the Nevada Tennis Association, which allowed state and national accreditation for junior tennis players.

In addition to his work, politics, and athletics, Zenoff contributed to many civic groups, such as the Kiwanis, Anti-Defamation League, American Legion, and Marine Corps League. He supported many Jewish causes and was recognized for his leadership in founding places of worship, inspiring Temple Emanu-El to describe him as "an individual who has given extraordinary service to Israel and to mankind."

In 1976, he announced his retirement from the Supreme Court. He explained that though he had expected to serve his full term and was not looking for other opportunities, he had been made an offer to serve as a legal consultant and wanted to "enjoy a more relaxed and reduced lifestyle." One might say that he had fought the good fight, was proud of his service, and was anxious to retreat from the public spotlight.

His public service continued, however, when he accepted an appointment as the first senior justice and helped resolve a politically controversial prosecution of several athletes at the University of Nevada, Reno. He also accepted several board positions, including the boards of Southwest Gas, the Golden Nugget Hotel, and Irwin Molasky's Paradise Development and Realty Holdings.

He divided his retirement time between Las Vegas and Carlsbad, California. After an unwavering commitment to his wife of sixty-five years and their three accomplished children, he died in California in 2005 at age eighty-nine. True to his career passion, the lead sentence of his obituary reads: "Former Nevada Supreme Court Justice David Zenoff long felt that many bad kids could become good kids if shown the proper path in life." He was publicly recognized by several colleagues. Justice Gunderson wrote: "David believed children who had gone wrong had the potential to be shaped in a corrective manner—that was what he focused on very heavily. He was very much a pioneer in improving all aspects of the juvenile system and you could always count on him to be fair." Justice Young commented that Justice Zenoff "was a good leveling influence on the court. He was a credit to the judiciary." Justice Becker added her own observation that Zenoff "was a caring, intelligent and dedicated individual. He worked hard for the children of this State and I remember thinking, as a young lawyer and judge, 'that's the type of person I want to be.'"

The Nevada Supreme Court published a moving memorial in which it noted that Justice Zenoff "demonstrated dedication, ability, and leadership in all areas of his life—in his legal career, in his involvement in his community, and in his family." Even though he might have smiled at his own occasional zeal, Zenoff was a serious jurist who endeavored to improve Nevada law. In so doing, he left a personal mark that shall remain timeless.

Jon R. Collins

1966–1971

FOR A TIME, LIONEL SAWYER & Collins was the largest law firm in Nevada and viewed by many as the most prestigious. Grant Sawyer, who had served as Nevada governor, and Sam Lionel were larger-than-life lawyers, but it seems that Justice Collins faded into history as his founding law partners increased in visibility. A review of the historical records, however, reveals that Collins's imprint on the Nevada judiciary is deep and enduring.

Jon R. Collins was born in Ely in 1923. He attended public schools and graduated from White Pine High School. Two future Nevada governors were editors of opposing newspapers during Collins's youth. Vail Pittman published the *Ely Daily Times,* and Charles Russell owned the *Ely Record.* In Collins's first job, he sold newspapers for both of them, and he often reflected on how essential this early experience was in shaping his character: "Dealing with the public in those days was the foundation for my attitude in public life. Everything I learned then has in some way affected my actions today. That's a boy's first effort to sell himself to the public."

Collins graduated from the University of Pennsylvania in 1941 and enlisted in the navy during World War II, serving two years in the Pacific theater. After the war, he attended Georgetown Law School, working as an elevator operator, capitol policeman, and member of Senator Patrick McCarran's staff. These were fond times for him, as there he met his wife Rita and lifelong friend and fellow Nevadan Grant Sawyer. He worked for the justice department before returning to Ely in 1950, where

Jon R. Collins

he was elected White Pine County district attorney—shortly after Sawyer was elected Elko County district attorney. The two continued their friendship as rural county prosecutors, and each became involved in Democratic Party politics. Sawyer would eventually serve as governor, being first elected in 1952. Collins was a delegate to the National Democratic Convention for several election cycles, and he later chaired Jimmy Carter's 1976 presidential campaign in Nevada.

In 1958, Collins ran for district judge in the Seventh Judicial District against incumbent Judge Harry Watson. He almost won by default when Watson filed for reelection in the wrong location, but the Nevada Supreme Court extended the filing period to accommodate Watson's mistake. Collins defeated Watson by a mere nineteen votes, which led to litigation for a year about recounting ballots that had been lost.

Many lawyers spoke highly of Collins's work as a trial judge. He was formal, dignified, and made decisions "firmly and without hesitation." Despite enjoying this stellar reputation among his peers, an unfounded perception of misconduct would lead to tragedy.

In 1960 he presided over a property dispute involving a husband, wife, and the wife's mother in the Washoe County courthouse. As he was issuing his oral pronouncement, the husband pulled a gun from his waistband and shot at his wife, her attorney, and Collins. Two attorneys were killed. Collins was a percipient witness in the husband's subsequent criminal trial prosecuted by William Raggio, where among other things, the husband argued that Collins had conspired with the attorneys against him.

In May of 1966, Nevada Supreme Court justice Milton Badt died of a heart attack. The Board of Bar Governors considered several possible successors before forwarding Collins's name to Governor Sawyer, who appointed him to the position. Sawyer was worried about the appearance of appointing his good friend, whom he knew to be "totally incorruptible and independent," and also knew "almost too well," but the bar's neutral recommendation persuaded him it was the right appointment to make. Shortly after receiving the appointment, Collins successfully retained his seat in the 1966 election.

As a supreme court jurist, Justice Collins indicated he did not want to be a "liberal or conservative judge, although his sincere feelings are that the pendulum has swung too far in favor of the law breaker as against a safe, orderly society." Instead, his "philosophy of government lies in the solid middle ground, with a safe cushion against either of those two extremes—conservatism and liberalism. Or to put it another way—freedom as we know it has a price and that price is responsibility."

Collins put his ideas to action by devoting his first few years to the substantive work of the court. He authored 163 opinions and was known for his brief, concise writing style. In 1969, on becoming chief justice, he conceded some personal pride: "One factor I admired about McCarran, prior to his becoming a senator, was that he had once been chief justice of Nevada. It's extremely pleasing to me to be able to follow in his footsteps, because most, if not all, of my legal training was acquired through him—a man that I admired very much and a man who helped innumerable Nevadans become lawyers."

In his new role as chief justice, he engaged in efforts to modernize the judiciary, which he often described as antiquated machinery built for an earlier time. He used several metaphors to make the point, such as driving a 1970 car with a 1900 engine and "run[ning] General Electric or IBM with business practices of 1865," and argued that it was "vitally urgent we devise new machinery to deal with the problems we face in the near future."

To this end, he prepared an ambitious reform agenda for the 1969 legislative session that included (1) organizing the various courts and judicial districts under the supreme court's supervision, (2) hiring a statewide court administrator, (3) modifying the justice and municipal courts, (4) developing consistent judicial education through a National College of State Trial Judges on the UNR campus, (5) starting a Nevada law school, (6) increasing judicial salaries, (7) empowering the state bar to investigate and discipline lawyers, (8) converting judicial election to merit selection, (9) creating a statewide office of public defenders, (10) authorizing an intermediate court of appeals, and (11) recalling retired judges back into service to address growing and unmanageable caseloads.

Unfortunately, Justice Collins was ahead of his time. The preceding years of civil unrest and factional divides had stretched our nation's social fabric, and judicial reform was not a legislative priority. Proposal after proposal ended in the Senate Finance Committee, causing Collins to say: "I have said before and repeat my statement, that there can be no improvement in the judicial system of Nevada unless you gentlemen will give those of us in the judiciary the authority and opportunity of improving judicial administration in Nevada. The situation simply cannot improve, and it might well get worse than it now is, because of the increasing judicial business which we are attempting to administer through a totally inadequate system."

Defeated and likely deflated, Collins gave a speech at UNR shortly after the legislative session ended. He lamented the length of the session, the unrestricted number of proposed bills, and the power of committee chairmen who operated in secret: "There is far too much legislating done behind closed doors and from individual legislators' hip pockets. It is almost impossible to find out the current status of a bill until the decisions are all made; then it is usually too late." He went so far as to suggest the bicameral legislature be replaced with a unicameral legislature with thirty to forty members. His speech ended with a concession that the "problems and challenges we bequest to you are not easily solved. I hope you will be wildly successful. . . . Our generation has been only modestly successful."

A month later, he sat for a press interview and said: "Unless the next Legislature recognizes our pressing need for in-depth judicial reform, including a statewide court administrator, statewide court integration, and authorization to call back retired and former judges to temporary active judicial service, we are in serious trouble. . . . Hopefully, the pressing need for improvement in judicial administration can be made clearly known to the people of Nevada before an insoluble crisis develops."

The difficult legislative session affected his health during the latter part of 1969. It was during this time that he reflected on his future and became more stately in his public comments. At the governor's prayer brunch in February 1970, he acknowledged the country was "raging in controversies that could engulf and destroy us unless we re-assess ourselves." He continued this theme at a Memorial Day speech, urging his fellow citizens to remember that "arguable opinion" is not "final judgment" and implored:

> Each of us must reassess his own attitude toward his brother and realize that only God can know truth while man must be content with fallible arguments that only approach truth. This concept of brotherhood for which many veterans died has been set up on a shelf to be looked at, talked about and admired, but not to be touched, used, or practiced. The controversies rage on and on until one almost thinks there are no brothers anywhere in the world. Only when men reassess their arguments and realize they are only separated by shades of difference can they again become brothers seeking ultimate truth for which veteran patriots have died and are dying every day.

A few days later he announced he would not seek reelection "for personal reasons, principally economic." He admitted it was "very hard to leave judicial service because I see so much to be done. I see the growth of this State and the need for understanding of judicial problems. I urge the judges on this court to work toward improvement in judicial administration. I hope that the people of Nevada will find it in their hearts to concern themselves with problems which exist and help in the solution of them." Although some speculated he might run for governor, he instead announced he would be joining former governor Sawyer in the law firm that became Lionel Sawyer & Collins.

In his personal life, Justice Collins was a devoted husband and father. He adored his wife, Rita, and their four daughters. One colleague and friend said, "Both Rita and Jon Collins just simply blend in with all of us. You don't just meet the Collinses—you immediately like them, and they take to you as we take to them." He enjoyed spending time in the Nevada mountains and woodworking in his garage, "where [he made] anything and everything for the house." He was deeply respected by court employees throughout the state because of his genuine inquiries and kind gestures.

He died in 1987. The supreme court's memorial ended with former governor Sawyer's personal tribute:

> I should confess that I am entirely incapable of putting into words what should be said about Jon Collins. Given the fact that he was a

distinguished Nevadan, that he was an outstanding jurist, a highly respected attorney, the more personal side of Jon is what I would really like to talk about. He was so real; no artifice, no guile, no con. What you saw was what you got with Jon. He was totally unaffected and unassuming, dead honest, but probably the most important fact of Jon's character was his abiding concern about other people. He had friends in all walks of life, and he spent a lot of his life trying to help others. He knew and was close to people in highest government circles and he was friend and counselor to the poor and the needy and the disadvantaged. His girls were the basis of his life as he was theirs. He gloried in the successes and achievements of others and he was totally selfless. Jon was one of the few people that I've known who never in my presence made a mean, petty or unkind remark about another person. That rare quality of Jon's was felt, if not understood, by people throughout this State. I never went anywhere in the State of Nevada but that someone, usually a number of people, did not ask about Jon Collins. He knew and was respected by everyone, and loved by all those who knew him well. He leaves a void in our lives and we will miss him.

Washoe County district judge Thomas Craven spoke at Justice Collins's investiture and predicted he "will leave an indelible and constructive imprint on the legal annals of this state." These words could have been hyperbole at a time fitting for the ceremonial occasion. However, much of Collins's 1969 legislative agenda has now been implemented in the modern Nevada court system. Nevada is indebted to the wisdom and efforts of Jon Collins, who indeed left "an indelible and constructive imprint on the legal annals of this state."

Cameron M. Batjer

1967–1981

Justice Cameron Batjer demonstrated throughout his life the influences of his youth: inspirational women, rural values, and civic duty. He was a loyal friend, often noted for his humility and gentle presence. While active in party politics and a fierce legal advocate, he was apolitical and impartial as a judge and a peacemaker among colleagues during a divisive time for the Nevada Supreme Court. He is remembered fondly by those who knew him, and the Nevada judiciary is better because of his service.

Batjer's uncle first came to Nevada as a miner in the late 1850s. Shortly after statehood, his grandparents emigrated from Canada to join their son on 480 acres of fertile ranch land in Smith Valley, just south of Yerington. It was there, in his grandparents' small ranch home, that Batjer was born in 1919. Shortly after birth, he moved with his parents to Shoshone, Idaho, where they resided for four years before returning to Smith Valley to live within a tight-knit ranching family. Indeed, his extended family composed his village, as his parents were often absent for work. His father Robert Wilhelm Batjer, who emigrated from Germany to Nevada in the 1890s, worked as a cattle rancher and trucker delivering dry goods to mining camps throughout rural Nevada. He died in the 1930s during the difficult days of the depression. Despite this tragedy, Batjer's earliest memories of ranch life were of family, dusty roads, pre-motorized farm equipment, and stubborn horses he never learned to love.

While the men brought the family to Nevada, it was the trailblazing

Justice Cameron M. Batjer

women in his family who inspired him throughout his life. A source of pride for Batjer was his great-grandmother, who graduated from the University of Edinburgh in 1850 and qualified to be a lawyer. Regrettably, gender limited her legal options, and she worked as a governess until immigrating to Canada.

While he was proud of his great-grandmother, his mother was his hero and the singular influence in his life. Mary Belle McVicar Batjer had already graduated from the University of Nevada and was a schoolteacher in Smith Valley before her 1916 marriage to Batjer's father. She worked throughout Batjer's life and was highly regarded as a teacher at several rural schools. She even found time to serve on the school board.

His sister Helene Batjer briefly taught school in Virginia City before beginning a foreign service career in 1945. She enjoyed positions in Berlin, Sofia, Rome, Athens, Belgrade, and Stockholm before becoming the lead diplomat at the American consulate in Istanbul, Turkey. She was named officer in charge of Czechoslovakian affairs in 1967, and between 1970 and 1972 she was the financial economist for the American embassy in Pakistan. She ended her career as the diplomat in residence at Reed College in Portland, Oregon.

Batjer met his wife Lura Gamble briefly during his UNR years but fell in love with her when they were both public school teachers in Dayton. Also the child of rural Nevada pioneers, Lura was raised on the family ranch in Hazen and attended Churchill County schools, where she was recognized as an outstanding student and athlete. She and Batjer were the parents of three daughters.

Batjer enjoyed high-level positions in state and federal governments, but he never lost the connection with his rural roots and accomplished women who inspired him throughout his life. He remembered fondly (and by name) his grammar school teachers and classmates. He attended first through fifth grades in a small schoolhouse across the street from his home and was one of thirteen students in his class. He enjoyed school "from the first day, and learning was a continuing great experience." Equally important to him were his early memories of traveling to church with his grandmother in a horse-driven buggy. They attended the Methodist Church in Smith Valley—the only church in town—where a congregation of twenty to thirty, most of them part of his family, worshipped together. He continued to value faith throughout his life, and for more than sixty years was a member of the First Presbyterian Church of Carson City.

Smith Valley was small but progressive, and the desire for knowledge was embedded into Batjer early. His childhood friend Mary Arentz was the daughter of US Congressman Samuel Arentz, and Batjer's lifelong love of country and civic duty were borne of his observations of Congressman Arentz. His uncle Robert McCall, an assemblyman from Esmeralda County who died while serving in Carson City, contributed to Batjer's commitment to community. And during his frequent trips to

Yerington, he occasionally stopped at the courthouse to watch District Attorney Jack Ross in court proceedings.

Batjer's small Smith Valley world expanded in size throughout his childhood. When he passed through Carson City, he enjoyed seeing the capitol complex that housed all three branches of government, and he was particularly enamored by the portraits of governors hanging in the hallways. But one trip in particular had a lasting impression on him. In 1927, he traveled to Reno to celebrate the completion of the Victory and Lincoln Highways. This was an "eye-opening" trip for the seven-year-old from Smith Valley. He walked the UNR campus with his mother and described Idlewild Park and the California Building with awe. He saw the stately homes along Riverside Drive and knew his life could be larger than Smith Valley ranching.

Batjer's primary education introduced him to more of his home state than the family ranch. In the sixth, seventh, and eighth grades, he accompanied his mother as she taught at various schools in northern Nevada. She was one of his teachers, and he considered her to be particularly hard on him—especially during English lessons. Eventually, he returned to Smith Valley to live with his grandmother and uncle during his high school years. He loved history and tolerated the sciences; and the seeds of law were sown when he briefly studied commercial law.

He enrolled at UNR after graduating from high school. He worked at a grocery store and lumberyard in Reno during the school years and returned to the ranch to work every summer. With the shadow of war hanging over campus, he knew he was destined for military service. However, he was declined for ROTC because of color blindness. He then received several medical deferments because of whooping cough, poor eyesight, and frailty. He graduated with a degree in history and minors in education and economics. He was certified as a teacher when he graduated in 1941, and accepted a job teaching elementary school in Dayton. But as he extended his family's long tradition as educators, on December 7, 1941, the Imperial Japanese Navy Air Service attacked Pearl Harbor and plunged the United States into World War II.

Batjer enlisted in the navy in February 1942. He completed the school year as a teacher and married Lura before his military induction in San Francisco. Initially assigned to a Seabee construction battalion in the South Pacific, he endured many nights in a foxhole during the bombing raids on Guadalcanal before receiving an officer's commission while stationed in New Zealand. Unable to remain with the Seabees because he did not have a degree in civil engineering, he attended Japanese language school and was later assigned to General MacArthur's Seventh Fleet in Brisbane, Australia. His service continued through the duration of the war, and he was released from military service in November 1945.

On returning to Nevada, he was unsure about his immediate future, so he did what was familiar to him: he called the superintendent of education in Carson City and obtained a midyear teaching position in McGill, Nevada. In 1947, he was hired as the football and basketball coach at Fernley High School, which he found ironic because he was a self-described "lousy athlete." While in Fernley he resolved to attend law school and selected the University of Utah because of its proximity to Nevada. He began law school in 1948 and graduated in 1950. He did well and was selected for Order of the Coif. He passed the Utah bar exam and worked for the Utah Senate during its 1951 session.

Batjer was then hired to work in Washington, DC, for newly elected Nevada senator George "Molly" Malone. He worked closely with committees important to Nevada (Interior, Mine and Mining, and Insular Affairs) and quickly became exhausted with politics and bureaucracy. He and Lura yearned to return to Nevada, which they did in 1952. They arrived in March so Batjer could satisfy the six-month residency requirement before the bar exam in September. He again returned to his education roots by accepting a position to teach seventh and eighth grades in Carson City for the remainder of the school year.

After passing the bar, he began working in Carson City with Frank Gregory and Dick Hanna. During this time he became friendly with Paul Laxalt, who was then serving as Ormsby County district attorney. Batjer and Laxalt remained close friends for the duration of their lives.

Laxalt hired Batjer as a deputy district attorney, and when Laxalt resigned in 1954 to return to a full-time law practice, the Board of County Commissioners appointed Batjer in his place. This was a busy time for him; not only was he the Ormsby County district attorney, he advised the Carson City Council and school district, and maintained a small private practice. He was elected to his own term as Ormsby County district attorney without opposition in November 1954.

In 1958, at age thirty-nine, Batjer ran for Nevada attorney general as a Republican. His opponent was Roger Foley, a friend and former fraternity brother. Democrats exceeded Republicans in statewide registration, and Batjer was horribly underfunded. He later described his decision to be a candidate as "stupid." Yet four years later, in 1962, he ran for the same office. He was then serving as chair of the Ormsby County Republican Party and was escorted to the filing office by the chair of the state Republican Party. When nobody else filed to run as a Republican, Batjer became a candidate at 4:55 p.m. He described himself as a "most hesitant candidate" and his decision an "absolute stupid move" that he agreed to only because the Republicans "needed someone to carry the torch." Again, he lost the statewide election.

Batjer completed his term as Ormsby County district attorney and returned to private practice in loose association with Laxalt. He became active in the profession, including volunteer work for the state bar and American Judicature Society. Paul Laxalt was elected governor in 1966, and Batjer advised him during the 1967 legislative session. During this session, the supreme court expanded from three to five justices to accommodate the overwhelming amount of work, immediately creating two vacancies. When Governor Laxalt approached his trusted friend about an appointment to the court, Batjer expressed an interest and willingness to serve. In October 1967, Laxalt appointed him and John Mowbray to the Nevada Supreme Court.

Justice Batjer was opposed in his 1968 election by a strong candidate from Las Vegas. Governor Laxalt publicly endorsed Batjer, and when criticized, responded that "absolutely nothing precludes me, either as a private citizen or as governor of this state, from speaking out in important election contests. What is significant to me is the fact there is a basic unfairness in expecting a quiet and retiring man like Cameron Batjer to out-campaign a rugged, political in-fighter like John Mendoza.

With Laxalt's endorsement, Batjer was elected in 1968, reelected against a nominal opponent in 1972, and reelected without opposition in 1978. He enjoyed the studious work of an appellate judge and wrote several significant opinions. As noted by Justice Kristina Pickering upon his death, Batjer was a "great scholar and jurist who understood the virtue of brevity, common sense, and kindness."

Batjer was on the court during a time of increasing work, politically difficult decisions, and internal feuding among the justices. He and his colleagues were severely criticized when they reversed capital sentences in response to jurisprudence from the US Supreme Court. He was publicly gracious and unwilling to speak of internal affairs, but privately attempted to intervene in the growing frictions among his colleagues. He was criticized in the press for his efforts to resolve judicial ethics complaints his colleagues had filed against each other. He attempted to downplay the divisiveness, saying at one point: "There are always disagreements. You arrive at decisions by kicking cases around." At one point the press reported he might even resign if the "infighting gets any worse." This desire for cooperation informed his approach to every aspect of his work. In retirement, he reminisced that he had even been reluctant to write dissents: "You know, the supreme court is supposed to be a collegial body, where you get together and hear the arguments of the lawyers and then the position of the judges and come up with the best answer."

By 1981, his friend Paul Laxalt was in the US Senate and a close, personal confidant of President Reagan. Through Laxalt, President Reagan came to know Justice Batjer, who resigned his position on the Nevada Supreme Court in 1981 to accept a presidential appointment as chair of the US Parole Commission, with concomitant duties as chair of the National Appeals Board. He relocated to Washington, DC, and was well regarded for his service. He again yearned for Nevada and retired after nine years because it was the "prudent thing to do" and "Washington is a town for the upward bound."

He and his wife enjoyed their retirement years, dividing time between Reno and Maui. Lura died in 1997, and Batjer himself on June 1, 2011. Many colleagues mourned his death, describing him as even-tempered, bright, humble, self-reliant, persistent, and compassionate.

In 2002, Justice Batjer sat for his oral history as part of the Nevada Legal Oral History Project, a joint effort of the Nevada Judicial Historical Society, the Ninth Judiciary Circuit Historical Society, and the University of Nevada Oral History Program. His endearing personality and personal reminisces are woven throughout the transcript. The editors noted that readers "will be struck by his intelligence, humility, pragmatism, and gentle humor." He was a "gifted storyteller" and "teacher at heart," demonstrating by example the best qualities that bind us together.

Thomas L. Steffen

1982–1997

Justice Thomas Steffen was known for many qualities, yet he may best be remembered for a powerful writing style that unlocked appellate decisions from their typically analytical and dispassionate form. The best example is found in a right-to-die decision issued after the US Supreme Court's opinion in *Cruzan v. Director, Missouri Department of Health*. Steffen's decision is legally persuasive, but more importantly, written with prose that speaks to the public's consciousness. A few excerpts illustrate:

> At the tender age of ten, Kenneth suffered the fate of a quadriplegic as the result of a swimming accident. Twenty-one years later, faced with what appeared to be the imminent death of his ill father, Kenneth decided that he wanted to be released from a life of paralysis held intact by the life-sustaining properties of a respirator. Although Kenneth was able to read, watch television, orally operate a computer, and occasionally receive limited enjoyment from wheelchair ambulation, he despaired over the prospect of life without the attentive care, companionship and love of his devoted father. . . .
>
> One of the verities of human experience is that all life will eventually end in death. As the seasons of life progress through spring, summer and fall, to the winter of our years, the expression unknown to youth is often heard evincing the wish to one night pass away in the midst of a peaceful sleep. It would appear, however, that as the scientific community continues to increase human longevity

and promote "the greying of America," prospects for slipping away during peaceful slumber are decreasing. And, for significant numbers of citizens like Kenneth, misfortune may rob life of much of its quality long before the onset of winter. . . .

It must nevertheless be conceded, as noted above, that death is a natural end of living. There are times when its beckoning is sweet and benevolent. Most would consider it unthinkable to force one who is wracked with advanced, terminal, painful cancer to require a therapy regimen that would merely prolong the agony of dying for a brief season. In allowing such a patient to refuse therapy could it seriously be argued that he or she is committing an act of suicide?

Justice Steffen was tireless in effort, incorruptible in action, and endlessly graceful in person. And he was the wordsmith the above excerpt reveals him to be.

Thomas L. Steffen was born in Tremonton, Utah, in 1930. His childhood in rural Utah was defined by family, faith, and work. His father was an accountant and part owner of an automobile dealership. Consistent with the times, his mother was a homemaker who taught him the values of education and industry. Steffen remained attentive to his parents throughout their lives, largely because his oldest brother did not survive infancy and his only other sibling was killed in Germany during the last days of World War II. His brother had been named outstanding senior boy at Bear River High School and planned a career in law. Steffen was fourteen years old when his brother died, and he sought to honor his brother's memory throughout his lifetime—including his decision to become a lawyer.

In high school, Steffen was a gifted student who enjoyed athletics (football, baseball, and boxing) but was often unable to participate because of his employment at the local grocery store. He was also a proud Eagle Scout who remained devoted to the Boy Scouts of America through his adulthood. Although he matriculated at the University of Utah immediately after high school, he interrupted his studies after his first year to volunteer for his church in Western Canada.

After returning to the University of Utah, Steffen started working for Household Finance Corporation, where he quickly assumed greater management responsibilities. More importantly, it was during this time that he met LaVona, his lifelong love and wife of sixty-two years. Household

Thomas L. Steffen

Finance soon transferred him to Southern California, where he studied at the University of Southern California for two semesters. Again promoted at a young age, Steffen returned to Utah to manage the Household Finance office in Provo. While working full time, he completed his undergraduate degree by taking night classes at the University of Utah. He and LaVona were growing their young family at the time, but he found an outlet through collegiate boxing competitions. (His admiration for boxing explains why he was a zealous advocate for his clients—yet always civil, complying with rules, and respecting the courts and law.)

Steffen's career reached an inflection point during this time. He had planned to pursue a career in politics, but was dissuaded after observing his lifelong friend Ralph Harding, a young congressman from Idaho, sacrifice so much of his privacy and family to the demands of public office. Meanwhile, Household Finance offered a transfer to the San Francisco office. But Steffen and LaVona took a different path. They sold their home in Utah and moved with their four young children to Washington, DC, where he began his studies at George Washington Law School. He worked one semester as a capitol policeman but soon learned he could not work all night and attend school during the day, so he obtained a full-time job as a contract negotiator with the Bureau of Naval Weapons while continuing his legal studies as a night student. He performed well in law school and served as editor of the law review.

Steffen intended to return to Utah but was unable to sit for the Utah bar exam because of a delay in his law school finals exam schedule. During this same time, he began to wonder if the Utah market was too crowded; he saw Las Vegas as a town of opportunity and Nevada as a state worthy of his family. He passed the Nevada bar exam in 1964 with the highest score of all applicants and began practicing with his friend Lloyd George, who later served as a US district court judge.

During the next eighteen years Steffen was active in the legal community, serving as director of the Nevada Trial Lawyers Association, while primarily representing plaintiffs in personal injury actions. He later developed a commercial litigation practice representing contractors and subcontractors in their disputes with banks. During this time he balanced the responsibilities of family, church, community, and professional volunteerism.

Steffen's law practice was successful by all measures. He never aspired to be a judge and could have happily remained in private practice for the duration of his career. Yet with the broad encouragement of lawyers and judges, he applied to fill the vacancy on the Nevada Supreme Court created by the resignation of Justice Cameron Batjer. Governor Robert List appointed him to the court in 1982.

During his fifteen-year tenure, Justice Steffen considered his judicial service to be a sacred public duty and believed that "above all else every judge should be scrupulously and fearlessly honest." He retired from the supreme court in 1997, having served as its chief justice and earning broad respect for his diligence, impartiality, keen mind, and superior writing. In retirement, he served "of counsel" with his son's law firm Hutchinson & Steffen, followed collegiate football, and enjoyed time with his wife, five children, and eighteen grandchildren.

Steffen died in 2020, after being a widower for several years. As he aged he understood the very words he had written as an appellate jurist thirty years earlier: "As the seasons of life progress through spring, summer and fall, to the winter of our years, the expression unknown to youth is often heard evincing the wish to one night pass away in the midst of a peaceful sleep." Justice Steffen died as he lived: with fidelity to family, faithful to convictions, dignified in presence, and heroic to all who had the privilege of working with him. His deep imprint on Nevada justice shall remain timeless.

Sources

SELECTED BIBLIOGRAPHY FOR INTRODUCTION

Primary Sources

An Act to Enable the People of Nevada to Form a Constitution and State Government. Ch. 36, 13 Stat. 30–32 (March 21, 1864).
An Act to Establish a Territorial Government for Utah. Ch. 51, 9 Stat. 453–458 (Sept. 5, 1850).
An Act to Extend the Territorial Limits of the Territory of Nevada. Ch. 173, 12 Stat. 575 (July 14, 1862).
An Act to Organize the Territory of Nevada. Ch. 83, 12 Stat. 209–214 (March 2, 1861).
Acts, Resolutions, and Memorials, Passed at the Several Annual Sessions of the Legislative Assembly of the Territory of Utah. Great Salt Lake City: Joseph Cain, Public Printer, 1855.
Acts, Resolutions, and Memorials, Passed by the First Annual, and Special Sessions of the Legislative Assembly. Great Salt Lake City: Brigham H. Young, Printer, 1851.
Address of R. M. Clarke, Attorney General, May 13, 1867. In *Reports of Cases Determined in the Supreme Court of the State of Nevada.* San Francisco: Towne & Bacon, 1866.
Appendix to Journals of Senate of the First Session of the Legislature of the State of Nevada. Carson City: John Church, 1865.
"The Ax Began to Fall." *Gold Hill Evening News,* July 21, 1864.
Bellows, Henry. Letter to US Attorney General Edward Bates, July 25, 1864. Bellows Papers, Massachusetts Historical Society, Boston.
"Brothers-in-Law." *Gold Hill Evening News,* July 30, 1864.
Cradlebaugh, John. Letter to General Sherman, Feb. 12, 1861. Vault Manuscript Collection, MSS 688, Harold B. Lee Library, Brigham Young University, Provo, UT.

Goldman v. Nevada Comm'n on Judicial Discipline. 108 Nev. 251, 256, 830 P.2d 107, 110 (1992).

Jones, Horatio M. Letter to US Attorney General Edward Bates, Nov. 30, 1862. In *Letters Received by the Attorney General 1809–1870: Western Law and Order*, edited by Fredrick S. Calhoun and Martin Schipper. Bethesda, MD: University Publications of America, 1995, reel 8, Nevada, box 1, folder 3.

Jones, Horatio. Letter to US Attorney General Edward Bates, July 30, 1863. In Russell W. McDonald, "Biographical Summaries: Nevada's Territorial, District, Supreme Court, and Federal Judges: 1856–1993" (unpublished ms.). Reno: Nevada Historical Society.

The Journal of the Senate During the First Session of the Legislature of the State of Nevada. Carson City: State Printer, 1865.

Lincoln, Abraham. "By the President of the United States: A Proclamation [to Admit Nevada into the Union]," Proclamation No. 22, 13 Stat. 749–780 (Oct. 31, 1864).

Marsh, Andrew J. *Debates and Proceedings in the Constitutional Convention of the State of Nevada.* San Francisco: Frank Eastman, 1866.

Marsh, Andrew J. *Letters from the Nevada Territory: 1861–1862.* Edited by William C. Miller, Russell W. McDonald, and Ann Rollins. Carson City, NV: Legislative Counsel Bureau, 1972.

McDonald, Russell W. "Biographical Summaries: Nevada's Territorial, District, Supreme Court, and Federal Judges: 1856–1993" (unpublished ms.). Reno: Nevada Historical Society.

Miller, William C., and Eleanore Bushnell, eds. *Reports of the 1863 Constitutional Convention of the Territory of Nevada.* Carson City: Legislative Counsel Bureau, 1972.

"Official Report of Governor Cumming to General Cass." *Utah Territory: Message of the President of the United States Communication in Compliance with a Resolution of the House, Copies of Correspondence Relative to the Conditions of Affairs in the Territory of Utah.* 36th Cong., 1st Sess., House Exec. Doc. 78 (Serial 1056), Washington, DC: Thomas H. Ford, 1860.

"The Petition." *Gold Hill Evening News,* Aug. 11, 1864.

Reports of Cases Determined in the Supreme Court of the State of Nevada. San Francisco: Sumner Whitney, 1866.

Robinson v. First Judicial District Court, 73 Nev.169, 313 P.2d 436 (1957).

Rothman, Hal K. "Utah: The Territorial and District Courts." In Rothman, *The Making of Modern Nevada.* Reno: University of Nevada Press, 2010.

Russell McDonald Papers. "Nevada Territorial Supreme Court Opinions," box 4, Nevada Historical Society, Reno.

Territorial Transcripts Nevada Supreme Court. Carson City: Nevada Records Management Services, 1971.

Trench v. Strong, 4 Nev. 87 (1868).

Turner, George. Letter to US Attorney General Edward Bates. In *Letters Received by the Attorney General 1809–1870: Western Law and Order,* edited by Fredrick S. Calhoun and Martin Schipper. Bethesda, MD: University Publications of America, 1995, reel 8, Nevada, box 1, folder 3.

Welliver, Andy, ed. "First Records of Carson Valley; Utah Ter. 1851." *Nevada Historical Society Quarterly* 9, nos. 2–3 (1966), https://epubs.nsla.nv.gov/statepubs/epubs/210777-1966-2-3Summer-Fall.pdf.

Newspapers

Carson Daily Appeal
Daily Missouri Republican
Eastern Slope
Elko Daily Free Press
Esmeralda Union
Gold Hill Evening News
Humboldt Register
Las Vegas Sun
Liberty Tribune
Los Angeles Times
Mason Valley News
Morning Appeal
Nevada State Journal (Reno)
Pioche Record
Reese River Reveille
Reno Evening Gazette
Reno Gazette-Journal
Sacramento Bee
Sacramento Daily Union
San Francisco Evening Bulletin
San Francisco Examiner
San Luis Obispo Tribune
Silver State
Territorial Enterprise
Tonopah Daily Bonanza
Vermontville Echo (formerly *Enterprise*)
Virginia Daily Union
White Pine News (Cherry Creek)

Secondary Sources

Alverson, Bruce. "The Limits of Power: Comstock Litigation, 1859–1864." *Nevada Historical Society Quarterly* 43, no. 1 (Spring 2000): 74–79.

"AN ACT Defining the Boundaries of Counties." In *Acts, Resolutions, and Memorials, Passed at the Several Annual Sessions of the Legislative Assembly of the Territory of Utah*. Great Salt Lake City, UT: Joseph Cain, Public Printer, 1855.

Angel, Myron, ed. *History of Nevada*. Oakland, CA: Thompson & West, 1881.

Armstrong, Robert D. *Nevada Printing History: Bibliography of Imprints and Publications, 1858–1880*. Reno: University of Nevada Press, 1981.

Bakken, Gordon Morris. *The Development of the Law of the Rocky Mountain Frontier: Civil Law and Society*. Westport, CT: Greenwood Press, 1983.

_____. *Rocky Mountain Constitution Making, 1850–1912*. Westport, CT: Greenwood Press, 1987.

Bancroft, Hubert Howe. *History of Nevada, Colorado, and Wyoming, 1540–1888*. San Francisco: History Co., 1890.

_____. *History of the Pacific States of America*. San Francisco: History Co., 1890.

BeDunnah, Gary. *Nevada: Our Home*. Salt Lake City, UT: Gibbs-Smith, 2006.

Bowers, Michael W. Foreword to *Nevada Historical Quarterly* 43, no. 1 (2000): 3–4.

_____. "Judicial Selection in Nevada: Choosing the Judges." *Halcyon: A Journal of the Humanities* 11 (1989): 86–103.

_____. *The Nevada State Constitution: A Reference Guide*. Westport, CT: Greenwood Press, 1993.

_____. *The Sagebrush State*, 3rd ed. Reno: University of Nevada Press, 2006.

Bowers, Michael W., and Larry D. Strate. "Judicial Selection in Nevada: An Historical, Empirical, and Normative Evaluation." *Nevada Historical Society Quarterly* 36, no. 4 (Winter 1993): 227–245.

Browne, J. Ross. "A Peep at Washoe." *Harper's Monthly Magazine*, January 1861.

Bushnell, Eleanore. *The Nevada Constitution: Origin and Growth*, rev. ed. Reno: University of Nevada Press, 1968.

Bushnell, Eleanore, and Don W. Driggs. *The Nevada Constitution: Origin and Growth*, 6th ed. Reno: University of Nevada Press, 1980.

Dequille, Dan. *The Big Bonanza*. New York City: Knopf, 1947.

_____. *History of the Big Bonanza*. Hartford, CT: American Publishing, 1876.

Elliott, Russell R., with the assistance of William D. Rowley. *History of Nevada*, 2nd ed., rev. Lincoln: University of Nebraska Press, 1987.

_____. *Servant of Power: A Political Biography of Senator William M. Stewart*. Reno: University of Nevada Press, 1983.

Ellison, Marion. *An Inventory & Index to the Records of Carson County, Utah & Nevada Territories, 1855–1861*. Reno: Grace Dangberg Foundation, 1984.

Ellison, Robert W. *Territorial Lawmen of Nevada*. Vol. 1. Minden, NV: Hot Springs Mountain Press, 1999.

Fletcher, Galen LeGrande. "200 Nevada Legal History References: A Selective Annotated Bibliography and Introduction." *Nevada Law Review*, Spring 1998: 101–130.

Fletcher, Galen LeGrand, and Ann S. Jarrell. "Territorial Legal Research for

Nevada." In *Prestatehood Legal Materials: A Fifty State Research Guide,* edited by Michael Chiorazzi and Marquerite Most. Binghamton, NY: Haworth Information Press, 2006.

Hardy, David A. "The Nevada Territorial Supreme Court: A Transitional Influence from Frontier Lawlessness to Statehood." PhD diss., University of Nevada, Reno, 2015. ProQuest (UMI 3707834).

Hawthorne, Nathaniel. *The Scarlet Letter.* 1850. Reprint, Bronxville: Cambridge Book Co., 1968.

Heller, Dean. *Political History of Nevada,* 10th ed. Carson City, NV: State Printing Office, 1997.

Homer, Michael W. "The Judiciary and Common Law in Utah Territory, 1850–61." *Dialogue: A Journal of Mormon Thought* 21, no. 1 (Spring 1988): 97–108.

Hulse, James W. *The Silver State: Nevada's Heritage Reinterpreted,* 3rd ed. Reno: University of Nevada Press, 2004.

James, Ronald M., and Raymond Elizabeth, eds. *Comstock Women: The Making of a Mining Community.* Reno: University of Nevada Press, 1998.

Johnson, David A. "A Case of Mistaken Identity: William M. Stewart and the Rejection of Nevada's First Constitution." *Nevada Historical Society Quarterly* 22, no. 2 (Fall 1979): 186–198.

———. "The Courts and the Comstock Lode: The Travail of John Wesley North." *Pacific Historian* 27, no. 2 (1983): 31–46.

———. *Founding the Far West: California, Oregon, and Nevada, 1840–1890.* Berkeley: University of California Press, 1992.

Kintop, Jeffrey M. "Mining Nevada's Legal History: Going to the Sources." *Western Legal History* 20, nos. 1–2 (2007): 99–118.

"Legendary Mormon Curse Blamed for Washoe Disasters." Available at http://www.lvrj.com/news/legendary-mormon-curse-blamed-for-washoe-disasters-138767239.html.

Lord, Eliot. *Comstock Mining and Miners.* Washington, DC: Government Printing Office, 1883.

Nevada's Court Structure. Carson City, NV: Legislative Counsel Bureau, 1968.

O'Brien, J. P., ed. *History of the Bench and Bar of Nevada.* San Francisco: Bench and Bar Publishing, 1913.

Purkitt, J. H. "Nevada Territory." *San Francisco Evening Bulletin,* Feb. 15, 1860.

Shinn, Charles Howard. *The Story of the Mine: As Illustrated by the Great Comstock Lode of Nevada.* New York: D. Appleton, 1896.

Smith, Grant H. *The History of the Comstock Lode.* Reno: University of Nevada Press, 1998.

Stewart, William M., and George Rothwell Brown. *Reminiscences of Senator William M. Stewart of Nevada.* New York: Neale Publishing, 1903.

Stone, Wilbur Fisk, ed. *History of Colorado.* Chicago: S. J. Clarke, 1918.

Stonehouse, Merlin. *John Wesley North and the Reform Frontier.* Minneapolis: University of Minnesota Press, 1965.

Swackhamer, Wm. D. *Political History of Nevada*, 8th ed. Carson City, NV: The Secretary, 1986.

Watkins, T. H. *Gold and Silver in the West: The Illustrated History of an American Dream.* Palo Alto, CA: American West Publishing, 1971.

Zanjani, Sally Springmeyer. *Devils Will Reign: How Nevada Began.* Reno: University of Nevada Press, 2006.

———. *Goldfield: The Last Gold Rush on the Western Frontier.* Las Vegas: Nevada Publications, 1992.

SELECTED SOURCES FOR BIOGRAPHIES

Nevada Territorial Supreme Court Justices

GEORGE E. TURNER

George Turner to Abraham Lincoln, May 28, 1863, in General Records of the Department of Justice, Appointment File—Nevada 1861–1865, National Archives.

Gold Hill Daily News, Feb. 21, 1867.

Humboldt Register, Feb. 25, 1865.

"Meeting of the Bar and Citizens of Ormsby County," *Virginia Daily Union,* Aug. 27, 1864.

Nevada State Journal, Aug. 28, 1923.

San Francisco Examiner, Aug. 13, 1885.

Merlin Stonehouse, *John Wesley North and the Reform Frontier* (Minneapolis: University of Minnesota Press, 1965).

GORDON N. MOTT

"Territorial Supreme Court," *Humboldt Register,* May 2, 1863.

Eliot Lord, *Comstock Mining and Miners* (Washington, DC: Government Printing Office, 1883), 132.

"How Judge North Got His Seat," *Gold Hill Evening News,* July 26, 1864.

HORATIO M. JONES

Russell W. McDonald, "Biographical Summaries: Nevada's Territorial, District, Supreme Court, and Federal Judges: 1856–1993" (unpublished ms.) (Reno: Nevada Historical Society).

G. W. Beattie memoirs: cited in McDonald, "Biographical Summaries."

Horatio Jones to Abraham Lincoln, July 30, 1863, in General Records of the Department of Justice, Appointment File—Nevada 1861–1865.

"Thunder in the Sky," *Gold Hill Evening News,* July 19, 1864.

Vermontville Echo, June 20, 1906.
"A Strange Story," *Virginia Daily Union,* May 11, 1864.

Powhattan Locke
"Judge Locke's Case," *Gold Hill Evening News,* May 11, 1864.
"Unpublished Chapters," *Gold Hill Evening News,* August 3–4, 1864.
"Judge Locke's Case," *Daily Union,* May 11, 1864, qtd. in "Judge Locke's Case," *Gold Hill Evening News,* May 11, 1864.
Daily Missouri Republican, Oct. 9, 1868.
"Judge Locke," *Gold Hill Evening News,* May 27, 1864.
"A Stampede," *Gold Hill Evening News,* Aug. 9, 1864.
William M. Stewart and George Rothwell Brown, *Reminiscences of Senator William M. Stewart of Nevada* (New York: Neale Publishing, 1903), 162.
Daily Missouri Republican, Oct. 9, 1868.
Resolution of State Bar of Louisiana. *The Weekly Caucasian* (Lexington, MO), June 27, 1868.
Virginia Daily Union, Aug. 25, 1864.

John W. North
"District Court," *Gold Hill Evening News,* May 23, 1864.
"More Facts for Consideration," *Gold Hill Evening News,* July 25, 1864.
"How Judge North Got His Seat," *Gold Hill Evening News,* July 26, 1864.
"A Card," *Virginia Daily Union,* July 24, 1864.
"Lame and Shuffling Defenses," *Gold Hill Evening News,* Aug. 5, 1864.
David Alan Johnson, *Founding the Far West* (Berkeley: University of California Press, 1992), 317.
Henry Bellows to US Attorney General Edward Bates, July 25, 1864, Bellows Papers, Massachusetts Historical Society, Boston.
Eliot Lord, *Comstock Mining and Miners* (Berkeley, CA: Howell-North Books, 1959).
Judge North, qtd. in Lord, *Comstock Mining and Miners,* 144.
"Meeting of the Bar and Citizens of Ormsby County," *Virginia Daily Union,* Aug. 27, 1864.

Nevada Supreme Court Justices

James F. Lewis
Carson Daily Appeal, May 17, 1867.
The Administrative Office of Courts has compiled some information in the Nevada Judicial History Database. See https://nvcourts.gov/aoc/judicialhistory, accessed March 22, 2016.
"James F. Lewis," Online Nevada Encyclopedia, accessed March 22, 2016, http://onlinenevada.org/articles/james-f-lewis.

Patty Cafferata, "Nevada's Original Jurists Flitted Through Nevada," *Nevada Lawyer*, Aug. 2010.
Sam Post Davis, ed., *The History of Nevada*, vol. 1 (Elms Publishing, 1913).
State of Nevada v. Duffy, 7 Nev. 342 (1872).
State of Nevada v. Rhodes, 3 Nev. 240 (1867).
"In Memoriam, James F. Lewis," 19 Nev. 449 (1886).

Henry O. Beatty

Gold Hill Daily News, Oct. 27, 1864.
Russell W. McDonald, "Biographical Summaries: Nevada's Territorial, District, Supreme Court, and Federal Judges: 1856–1993" (unpublished ms.) (Reno: Nevada Historical Society).
Cornelius Cole, *Memoirs of Cornelius Cole: Ex-Senator of the United States from California* (New York: McLoughlin Brothers, 1908).
Morning Appeal, Feb. 17, 1892.
"Henry O. Beatty," Online Nevada Encyclopedia, accessed March 22, 2016, http://onlinenevada.org/articles/henry-o-beatty.
Robert D. Armstrong, *Nevada Printing History: A Bibliography of Imprints and Publication 1858–1880* (Reno: University of Nevada Press, 1981).
Sam Post Davis, ed., *The History of Nevada*, vol. 1 (Elms Publishing, 1913).
State of Nevada v. Rhodes, 3 Nev. 240 (1867).

Cornelius M. Brosnan

Carson Daily Appeal, May 17, 1867.
Eastern Slope, January 27, 1866.
Esmeralda Union, October 29, 1864.
Gold Hill Daily News, July 1864.
Russell W. McDonald, "Biographical Summaries: Nevada's Territorial, District, Supreme Court, and Federal Judges: 1856–1993" (unpublished ms.) (Reno: Nevada Historical Society).
"Cornelius M. Brosnan," Online Nevada Encyclopedia, accessed April 25, 2016, http://onlinenevada.org/articles/cornelius-m-brosnan.
Milliken v. Sloat, 1 Nev. 573 (1865).

J. Neely Johnson

Carson Daily Appeal, May 12, 1867.
California State Legislature, "Journal of the Eighth Session of the Senate of the State of California," American Legislation Project, accessed July 25, 2024, https://kellenfunk.org/legislation/items/show/1211.
Russell W. McDonald, "Biographical Summaries: Nevada's Territorial, District, Supreme Court, and Federal Judges: 1856–1993" (unpublished ms.) (Reno: Nevada Historical Society).

"J. Neely Johnson Explained," accessed May 11, 2016, http://everything.explained.today/J._Neely_Johnson.

"J. Neely Johnson." *The National Cyclopedia of American Biography* (New York: James T. White & Company, 1904), 188.

Andrew Jackson Marsh, *Official Report of the Debates and Proceedings in the Constitutional Convention of the State of Nevada, Assembled at Carson City, July 4th, 1864, to Form a Constitution and State Government* (1866), 5.

Sacramento Daily Union, Sept. 2, 1872.

BERNARD CROSBY WHITMAN

"Modest and Retiring," *Gold Hill Daily News*, Dec. 8, 1864.

"In Memoriam, Bernard Crosby Whitman," 19 Nev. 445 (1885).

Virginia Union, Dec. 8, 1864.

JOHN GARBER

John P. O'Brien, ed., *History of the Bench and Bar of Nevada* (San Francisco: Bench and Bar Publishing, 1913).

"The Opposing Candidates for Supreme Judge," *Gold Hill Daily News*, Oct. 12, 1870.

"In Memoriam, John Garber," 30 Nev. 507 (1908).

"The Mass Meeting Saturday Night," *Reese River Reveille*, Aug. 23, 1864.

Oscar T. Shuck, ed., *History of the Bench and Bar of California* (Los Angeles: Commercial Printing House, 1901).

Sacramento & Meredith Min. Co. v. Showers, 6 Nev. 291 (1871).

CHARLES HENRY BELKNAP

John P. O'Brien, ed., *History of the Bench and Bar of Nevada* (San Francisco: Bench and Bar Publishing, 1913).

Thomas Wren, *A History of the State of Nevada, Its Resources and People* (New York: Lewis Pub., 1904).

"In Memoriam, Charles Henry Belknap," 50 Nev. 443 (1926).

National Register of Historic Places Registration Form for the "Belknap House," Oct. 30, 1997, https://npgallery.nps.gov/pdfhost/docs/NRHP/Text/97001302.pdf.

THOMAS PORTER HAWLEY

John P. O'Brien, ed., *History of the Bench and Bar of Nevada* (San Francisco: Bench and Bar Publishing Co., 1913).

Thomas Wren, *A History of the State of Nevada, Its Resources and People* (New York: Lewis Pub., 1904).

"In Memoriam, Thomas P. Hawley," 29 Nev. 597 (1907).

"Judge Hawley's Candidature," *Nevada State Journal*, July 31, 1902.

Warner Earll

John P. O'Brien, ed., *History of the Bench and Bar of Nevada* (San Francisco: Bench and Bar Publishing, 1913).

Thomas Wren, *A History of the State of Nevada, Its Resources and People* (New York: Lewis Pub., 1904).

"In Memoriam, Warner Earll," 19 Nev. 453 (1888).

San Luis Obispo Tribune, July 13, 1888.

State v. Rogers, 10 Nev. 319 (1875).

William H. Beatty

John P. O'Brien, ed., *History of the Bench and Bar of Nevada* (San Francisco: Bench and Bar Publishing, 1913).

Thomas Wren, *A History of the State of Nevada, Its Resources and People* (New York: Lewis Pub., 1904).

Russell W. McDonald, "Biographical Summaries: Nevada's Territorial, District, Supreme Court, and Federal Judges: 1856–1993" (unpublished ms.) (Reno: Nevada Historical Society).

Nevada State Journal, April 22, 1874; June 1, 1975; July 4, 1899.

"In Memoriam, William Henry Beatty," 37 Nev. 511 (1914).

"In Memoriam, William Henry Beatty," 168 Cal. 799 (Cal. 1915).

Oscar T. Shuck, ed., *History of the Bench and Bar of California* (Los Angeles: Commercial Printing House, 1901).

Reese River Reveille, Oct. 7, 1864; June 17, 1868.

Sacramento Daily Union, Oct. 31, 1874.

Orville Rinaldo Leonard

Nevada State Journal, Sept. 19, 1882; Sept. 23, 1882.

"Eliza Sylvester Leonard," Find a Grave, accessed July 14, 2017, https://www.findagrave.com/memorial/121417444/eliza-leonard.

Horace Stuart Cummings, *Dartmouth College: Sketches of the Class of 1862* (Washington, DC: H. I. Rothrock, Printer, 1884), 101.

John P. O'Brien, ed., *History of the Bench and Bar of Nevada* (San Francisco: Bench and Bar Publishing, 1913).

Thomas Wren, *A History of the State of Nevada, Its Resources and People* (New York: Lewis Pub., 1904).

Michael Augustus Murphy

"Michael A. Murphy—Republican, Elected," NV.gov, accessed July 14, 2017, http://ag.nv.gov/Bios/Biographies/05_-_Michael_A__Murphy/.

"In Memoriam, Michael A. Murphy," 31 Nev. 541 (1910).

Nevada State Journal, Sept. 19, 1882; Oct. 27, 1909.

John P. O'Brien, ed., *History of the Bench and Bar of Nevada* (San Francisco: Bench and Bar Publishing, 1913).
Thomas Wren, *A History of the State of Nevada, Its Resources and People* (New York: Lewis Pub., 1904).

Rensselaer R. Bigelow
R. R. Bigelow, "Chief Justice Bigelow, of Nevada, Against Free Coinage" (Home Market Club, 1896).
"In Memoriam, Rensselaer R. Bigelow," 29 Nev. 597 (1907).
The Law Notes, vol. 11: April 1907 to March 1908 (Edward Thompson, 1908).
John P. O'Brien, ed., *History of the Bench and Bar of Nevada* (San Francisco: Bench and Bar Publishing, 1913).
Thomas Wren, *A History of the State of Nevada, Its Resources and People* (New York: Lewis Pub., 1904).

McKaskia Stearns Bonnifield
Andy Osterdahl, "McKaskia Stearns Bonnifield (1833–1913)," The Strangest Names in American Political History, Jan. 3, 2012, accessed July 14, 2017, https://politicalstrangenames.blogspot.com/2012/01/mckaskia-stearns-bonnifield-1833-1913.html.
"In Memoriam, M. S. Bonnifield," 36 Nev. 647 (1913).
John P. O'Brien, ed., *History of the Bench and Bar of Nevada* (San Francisco: Bench and Bar Publishing, 1913).
Thomas Wren, *A History of the State of Nevada, Its Resources and People* (New York: Lewis Pub., 1904).
Cari M. Carpenter and Carolyn Sorisio, eds., *The Newspaper Warrior: Sarah Winnemucca Hopkins's Campaign for American Indian Rights, 1864–1891* (Lincoln: University of Nebraska Press, 2015).
Silver State, March 29, 1875.
"A Notable Conversion," *White Pine News,* Nov. 3, 1894.

William A. Massey
William Alexander Massey, Find a Grave, accessed July 30, 2024, https://www.findagrave.com/memorial/7125926/william-alexander-massey.
"Documenting Nevada's Long History of Intraparty Squabbles," *Vegas Seven,* July 1, 2015, 16, accessed May 9, 2024, https://issuu.com/vegasseven/docs/lv19275_vegas_seven_07_02.
"In Memoriam, William A. Massey," 37 Nev. 507 (1914).
John P. O'Brien, ed., *History of the Bench and Bar of Nevada* (San Francisco: Bench and Bar Publishing, 1913).
Thomas Wren, *A History of the State of Nevada, Its Resources and People* (New York: Lewis Pub., 1904).

Nevada State Journal, Nov. 8, 1901; March 6, 1914.

"Massey, William Alexander," Biographical Directory of the U.S. Congress, accessed Aug. 15, 2017, http://bioguide.congress.gov/scripts/biodisplay.pl?index=M000229.

"Hon. W. A. Massey," *Nevada Genealogy Trails,* accessed Aug. 15, 2017, https://genealogytrails.com/nev/carson/bios1.html.

Adolphus Leigh Fitzgerald

"In Memoriam, Adolphus Leigh Fitzgerald," 45 Nev. 453 (1921).

"Hon. Adolphus Leigh Fitzgerald," Nevada Genealogy Trails, accessed Sept. 17, 2024, https://genealogytrails.com/nev/eureka/bios.html.

John P. O'Brien, ed., *History of the Bench and Bar of Nevada* (San Francisco: Bench and Bar Publishing, 1913).

Thomas Wren, *A History of the State of Nevada, Its Resources and People* (New York: Lewis Pub., 1904).

"Nevada Confederate Veterans," Sons of Confederate Veterans, accessed Aug. 15, 2017, https://web.archive.org/web/20161209135425/http:/www.dixon-hunley.org/nevada_vets.php.

Tasker L. Oddie, *Letters from the Nevada Frontier: Correspondence of Tasker L. Oddie, 1898–1902,* ed. William A. Douglass and Robert A. Nylen (Reno: University of Nevada Press, 1992), 359n.

Thomas Van Camp Julien

John P. O'Brien, ed., *History of the Bench and Bar of Nevada* (San Francisco: Bench and Bar Publishing, 1913).

Nevada State Journal, July 23, 1890; Nov. 8, 1901.

Thomas Wren, *A History of the State of Nevada, Its Resources and People* (New York: Lewis Pub., 1904).

Russell W. McDonald, "Biographical Summaries: Nevada's Territorial, District, Supreme Court, and Federal Judges: 1856–1993" (unpublished ms.) (Reno: Nevada Historical Society).

Reno Evening-Gazette, Oct. 28, 1880; Oct. 22, 1884; March 1, 1902.

George Frederick Talbot

"In Memoriam, George F. Talbot," 58 Nev. 483 (1938).

Sam Post Davis, ed., *The History of Nevada,* vol. 1 (Elms Publishing, 1913).

"Hon. George Frederick Talbot," Nevada Genealogy Trails, accessed Sept. 17, 2024, https://genealogytrails.com/nev/elko/biosNZ.html.

John P. O'Brien, ed., *History of the Bench and Bar of Nevada* (San Francisco: Bench and Bar Publishing, 1913).

Thomas Wren, *A History of the State of Nevada, Its Resources and People* (New York: Lewis Pub., 1904).

Russell W. McDonald, "Biographical Summaries: Nevada's Territorial, District, Supreme Court, and Federal Judges: 1856–1993" (unpublished manuscript) (Reno: Nevada Historical Society).
Pioche Record, April 18, 1914.

Frank H. Norcross
"Norcross, Frank Herbert," Federal Judicial Center, accessed Oct. 13, 2017, https://www.fjc.gov/history/judges/norcross-frank-herbert.
"Frank H. Norcross," Nevada Genealogy Trails, accessed May 9, 2024, https://genealogytrails.com/nev/washoe/biosLN.html.
"Judge Frank Herbert Norcross," Find a Grave, accessed Oct. 13, 2017, https://www.findagrave.com/cgi-bin/fg.cgi?page=gr&GRid=63591459.
"In Memoriam, Frank H. Norcross," 69 Nev. 357 (1938).
John P. O'Brien, ed., *History of the Bench and Bar of Nevada* (San Francisco: Bench and Bar Publishing, 1913).
Thomas Wren, *A History of the State of Nevada, Its Resources and People* (New York: Lewis Pub., 1904).
Press Reference Library (Western edition). *Being the Portraits and Biographies of the Progressive Men of the West* (International News Service, 1913).
Nevada State Journal, June 8, 1894; Nov. 5, 1952.

James G. Sweeney
Carson City Daily Appeal, July 7, 1917.
"James G. Sweeney—Democrat—Silver Party, Elected," NV.gov, accessed Oct. 13, 2017, http://ag.nv.gov/Bios/Biographies/13_-_James_G_Sweeney.
John P. O'Brien, ed., *History of the Bench and Bar of Nevada* (San Francisco: Bench and Bar Publishing, 1913).
Thomas Wren, *A History of the State of Nevada, Its Resources and People* (New York: Lewis Pub., 1904).
Press Reference Library (Western edition), *Being the Portraits and Biographies of the Progressive Men of the West* (International News Service, 1915).
"The Journal's Nevada Forum," *Nevada State Journal,* March 22, 1977.

Patrick A. McCarran
"In Memoriam, Patrick A. McCarran," 70 Nev. 561 (1953–54).
David Montero, "There Is a Renewed Push to Remove the McCarran Name in Nevada," *Los Angeles Times,* March 27, 2017, http://www.latimes.com/nation/la-na-mccarran-nevada-2017-story.html.
Jerome Edwards, "Patrick Anthony McCarran," Online Nevada Encyclopedia, accessed Sept. 8, 2010, http://www.onlinenevada.org/articles/patrick-anthony-mccarran.
"Patrick Anthony McCarran Statue," Architect of the Capitol, accessed

Jan. 3, 2017, https://www.aoc.gov/art/national-statuary-hall-collection/patrick-anthony-mccarran.

"McCarran, Patrick Anthony (Pat)," Biographical Directory of the United States Congress, accessed Jan. 3, 2017, http://bioguide.congress.gov/scripts/biodisplay.pl?index=M000308.

Benjamin W. Coleman

"In Memoriam, Benjamin Wilson Coleman," 58 Nev. 485 (1937–38).
"Judge B. W. Coleman Dies at Home in Carson While Treating Injury to Neck," *Reno Gazette-Journal*, Feb. 27, 1939.
Russell W. McDonald, "Biographical Summaries: Nevada's Territorial, District, Supreme Court, and Federal Judges: 1856–1993" (unpublished manuscript) (Reno: Nevada Historical Society).

John Adams Sanders

"In Memoriam, John Adams Sanders," 65 Nev. 789 (1948).
"John Adams Sanders," Prabook.com, accessed March 12, 2018, https://prabook.com/web/john_adams.sanders/937755.
"Justice Sanders Is Visitor in Richmond," *Nevada State Journal*, June 10, 1923.
"J. A. Sanders Noted Jurist Dies in Reno," *Nevada State Journal*, Aug. 16, 1948.
"Nevada Supreme Court Justice Will Not Run Again," *Reno Evening Gazette-Journal*, April 12, 1934.
Stockgrowers' & Ranchers' Bank of Reno v. Milisich, 52 Nev. 178, 283 P. 913 (1930).

Edward Augustus Ducker

"Judge Ducker Seeks Office," *Nevada State Journal*, April 1, 1942.
S.J. Res. 7, 41st Leg. Sess. (Nev. 1943).
"In Memoriam, Edward Augustus Ducker," 63 Nev. 477 (1946).
Russell W. McDonald, "Biographical Summaries: Nevada's Territorial, District, Supreme Court, and Federal Judges: 1856–1993" (unpublished manuscript) (Reno: Nevada Historical Society).
Reno Gazette Journal, Sept. 13, 1937.

Erroll James Livingston "E. J. L." Taber

"In Memoriam, E. J. L. Taber," 63 Nev. 497 (1945–46).
"Mrs. Farrington Dies Today at Age of 87," *Reno Gazette-Journal*, Jan. 21, 1938, 18.
"Justice Taber Dies Suddenly in Reno Today," *Reno Gazette-Journal*, Feb. 6, 1947, 20
"E. J. L. Taber of Supreme Court Dies," *Nevada State Journal*, Feb. 7, 1947, 14.
Heather Kennison, "*Local Architect Plans Historic Restoration of Downtown Building*," *Elko Daily*, April 4, 2015, https://elkodaily.com/news/local-architect-plans-historic

-restoration-of-downtown-building/article_ab93e249-d3d0-5b1b-bd2f
-17b983264f2f.html.
"Hatton Dons Silken Robes for Hearing," *Nevada State Journal,* April 29, 1937.
"They Served," *Nevada State Journal,* Feb. 7, 1947.
"Court Adjourns to Honor Taber," *Nevada State Journal,* Feb. 11, 1947.
"Justice E. J. L. Taber," *Reno Gazette-Journal,* Feb. 7, 1947.

William E. Orr

"Namesake," William E. Orr Middle School, accessed May 9, 2024, https://
www.orrmiddleschool.org/apps/pages/index.jsp?type=d&uREC
_ID=552352&pREC_ID=105883.
"In Memoriam, Honorable William E. Orr," 351 F.2d 1, 5–15 (9th Cir. 1965).
"Judge W. E. Orr Is New Justice," *Nevada State Journal,* March 3, 1939.
Sheldon Goldman, *Picking Federal Judges: Lower Court Selection from Roosevelt Through Reagan* (New Haven, CT: Yale University Press, 1999), 80–81.
Proceedings of the Twenty-Second Annual Meeting of the State Bar of Nevada, 15 Nev. St. B.J., 60, 65 (April 1950).
"Orr, William Edwin," Federal Judicial Center, accessed Aug. 14, 2018, https://
www.fjc.gov/history/judges/orr-william-edwin.
Proceedings of the Thirty-Fourth Annual Meeting of the State Bar of Nevada, 27 Nev. St. B.J., 1, 12–13, 41 (Jan. 1962).

Charles Lee Horsey

"In Memoriam, Charles Lee Horsey," 73 Nev. 355 (1958).
Southwestern Publishing Co. v. Horsey, 230 F.2d 319, 321–22 (9th Cir. 1956).
"Meet the Candidates—Supreme Court," *Reno Gazette-Journal,* Nov. 1, 1950.
"Horsey Files for Supreme Court Post," *Nevada State Journal,* June 15, 1946.
"Judge Clark Lee Horsey Announces Candidacy for the Supreme Court," *Mason Valley News,* Oct. 4, 1946.
"The News of Seaford," *Evening Journal,* Feb. 23, 1899.
"Judge Horsey To Be Named to Nevada Supreme Bench," *Reno Gazette-Journal,* Oct. 3, 1945.
"An Endorsement of Mr. Horsey," *Pioche Record,* July 23, 1910.
"Republicans Won Sweeping Victory in Nevada Last Tuesday," *Pioche Record,* Nov. 12, 1910.
"Death Takes Judge Horsey," *Reno Gazette-Journal,* March 31, 1958.
"Justice Charles Lee Horsey of Las Vegas Is a Candidate for Reelection to the Nevada Supreme Court," *Reno Gazette-Journal,* June 14, 1946.
"Senate Passes Lottery Repeal Resolution After Terms Are Assailed by Senator Horsey," *Reno Gazette-Journal,* Jan. 23, 1939.
"Elect Charles Lee Horsey (Incumbent) Justice of Supreme Court," *Reno Gazette-Journal,* Nov. 2, 1946.

"Former Jurist Wins Libel Trial," *Reno Gazette-Journal*, Sept. 29, 1954.
"Former Justice Sues Vegans on Charge of Libel," *Nevada State Journal*, July 23, 1952.
"Attorney Says He Didn't See Money Passed in Mullen," *Reno Gazette-Journal*, Nov. 4, 1977.
"In Memoriam," *UVA Lawyer*, Spring 2008, https://www.law.virginia.edu/static/uvalawyer/html/alumni/uvalawyer/spro8/memoriam.htm.
"Foley Grants Horsey Motion for New Trial," *Reno Gazette-Journal*, March 13, 1954.

Edgar Eather

"In Memoriam, Honorable Edgar Eather," 85 Nev. 725 (1970).
"Eureka-Lander Judge Retiring," *Reno Gazette-Journal*, April 4, 1946.
"Eureka Officials Trade Jobs and Judge Is Now Prosecutor," *Reno Gazette-Journal*, Nov. 5, 1929.
"Law Enforcement Occupies Center of Political Stage," *Reno Gazette-Journal*, Oct. 27, 1923.
"Eureka County Lawyer Files His Application for U.S. Appointment," *Reno Gazette-Journal*, Jan. 30, 1926.
"Gambling Debt Lawsuit Lost by Reno Man," *Reno Gazette-Journal*, Jan. 10, 1942.
"The Curious, Extravagant Life of George Whittell Jr.," *Auto Week*, Nov. 10, 2017, https://autoweek.com/article/car-life/thats-duesy.
"Edgar Eather New Supreme Court Justice," *Nevada State Journal*, Sept. 6, 1946.
"Judge Eather Fills Vacancy on High Court," *Reno Gazette-Journal*, Sept. 6, 1946.
"Justices Eather, Badt File for Reelection to Positions," *Nevada State Journal*, June 17, 1948.
"Report Eather to Leave Court," *Reno Gazette-Journal*, Nov. 29, 1958.
"Justice Eather Announces Plan to Leave Court," *Reno Gazette-Journal*, Dec. 1, 1958.
"Justice Edgar Eather Dead in Reno, Aged 81," *Reno Gazette-Journal*, Sept. 2, 1968.
"Area Deaths—Edgar Eather," *Reno Gazette-Journal*, Sept. 3, 1968.

Milton B. Badt

"In Memoriam, Honorable Milton B. Badt," 82 Nev. 465 (1966).
"Interview with Milton Badt," by Mary Ellen Glass, University of Nevada Oral History Program, available at https://archive.org/details/BadtMilton.
"Items About People You Know," *Reno Gazette-Journal*, Sept. 28, 1971.
"Milton B. Badt Named President State Bar Ass'n," *Nevada State Journal*, Feb. 4, 1933.
"Nevada Politics by the Observer," *Nevada State Journal*, June 6, 1948.
"Pardons Board Problems Told," *Reno Gazette-Journal*, Nov. 9, 1948.

"State's Judges Confer on New Probation Act," *Nevada State Journal,* Oct. 2, 1951.
"Civil Practice Rules Accepted by High Court," *Reno Gazette-Journal,* Aug. 29, 1952.
"Revision of Nevada Laws Proves to Be Titanic Job," *Reno Gazette-Journal,* Dec. 19, 1952.
"Contests Set in All but One State Race," *Reno Gazette-Journal,* July 14, 1964.
"Badt Denies He'll Retire," *Reno Gazette-Journal,* March 11, 1966.

Charles M. Merrill

"In Memoriam, Charles M. Merrill," 117 Nev. 997 (2003).
"Price, Merrill in Partnership," *Reno Gazette-Journal,* Jan. 3, 1935, 2.
"Charles M. Merrill, John E. Robinson, Leslie B. Gray Announce That They Have Formed a Partnership," *Reno Gazette-Journal,* July 27, 1946.
"Judge Merrill Nominated to Appeals Court," *Reno Gazette-Journal,* Aug. 28, 1959.
"Merrill Is High Court Candidate," *Nevada State Journal,* Feb. 28, 1950.
"Charles Merrill to Seek Seat on High Court," *Reno Gazette-Journal,* March 1, 1950.
"Merrill Wins High Tribunal Over Horsey," *Nevada State Journal,* Nov. 9, 1950.
"Political Races Under Way," *Reno Gazette-Journal,* July 17, 1956.
"Judge Merrill Urged for Post on High Court, *Reno Gazette-Journal,* Sept. 22, 1971.
"Jason P. Steed, The Most Important Election Ever," *Federal Lawyer,* Dec. 2014.
"U.S. Justice: The Law Called Expression of Public Conscience," *Reno Gazette-Journal,* May 25, 1973, 12.
"Merrill Dies," *Elko Daily Free Press,* April 4, 1996.
Obituary, *Sacramento Bee,* April 4, 1996.

Frank McNamee

"In Memoriam, Honorable Frank McNamee," 85 Nev. 729 (1970).
"Cause of Injury Unknown; Judge Found at Tahoe," *Reno Gazette-Journal,* Feb. 16, 1965.
"Justice Frank McNamee Dies in Vegas Rest Home," *Nevada State Journal,* Nov. 5, 1968.
Jean Reid Norman, "McNamee, Member of Pioneer Family of Attorneys, Dies at 68," *Las Vegas Sun,* Dec. 10, 2003, https://lasvegassun.com/news/2003/dec/10/mcnamee-member-of-pioneer-family-of-attorneys-dies.
"Mrs. Gable in Las Vegas," *Reno Gazette-Journal,* Jan. 21, 1939.
"Frank J. McNamee, Jr., Republican for Lieutenant Governor," *Reno Gazette-Journal,* Nov. 5, 1938.
"Leo A. McNamee Will Succeed Judge Brown," *Reno Gazette-Journal,* Aug. 12, 1943.
"Clark Election Cases Reach High Court," *Reno Gazette-Journal,* Aug. 10, 1940.
"Frank McNamee Named to Bench," *Reno Gazette-Journal,* July 11, 1946.

"Vegas Judge Doesn't Want a Fourth One," *Nevada State Journal*, Sept. 13, 1957.
"Watson's Perjury Counts Dismissed," *Reno Gazette-Journal*, Nov. 18, 1953.
"Freelance Pastor Faces Crackdown," *Reno Gazette-Journal*, Oct. 7, 1957.
"Statewide Races Set in Nevada," *Reno Gazette-Journal*, Nov. 5, 1960.
"Jurist Named 'Man of Year,'" *Reno Gazette-Journal*, Jan. 26, 1959.
"Late Senator Is Eulogized by Colleagues," *Reno Gazette-Journal*, Nov. 9, 1954.
"McNamee Beating—Justices: 'A Horrible Thing . . . ,'" *Reno Gazette-Journal*, Feb. 17, 1965.
"Jurist Remains Critical," *Reno Gazette-Journal*, Feb. 19, 1965.
"Jurisdiction Given Nevada in McNamee Case," *Reno Gazette-Journal*, March 12, 1965.
"Suspect Seized Here in Beating of Nevada Judge," *St. Louis Post-Dispatch*, Feb. 18, 1965.
"Held in Attack on Chief Judge," *Kansas City Times*, Feb. 18, 1965.
"McNamee Still in Coma," *Reno Gazette-Journal*, Feb. 20, 1965.
"Judge McNamee Showing Signs of Emerging from Deep Coma," *Reno Gazette-Journal*, Feb. 22, 1965.
"Denning Skips Hearing in McNamee Case," *Reno Gazette-Journal*, March 17, 1965.
"Grand Jury Indicts Denning," *Reno Gazette-Journal*, March 25, 1965.
"Denning Asks for a Hearing on Charges in McNamee Case," *Reno Gazette-Journal*, April 9, 1965.
"Denning Denied Motion for Hearing," *Reno Gazette-Journal*, April 23, 1965.
"Denning Pleads Innocent in McNamee Case," *Reno Gazette-Journal*, May 6, 1965.
"Denning Sent to Hospital for Tests," *Reno Gazette-Journal*, June 19, 1965.
"Denning Might Never Face Trial in Beating," *Reno Gazette-Journal*, July 30, 1965.
"Jurist Halts Unescorted Denning Trips," *Reno Gazette-Journal*, Oct. 18, 1965.
"Denning Mentally Fit to Stand Trial Now, Hughes Tells Judge," *Reno Gazette-Journal*, Oct. 23, 1965.
"Denning Case: 'A Political Football,'" *Reno Gazette-Journal*, Oct. 23, 1965.
"Suspect Calm; Psychiatrists Say He's Sane," *Reno Gazette-Journal*, Feb. 1, 1966.
"Denning Preliminary Hearing Planned," *Reno Gazette-Journal*, Feb. 2, 1966.
"Denning Hearing Postponed," *Reno Gazette-Journal*, Feb. 17, 1966.
"Judge Approves Change of Trial for Denning from Douglas to Lyon," *Reno Gazette-Journal*, March 11, 1966.
"Denning Trial Is Suspended," *Reno Gazette-Journal*, May 24, 1966.
"One-five Year Term in Beating," *Nevada State Journal*, June 1, 1966.
"Phillippe Denning Asks to Go Free on Parole," *Reno Gazette-Journal*, March 1, 1967.
"Denning Fails in Parole Bid," *Reno Gazette-Journal*, March 2, 1967.
"McNamee Suspect Denning is Released," *Reno Gazette-Journal*, March 29, 1969.

Miles N. "Jack" Pike

"Memorial, Honorable Miles N. Pike," 85 Nev. 735 (1970).
"Judge Willard H. A. Pike," Second Judicial District Court—A Historical Perspective, accessed April 8, 2019, https://www.washoecourts.com/Historical/1901/Pike.
"Miles Pike Files for District Judge," *Nevada State Journal*, July 22, 1938.
"M'Knight and Pike Leading," *Nevada State Journal*, Sept. 7, 1938.
"Politics—Parties and Candidates Preparing Now for State Conventions, Which Are Set for September 27th," *Reno Gazette-Journal*, Sept. 10, 1938.
"Miles N. (Jack) Pike for District Judge," *Nevada State Journal*, Oct. 31, 1938.
"The District Judgeship," *Reno Gazette-Journal*, Nov. 4, 1938.
"Miles N. Pike Endorsed by Both Senators for U.S. Attorney Position," *Reno Gazette-Journal*, July 18, 1939, 16.
"Pike Is Slated for Boyle Post," *Nevada State Journal*, July 19, 1939.
"Editorially Speaking," *Nevada State Journal*, July 19, 1939.
"Labor Unions Attack Pike," *Nevada State Journal*, July 20, 1939.
"Politics—Appointment of Pike to U.S. Post Ends Year's Controversy," *Reno Gazette-Journal*, July 22, 1939.
"Pike Takes Office as U.S. Attorney Today," *Reno Gazette-Journal*, Aug. 7, 1939.
"Politics," *Reno Gazette-Journal*, Nov. 23, 1940.
"Young Democrat Leader Selected," *Nevada State Journal*, Nov. 27, 1940.
"A New Justice," *Reno Gazette-Journal*, Sept. 16, 1959.
"Well Known Men Honored at Reception," *Reno Gazette-Journal*, Feb. 11, 1942.
"Brown and Pike Leave for Army," *Reno Gazette-Journal*, Feb. 11, 1942.
"Miles N. Pike Returns to Reno," *Reno Gazette-Journal*, Sept. 7, 1944.
"Maj. Miles Pike Returns to Reno," *Reno Gazette-Journal*, Sept. 8, 1944.
"Craven Resigns US Attorney Post and Pike May Succeed," *Reno Gazette-Journal*, Jan. 9, 1945.
"Miles N. Pike Takes Office U.S. Attorney," *Nevada State Journal*, March 17, 1945.
"Judge Thomas O. Craven," Second Judicial District Court—A Historical Perspective, accessed April 8, 2019, https://www.washoecourts.com/Historical/1951/Craven.
"Miles Pike Resigns U.S. Attorney Post," *Nevada State Journal*, July 1, 1952.
"Miles N. Pike, Attorney, Dies," *Reno Gazette-Journal*, May 27, 1969.
"New Patriotic Group Formed," *Nevada State Journal*, Oct. 26, 1954.
"Miles Pike Named to Supreme Court," *Reno Gazette-Journal*, Sept. 15, 1958.
"Nevada Supreme Court Work Load Is Doubled," *Reno Gazette-Journal*, Jan. 12, 1961.
"Pike Declines to Comment on Resignation," *Reno Gazette-Journal*, May 15, 1961.
"Nevada Political Picture," *Reno Gazette-Journal*, May 20, 1961.

"Pike Resigns; Reno Attorney Fills Position," *Reno Gazette-Journal*, May 23, 1961.
"Pike Elected Head of State Historical Group," *Reno Gazette-Journal*, May 20, 1961.
"Hard Work Puts Reno Rotarian on the Board," *Reno Gazette-Journal*, Dec. 19, 1991.
"Retired Judge Pike Hospitalized," *Reno Gazette-Journal*, July 18, 1968.

Gordon R. Thompson

"A Memorial to the Honorable Gordon R. Thompson," 117 Nev. 993 (2003).
"Thompson Leaving High Court Feud Behind," *Reno Gazette-Journal*, Oct. 20, 1980.
"Bruce R. Thompson," interview by Jay Sourwine, University of Nevada Oral History Program, accessed May 14, 2019, https://archive.org/details/ThompsonBruce.
"Mabel Thompson, Mother of Judges Dies," *Reno Gazette-Journal*, Sept. 26, 1967.
"Washoe Delegates Elect Officers," *Reno Gazette-Journal*, Nov. 29, 1944.
"Supreme Court Justice Files for New Term," *Reno Gazette-Journal*, March 5, 1962.
"Legal Institute Elects Justice," *Reno Gazette-Journal*, Feb. 15, 1963.
Gordon R. Thompson, "Unconstitutional Search and Seizure and the Myth of Harmless Error," *Notre Dame Law Review* 42, no. 4 (1967): 457, 457–458.
"High Court Judge Finds Campaign Is Hard Work," *Reno Gazette-Journal*, Oct. 12, 1974.
"Public Speaks," *Reno Gazette-Journal*, Feb. 12, 1970.
"Free Press, Fair Trial Discussed," *Nevada State Journal*, Jan. 13, 1966.
"Law Officers Must Adjust to New Rules," *Reno Gazette-Journal*, Aug. 7, 1965.
"Justice Court Rules of Civil Procedure," Legislative Counsel Bureau, Court Rules of Nevada, accessed May 14, 2019, https://www.leg.state.nv.us/courtrules/JCRCP.html.
"Justice Speaks of Watergate," *Nevada State Journal*, March 2, 1973.
"Law 'n Order Overkill Worries Judge," *Reno Gazette-Journal*, May 1, 1972.
"Former Jurist Endorses a Merit System," *Reno Gazette-Journal*, Feb. 23, 1981.
"Open-Heart Surgery Today for Thompson," *Reno Gazette-Journal*, Oct. 6, 1977.
"Conspiracy Alleged in High Court Feud," *Reno Gazette-Journal*, Sept. 4, 1980.
"Memorializing the Former Chief Justice of the Nevada Supreme Court, Gordon R. Thompson," Senate Concurrent Resolution No. 47, 68th Leg. (1995), https://www.leg.state.nv.us/Session/68th1995/95bills/SCR47.TXT.
"Jurist Gordon Thompson Dead at 76," *Reno Gazette-Journal*, Feb. 5, 1995.

David Zenoff

"In Memoriam, David Zenoff," 123 Nev. 661 (2009).
"David Zenoff, 89, Nevada High Court Judge Married Presleys," Los Angeles Times, Oct. 6, 2005, https://www.latimes.com/archives/la-xpm-2005-oct-06-me-passings6.1-story.html.

"Zenoff, Former Justice of Supreme Court, Dies," Las Vegas Sun, Oct. 5, 2005, https://lasvegassun.com/news/2005/oct/05/zenoff-former-justice-of-supreme-court-dies.

"Memory," *Reno Gazette-Journal*, Oct. 29, 2005, 2A.

"Hearing Planned for DA Office's Role in UNR Case," *Reno Gazette-Journal*, Oct. 15, 1988.

"Death Penalty Law Hit by Court," *Reno Gazette-Journal*, Feb. 18, 1977.

"Nevada Justice Zenoff Plans April Retirement," *Reno Gazette-Journal*, Dec. 8, 1976.

"State Young Republicans Vote Resolution to Impeach Zenoff," *Reno Gazette-Journal*, March 9, 1976.

"Brazen Judge," *Reno Gazette-Journal*, March 8, 1976.

"Nevada High Court Tells Plans for Zenoff Inquiry," *Reno Gazette-Journal*, March 4, 1976.

"Ski Pass for Justice Zenoff Launches Dispute," *Reno Gazette-Journal*, Feb. 27, 1976.

"Zenoff Seeks Reelection to High Court," *Reno Gazette-Journal*, Jan. 24, 1974.

"Zenoff Says New Ethics Panel Inadequately Funded," *Reno Gazette-Journal*, Sept. 17, 1975.

"Law School: Regents Agree on Study, Avoid Location Question," *Nevada State Journal*, Jan. 13, 1973.

"New Tennis Group Will Help Players Gain Recognition," *Reno Gazette-Journal*, Nov. 1, 1972.

"Justice Zenoff Gets Juvenile Justice Award," *Reno Gazette-Journal*, July 17, 1972.

"Zenoff Files for Reelection to High Court, *Reno Gazette-Journal*, Jan. 28, 1972.

"Zenoff Named to Committee on Delinquents," *Reno Gazette-Journal*, March 6, 1971.

"Zenoff Comment Draws Criticism of GOP's Abbot," *Reno Gazette-Journal*, Nov. 2, 1970.

"Recall of Supreme Court Trio Urged by Petition," *Mason Valley News*, March 20, 1970.

"Recall Plan Against Court Being Started," *Reno Gazette-Journal*, Feb. 11, 1970.

"Show Crime," *Reno Gazette-Journal*, March 19, 1969, 4.

Justice David Zenoff, "Thou Shalt Honor Whom?," *Juvenile and Family Court Journal* 20, no. 3 (Fall 1969), https://onlinelibrary.wiley.com/doi/abs/10.1111/j.1755-6988.1969.tb01312.x.

"General Agreement," *Reno Gazette-Journal*, Dec. 20, 1969.

"Death Penalty Vote by People Needed—Zenoff," *Reno Gazette-Journal*, May 28, 1968.

"Middle East War Possible—Israeli Spokesman," *Reno Gazette-Journal*, May 22, 1967.

"Laxalt-Court Controversy Is Examined," *Reno Gazette-Journal*, April 20, 1967.

"Valley Forge Foundation Cites Nevadans," *Reno Gazette-Journal*, Feb. 22, 1967.

"Juveniles' Facilities Praised," *Reno Gazette-Journal*, Nov. 21, 1966.

"Judge David Zenoff Files for Supreme Court Bench," *Nevada State Journal*, Jan. 25, 1966.
"Judge Zenoff Likes Supreme Court. He'll Seek Election," *Reno Gazette-Journal*, May 26, 1965.
"Way Clear for Russell to Appoint Clark Judge," *Reno Gazette-Journal*, Dec. 23, 1958.
"Young Is Expected to Deny Part in Redfield Burglary. Las Vegas Lawyer Retained," *Nevada State Journal*, Aug. 8, 1952.
"4 Renoites Serve as Bar Examiners," *Nevada State Journal*, Feb. 17, 1951.
"David Zenoff," Southern Nevada Jewish Heritage Project, https://digital.library.unlv.edu/jewishheritage/people/david-zenoff.

Jon R. Collins

"Collins Scholar Chosen," *Reno Gazette-Journal*, June 18, 1990, 14.
"In Memoriam, Jon R. Collins," 105 Nev. 939 (1989).
"Collins Resigns Energy Job," *Reno Gazette- Journal*, July 25, 1976.
"Collins to Head Energy Board," *Reno Gazette-Journal*, July 14, 1988.
"Colleagues, Friends Honor Jon Collins on Retirement," *Reno Gazette-Journal*, Dec. 19, 1970.
"A Special Session of the Supreme Court of the State of Nevada," 86 Nev. 949 (1970).
"National Judges' Group Honors Justice Collins," *Reno Gazette-Journal*, July 3, 1970.
"Justice Collins Won't Seek Re-Election," *Reno Gazette-Journal*, June 10, 1970.
"Brotherhood Understanding Call by Collins," *Reno Gazette-Journal*, May 30, 1970.
"Pre-Legal Group Carries Name of Collins," *Reno Gazette-Journal*, March 12, 1970.
"Brotherhood Idea Shelved, Collins Claims," *Reno Gazette-Journal*, Feb. 28, 1970, 9.
"Freedom Medal Goes to Collins for Speech," *Reno Gazette-Journal*, Feb. 23, 1970.
"Nevada Ready to Suspend Collins' Driving License," *Reno Gazette-Journal*, Jan. 14, 1970.
"Collins Wants Judiciary Reorganized," *Reno Gazette-Journal*, Oct. 17, 1969.
"Collins Supports State Public Defender System," *Reno Gazette-Journal*, Sept. 3, 1969.
"Chief Justice Seeks Answers to Problems," *Reno Gazette-Journal*, Aug. 7, 1969.
"Solutions Elusive," *Reno Gazette-Journal*, May 20, 1969.
"Chief Justice Argues Need for Legislative Reform," *Reno Gazette-Journal*, May 17, 1969.
"Collins Praises Public Defender," *Reno Gazette-Journal*, May 6, 1969.
"Collins Traveled Long Road to Head of Tribunal," *Reno Gazette-Journal*, Jan. 6, 1969.

"New Chief Justice Jon Collins: Some Changes in Future," *Reno Gazette-Journal*, Jan. 4, 1969.
"Washoe Bar Endorses Collins," *Reno Gazette-Journal*, Oct. 21, 1966.
"Judge Collins Sworn as Justice," *Reno Gazette-Journal*, May 6, 1966.
"Jon Collins Takes Oath for Supreme Court Post," *Reno Gazette-Journal*, May 6, 1966.
"A Special Session of the Supreme Court of the State of Nevada," 82 Nev. 471 (1966).
"Accused Says 'Don't Recall Court Shooting,'" *Reno Gazette-Journal*, July 7, 1961.
"Accused Man's Property Is Ordered Sold," *Reno Gazette-Journal*, Jan. 19, 1961.
"Bullet Wound Is Fatal to E. C. Mulcahy," *Reno Gazette-Journal*, Nov. 28, 1960.
"Attorney Slain in Court," *Reno Gazette-Journal*, Nov. 25, 1960.

Cameron M. Batjer

"Cameron Batjer Obituary," *Reno Gazette-Journal*, https://www.legacy.com/us/obituaries/rgj/name/cameron-batjer-obituary?id=23076512.
"Former Supreme Court Chief Cameron Batjer Dies," Nevada Appeal, June 6, 2011, https://www.nevadaappeal.com/news/2011/jun/06/former-supreme-court-chief-cameron-batjer-dies.
Cy Ryan, "Former Nevada Supreme Court Justice Cameron Batjer Dies at 91," Las Vegas Sun, June 1, 2011, http://lasvegassun.com/news/2011/jun/01/former-nevada-supreme-court-justice-cameron-batjer.
"Cameron Batjer Seeks Ormsby Attorney Office," *Reno Gazette-Journal*, March 25, 1954.
"Know Your Candidates Attorney General," *Reno Gazette-Journal*, Oct. 28, 1958.
"Ormsby GOP Leader Files for Office," *Reno Gazette-Journal*, July 19, 1962.
"Enters Second Bid for Chief Legal Office," *Reno Gazette-Journal*, July 19, 1962.
"Cam Batjer Day Slated Tuesday in Lyon County," *Mason Valley News*, Oct. 11, 1968.
"Laxalt Defends Endorsement of Justice Cameron Batjer," *Reno Gazette-Journal*, Oct. 31, 1968.
"Cameron M. Batjer," *Mason Valley News*, Feb. 18, 1972.
"Three Justices File for Re-election Today," *Reno Gazette-Journal*, May 14, 1968.
"Batjer Wins High Court Seat in Nevada," *Reno Gazette-Journal*, Nov. 8, 1972.
Tim Anderson, "Nevada Supreme Court Race," *Reno Gazette-Journal*, Oct. 31, 1978.
"Manoukain Retains Seat on Supreme Court," *Reno Gazette-Journal*, Nov. 8, 1978.
"Search Begins for New Justice," *Reno Gazette-Journal*, Nov. 10, 1981.
"Batjer Cool Type," *Mason Valley News*, Oct. 4, 1968.
"Helene Batjer Consul General for Istanbul," *Mason Valley News*, July 6, 1976.
"Nevada High Court Faces Heavy Load," *Reno Gazette-Journal*, Sept. 9, 1980.
"Nevada High Court Judges Skeptical About Open Meeting Law," *Reno Gazette-Journal*, Sept. 16, 1977.

"Exclusion of Justices Overturned," *Reno Gazette-Journal,* Dec. 25, 1980.
"Ex-state Supreme Court Justice Coming Home," *Reno Gazette-Journal,* Sept. 3, 1986.
"Lura Gamble Batjer," obituary, *Reno Gazette-Journal,* Dec. 13, 1997.
Cameron M. Batjer, former Chief Justice of Nevada Supreme Court, in Reno, Nevada, interview by Brad Lucas, University of Nevada Oral History Project, Nov. 4, 2002.
Azbill v. State, 88 Nev. 240, 495 P.2d 1064 (1972) (rehearing denied).
Ennis v. State, 91 Nev. 530, 539 P.2d 114 (1975).
Levers v. Rio King Land & Inv. Co., 93 Nev. 95, 560 P.2d 917 (1977).
Price v. Sinnott, 85 Nev. 600, 460 P.2d 837 (1969).
Bean v. State, 86 Nev. 80, 465 P.2d 133 (1970) (rehearing denied).

Thomas L. Steffen

McKay v. Bergstedt, 106 Nev. 808, 801 P.2d 617 (1990).
Thomas L. Steffen, interview by author, Dec. 8, 2015.

Acknowledgments

THIS BOOK GREW OUT OF my dissertation research and monthly essays I published in the Washoe County Bar Association's monthly magazine. As a judge, I often receive credit I do not deserve. My work is possible only through the assistance of department staff and law clerks. I have been privileged to work with seventeen law clerks during my time on the bench. Each clerk contributed to my avocation as an amateur historian. To each I express my gratitude.

I wrote most of these pages during early morning and late evening hours, and I am ever grateful for a spouse who allowed me to indulge my interests long after my career was set. I am reminded of a passage from the Scarlet Letter: "[He] thought of those long-past days . . . when he used to emerge at eventide from the seclusion of his study, and sit down in the firelight of their home, and in the light of her nuptial smile. He needed to bask himself in that smile, he said, in order that the chill of so many lonely hours among his books might be taken off the scholar's heart." So too has the lonely chill of this book been warmed by my wife's steady presence and support. Similarly, my three daughters Alisa, Morgan, and Abigail patiently endured my absences and made our times together joyful.

I acknowledge the tremendous work of Russell McDonald and reliable assistance from various employees at the Nevada Historical Society.

I walked into the Nevada Supreme Court for the first time in 1993 to be Justice Thomas Steffen's law clerk. I later worked for the entire court as a staff attorney. I enjoyed the rare privilege of observing Nevada justices work in seclusion before joining together to reach difficult decisions that impacted Nevadans personally and developed Nevada jurisprudence.

Every day was a gift, and I left the Nevada Supreme Court with reverence for the institution and profound respect for the many judges who sat at its bench. Their work left an imprint in my mind that is the informing influence of my career. This book is a tribute to them.

Index

Page numbers in italics indicate illustrations.

A
abolitionists, 42–43
Adams, Brent, 171
Adams, Robert Taylor, 167–168
African American children, 53
African Americans, 44
alcohol prohibition, 143–144
American Bar Association, 118
American way of life, ix
An Act to Organize the Territory of Nevada, 3
Anderson, Rufus, 88–89
anti-gaming efforts, 105
Anti-Slavery Society, 42
appellate jurist, work of, 149–150
Arentz, Mary, 185
Arentz, Samuel, 185
attorneys general, 94
Austin, Nevada, 88, 89

B
Badt, Milton B., *147*, 147–151, *148*
   death, 178–179
   education, 128
   McNamee, F., attack against deplored by, 159
   Merrill, C. praised by, 153
Baldwin, Joseph G., 73
Balzer, Frederick, 144
Bancroft, Hubert Howe, 15–16
Bartlett, John, 167
Bates, Edward, 35, 36
Batjer, Cameron M., 145, *183*, 183–189, *184*, 193
Batjer, Helene, 185
Batjer, Lura (Gamble), 185, 187, 189
Batjer, Mary Belle McVicar, 184–185
Batjer, Robert Wilhelm, 183
Bean, Thomas Lee, 168
Beatty, Henry O., *52*, *56*, 56–58
   Brosnan, C., tribute to, 63
   son of, 56, 87, 88
   successor of, 71
Beatty, William H., 56, 87–91
Belknap, Charles (Charles Henry), 71–72, *78*, 78–80, *80*, 84
Bellows, Henry, 18–19
Bible, Alan, 130, 145, 153, 154–155
Bigelow, Rensselaer R., *96*, 96–97, 110
Bigler, John, 65
bimetallism, 97
Black, Hugo, 155

221

Black Panther Party, 154
Blasdell, H. G., 26, 68
Bonnifield, M. S. (McKaskia Stearns), 94, *98*, 98–100, 125
Bonnifield, Nellie (Lovelock), 99
Bowen, Grant, 145, 167
Boyle, William, 162
Bradley, L. R., 78
Breyer, Stephen, 128
Brosnan, Cornelius M., *52*, *59*, 59–63, 68
Brotherhood of Elks, 144
Brown, Caroline Belknap, 79–80
Brown, Edmund G. "Pat," Sr., 128
Brown, Ernest, 158
Buchanan, James, 3

C
Caldwell, Earl, 154
California, crime and corruption in, 65
California constitution, 6
California Militia, 65
California Supreme Court
  appeals before, 29, 64, 73, 75
  justices on, 89–90
  opinions concerning, 60
Cannon, Howard, 145, 153
capital sentences, reversing, 188
Carson City capitol complex, 186
Carson City Council, 187
Carson City School District trustees, 57
Carson County system of laws, 3
Carter, Jimmy, 178
Carville, Ted, 162
Catholics, 140
Cheney, Massey & Smith, 102
civil juries, composition of, 10
civil liberties, viii
civil rights, 169
Civil War, 1, 66

Clarke, Robert M., 60, 62–63
Clemens, Orion, 4, 23
Cole, Cornelius, 58
Coleman, Benjamin W., *119*, 119–122, *120*
  death, 134
  Hawley, P., tribute to, 82–83
  tributes to, viii
Collins, Jon R., 145, *177*, 177–182, *178*
Collins, Rita, 181
Comstock Lode, 4
Confederate army, 103, 123
Conness, John, 47
conscience, law and, 154
Constitutional Convention, first (Nevada Territory), 6–9, 46, 60–61
Constitutional Convention, second (Nevada Territory), 9–12, 61, 64, 65–68
Coolidge, Calvin, 113
county courts *versus* district courts, 10
Craven, Thomas, 162–163, 182
criminal concepts, controversial, 168
Cruzan v. Director, Missouri Department of Health, 190

D
Davis, Jefferson, 3
death penalty, 88–89, 96–97, 174, 188
death penalty cases, 168
deceased, memories and records of, viii
deceased justices, writing about, viii
decision, reversing earlier, 175
DeLong, Charles, 11
Democratic Anti-Lecompton Party, 56
Democratic Party, 64, 115, 123, 173, 178
Democrats
  in military, 28
  on Nevada Supreme Court, 74
Denning, Phillippe, 159–160
district courts *versus* county courts, 10

diversity, power of, vii
divorce, 124, 156, 175
Ducker, Edward Augustus, *125*, 125–127, 144
duels and dueling, 29, 45–46
Duniway, Ben C., 155

E
Earll, Warner, 78, *84*, 84–86, 92
Eather, Edgar, *143*, 143–146, 157
Eather, Rose (Tognoni), 143
Eighteenth Amendment, 143
Eighth Judicial District Court, 140, 157
Eisenhower, Dwight, 153
Elko, Nevada, 148, 149
Elko County, 96–97, 129
equality before the law, 53
equal protection, viii
Esmeralda County, 94
Eureka, 143
executions, 96–97
extra-judicial activism, 169

F
families, assembling and disassembling, viii
Farrington, E. S., 128
Faucett, Miles, 96
federal Circuit Court of Appeals, San Francisco, 82
federal lands grazing cases, 149
female justice, first, vii
Field, Stephen, 47
Fillmore, Millard, 64
First Amendment protections, 154
Fisher, Eddie, 175
Fitzgerald, Adophus Leigh, *80*, *103*, 103–104
Foley, Roger, 136, 187
freedom of the press, 154, 169
freedoms, preserving, ix

Freeman, William, 165
Free-Soil Party, 98
free speech, 174
Frémont, John, 1

G
Gable, Clark, wife of, 156
Garber, John, *73*, 73–77, *74*
gentlemanly honor, 29
geological theories, 4, 5, 7, 40
George, Lloyd, 193
Germany, Catholics and Jews in, 140
gold mining, 4
Goldwater, Barry, 173
government ethics, 174
Grant, Ulysses S., 48, 68, 92
Gray, Leslie, 152, 154–155
grazing cases, 149
Great Depression, 124
Gregory, Frank, 187

H
hagiographic biographies, vii, viii
Hamlin, Hannibal, 45
Hanna, Dick, 187
Harding, Ralph, 192
Harlan, John M., 155
Harris, William Torrey, 37–38
Harrison, Benjamin, 81
Harry Reid International Airport, 117
Hawley, Thomas Porter, *81*, 81–83, *82*, 97
Hewlett, William, 128
historic biography, vii
History of the Bench and Bar of Nevada, 125
honorific themes, purpose of, viii
Horsey, Charles Lee, *138*, 138–142, 144, 153
Household Finance Corporation, 191–192

Hug, Proctor, Jr., 155, 167
Humboldt County, 15
Hutchinson & Steffen, 193

I
individual liberties, defense of, 175
inspiring qualities of justices, viii
intellectual honesty, 175

J
Jay, John (Court justice's grandson), 43
Jay, John (US Supreme Court justice), 43
Jewish causes, 175–176
Jewish families, 148
Jews in Germany, 140
Johnson, Andrew, 105
Johnson, J. Neeley, 10, *64*, 64–68, *66*
Jones, America (Strong), 33, 36–37, 38
Jones, Horatio M., *33*, 33–38, *34*
    appointment to Nevada Territorial Supreme Court, 4, 34
    resignation of, 5, 13, 35–36, 39
    workload challenges faced by/appellate decisions made by, 16
judges. *See also name of individual judge*; territorial judges
    election of, 11
    merit selection of, 174
    Nevada Supreme Court, first, 15, 51
    Nevada Supreme Court chief justice, first, 15, 51, 55
    qualifications of, ix
Judicial District Court, First, 95
judicial education, 179
judicial ethics complaints, 189
judicial misconduct, 17
judicial normalcy, 2
judicial reform, 179–180
judicial salaries, 53, 57, 157, 179
judiciary
    corruption of, 2
    debates over, 6–7
    independence and integrity of, viii
    newspapers on, 12–14
    reform sought for, 12
    role of, ix
Julien, Mary (Brewer), 106
Julien, Thomas Van Camp, *105*, 105–109, 110
jurisdiction, disputes over, 24–25
jurors, corruption among, 2
jury(ies), composition of, 10
jury(ies), rules governing, 75
justices, portrayal of, vii
justicial system, administration of, ix
juvenile justice, 173, 174, 175

K
Kansas-Nebraska Act, 64
Know Nothing Party, 65, 69

L
law, court role in declaring, not making, 54
law, protecting and upholding, 154
"law and order" movement, 169
law clerks, 135
laws, impartial administration of, ix
lawyers
    corruption among, 2
    investigating and disciplining, 179–180
    mentorship of, 121–122, 127
    teaching of, 171
Laxalt, Paul
    Badt, M., tribute to, 151
    Batjer, C. relations with, 187, 188, 189
    speeches, ix
    Zenoff, D. criticized by, 175
Legal Tender Act, 62

Leonard, Orville Rinaldo, *92*, 92–93
Lerude, Warren, 169
Lewis, James F., *51*, 51–55, *52*, 81
libel cases, 141–142
"liberal warrior of the court," 166, 170
Lincoln, Abraham
    appointments made by, 4, 23, 31, 39, 44, 45, 47
    correspondence, 16, 25, 35, 47
    election, 1860, 44
    election, 1864, 1
    inauguration of, 3, 30, 45
    Nevada statehood backed by, 10, 15
Lincoln County, 133
Lionel, Sam, 177
Lionel Sawyer & Collins, 177, 181
List, Robert, 193
litigation, end to, 54
Locke, Morris, 40
Locke, Powhattan, 39–41
    alcoholism, 17
    criticism of, 18, 40–41
    health problems, 41
    Jones, H. replaced by, 5, 39
    press coverage of, 13–14, 39–40
Loomis, George, 43
Lovelock, Nevada, 99
Low, Frederick, 47

M

Malone, George "Molly," 187
manslaughter, attempted, 159–160
marriage ceremonies, 157
Marsh, Andrew, 6
Massey, William, 100, *101*, 101–102, 108, 110
McCall, Robert, 185
McCarran, Patrick A., *117*, 117–118
    death, 158
    Ducker, E. defeat of, 125
    Horsey, C. defeat of, 140
    Orr, W. promoted by, 134–135
    as Pike, M. supporter, 162
    staff, 177
    Sweeney, J., tribute to, 116
McCarran airport (*later* Harry Reid International Airport), 117
McClinton, J. Giles, 61
McKnight, William, 162
McNamee, Frank, *156*, 156–160, 173
Mendoza, John, 188
Merrill, Charles, *152*, 152–155
    Eather, E., tribute to, 145–146
    Horsey, C. defeated by, 141, 158
    resignation from Nevada Supreme Court, 164
Mexican-American War, 28
mining depression, 74
mining industry
    judiciary's impediment, perceived to, 10
    legislation impacting, 140
    productivity, decline in, 5
    revival of, 103
    support for, 124
mining lawyers, 123
mining litigation, 4–5, 12, 47
mining recession, 1860s, 10
mining suits, 15–16
mining taxation, 6, 7, 8, 31–32
money, seizing and awarding, viii
Moran, Thomas, 162
Mormons, 3
Mott, Gordon N., *28*, 28–32, *30*
    appointment to Nevada Territorial Supreme Court, 4, 30
    election to Congress, 35
    mining litigation brought before, 5
    press coverage of, 30–31
    resignation of, 13, 14, 31
    Turner, G. case, intervention in, 25
    workload challenges faced by, 16

Mowbray, John, ix, 145, 170, 188
multi-ledge mining companies, 7
multi-ledge theory, 4, 9, 18, 31
murder cases, 96
murder convictions, reversing, 89
Murphy, Michael Augustus, 80, 94, 94–95

N
National College of State Trial Judges, 179
Native American Party (Know Nothings), 65, 69
Native Americans, 105, 148, 149
Nevada as divorce state, 124
Nevada Civil Practice Act, 1866, 64
Nevada constitution, 6, 15, 60
    Constitutional Convention, first, 6–9, 46, 60–61
    Constitutional Convention, second, 9–12, 61, 64, 65–68
Nevada Gaming Commission, 164
Nevada jurisprudence, authors of, viii
Nevada law, evolution of, 150
Nevada Legal Oral History Project, 189
Nevada Reports, 57
Nevada State Bar, 107, 118, 135–136
Nevada statehood
    debates over, 11–12
    issues underlying, 7, 8–9
    overview of, 1–2
    rejection of, 6, 9
    supporters, 10, 57, 60, 61
    territorial judiciary influence on, vii
    vote on, 12, 15
Nevada Supreme Court
    administrative leadership of, 150
    appeals to, 47
    chief justice, first, 15, 51, 55
    establishment of, 1
    expansion of, 188
    judicial environment described by, 2–3
    size and composition of, 10
Nevada Supreme Court justices. *See name of individual judge*
Nevada Supreme Court justices, first, 15, 51
Nevada Territorial Supreme Court
    appeals to, 52
    creation of, 3–4
    litigation, 4–5
Nevada Territory
    constitution, work on drafting (*see* Constitutional Convention, first [Nevada Territory]; Constitutional Convention, second [Nevada Territory])
    creation of, 3–4, 6
    government, 12
    judges (*see* territorial judges)
    mining industry, 4–5, 60
    organization of, 2–3
Nevada Trial Lawyers Association, 193
Ninth Circuit Court of Appeals
    libel cases before, 141
    memorial sessions convened by, 136
    Merrill, C. appointment to, 153, 164
    Merrill, C. on, 154, 155
    Norcross, F. appointment to, 113
    Orr, W. appointment to, 134–135
Nixon, George, 102
Nixon, Richard, 154–155
"nonwhites," court testimony prohibited for, 66
Norcross, Frank H., 108, *112*, 112–114, 134
North, Ann (Loomis) (John North's second wife), 43, 46
North, Emma (Bacon) (John North's first daughter), 43
North, Emma (Bacon) (John North's first wife), 43

North, John, *42*, 42–48, *44*
　attitudes toward, 7–8, 18–19
　as constitutional convention president, 6, 46
　evaluation of, 17–19
　health problems, 10, 13, 14, 46–47
　judge difficulties described by, 16, 47
　Lewis, J. partnership with, 51, 54
　as Lincoln, A. supporter, 44–45
　Locke, P. siding with, 40–41
　mining taxation, views on, 7
　Mott, G. replaced by, 5
　press coverage of, 13
　resignation of, 14, 19, 47
　response to criticism, 14
　statehood vote as referendum on, 6
　Stewart, William, relations with, 7–8, 9
　surveying and mining activities, 45
Nye, James, 4, 10, 45

O
Oberlin College, 33
Oddie, Tasker, 102, 144
Oleander, California, 48
one-ledge theory. *See* single-ledge theory
Ormsby County Republican Party, 188
Orr, John, 113
Orr, William E., *133*, 133–137, *134*, 140–141

P
Panama Canal Commission, 76
Panic of 1837, 64
People's Party of California, 56
Pickering, Kristina, 188
Pike, Miles N. "Jack," *161*, 161–165, 167
Pike, Russell and Roy Robert, 162
Pike, W. H. A., 161

Pioche, Nevada, 133–134, 138–139, 140
Pittman, Key, 102, 162, 163
Pittman, Vail, 140–141, 144–145, 149, 155, 177
police interrogation tactics, 168
post-death memorials, challenges of, viii
postwar reconstruction, 1
Potts, Elizabeth, 96–97
Potts, Josiah, 96
Powell, Lewis, 155
predators, punishing, viii
Presley, Elvis and Priscilla, 175
Price, Robert, 152
professional courage, 175
property rights, defining, viii
public good, dedication of, ix
public safety, judiciary role in, viii–ix
public schools, integration of, 53

Q
quartz-crushing mill, 7
quartz veins, 4, 18

R
Raggio, William, 168
Rattazzi, James, 144
Raymond, Lizzie, 52
Reagan, Ronald, 189
Reconstruction, 47
Rehnquist, William, 155
Reno, Nevada
　attitudes concerning, 124
　public library, 1st in, 113
　trips to, 186
Reports of the 1863 Constitutional Convention of the Territory of Nevada, 6
Republican Party, 84, 97, 102
Republican Party of Minnesota, 43–44
Reynolds, Debbie, 175
Reynolds, W. R., 143, 145

right-to-die case, 190–191
Riverside, California, 48
Roosevelt, Franklin, 113, 162
Roosevelt, Theodore, 76, 128
Ross, Jack, 186
rule of law, 175
Russell, Charles, 157, 173, 177
Russia, blood purges in, 140

S
Sanders, John Adams, *123*, 123–124, 129
Sanders, Jon, 120
San Francisco earthquake, 1906, 148
San Francisco lawyers, 59–60
Sawyer, Grant
    Collins, J., tribute to, 181–182
    Collins, J. Nevada Supreme Court appointment by, 179
    as district attorney, 178
    as law firm member, 177, 181
    McNamee, F. Nevada Supreme Court selection confirmed by, 157
    McNamee, F. succession plan, role in, 159
    Nevada Gaming Commission appointment by, 164
    Thompson, G. Nevada Supreme Court appointment by, 167
    Zenoff, D., relations with, 173–174
school segregation, opposition to, 45, 53
Schwartz, Sidney, 147
Seabees, 186–187
Seward, William, 4, 45, 165
Shearing, Miriam, vii
Sherman, William Tecumseh, 65
Sierra Nevada Mountains, 3, 64
silver mines, 2–3
silver mining litigation, 4–5
Silver Party, 94
single-ledge theory
    evidence in favor of, 18
    interests, court rulings against, 7
    judges favoring, 31
    overview of, 4
    rulings against, 16
    state government and, 9
    support for, 31
slaves, aid to freed, 17, 47
social justice issues, 42–43, 47, 48
social order, judiciary role in, viii–ix
Southern Pacific Railroad, 85
Springer, Charles, 168
Stanford, Leland, 27
Steffen, LaVona, 191, 192
Steffen, Thomas L., *190*, 190–193, *192*
Stewart, William
    criticism of, 8–9
    Johnson, J. N., travels with, 68
    Locke, P. described by, 17
    mining interests represented by, 8
    mining litigation, earnings from, 5
    North, J., relations with, 7–8, 9, 47
    statehood, campaign for, 6
Stone, M. N., 93
Storey County, 10, 12
Summerfield, Sardis, 79
Swackhamer, Bill, 155
Sweeney, James G., *115*, 115–116

T
Taber, Erroll James Livingston (E. J. L.), *128*, 128–132, 149
Taber, Joseph M., 128
Talbot, George Frederick, 90–91, *110*, 110–111
Taylor, Elizabeth, 175
temperance movement, 43
territorial judges
    challenges and difficulties facing, 16, 47
    corruption, alleged among, 15–16, 25

critical material about, vii
distrust of, 2
election of, 10
historic perspective on, 15–19
impeachment and removal of, 10
press coverage of, 13–14
resignation of, 2
terms, length of, 6–7
territorial judiciary, statehood influenced by, vii
Texas, 28
Thirteenth Amendment, 1
Thompson, Bruce, 166
Thompson, Gordon R., 145, 159, *166*, 166–171, *169*
trial process, integrity of, 75
Truman, Harry, 134, 135, 173
Turner, George E., *23*, 23–27, *24*
    appointment to Nevada Territorial Supreme Court, 4, 23
    attitudes toward, 16–17, 18
    duration of term, 5
    Locke, P. siding with, 41
    North, J. distancing from, 14
    press coverage of, 13, 23–24, 25, 26
    resignation of, 16–17
Twain, Mark (Samuel Clemens)
    arrest warrant against, 45–46
    Brosnan, C. praised by, 60
    brother of, 4
    Reports of the 1863 Constitutional Convention notes compiled by, 6
    Turner, G. described by, 23, 24
    Unionville described by, 99

U
Uniform State Laws, 113
Union Army, 65, 101, 166
Union Party
    California Supreme Court candidates, 56
    Nevada Supreme Court candidates, 52
    statehood and, 6
    Storey County convention, 8
    supporters, 57, 68
Union soldiers, wounded, aid to, 18
Unionville, Nevada, 99
United States Constitution, 3
United Way, 18
University of Nevada, Reno
    graduating class, 1st, 112
    professors and deans at, 166
    visits to, 186
University of Nevada Oral History Program, 150, 189
US District Court, 54
US Parole Commission, 189
US Sanitary Commission, 18
US Senate, 69–70, 82, 118
US Senators, 141
US Supreme Court, 111, 149, 154–155, 188, 190
Utah Territory common law, 3

V
victims, protecting, viii
vigilance committee, 65
Virginia City
    judge duties at, 16
    litigation in, 11, 35
    mining litigation in, 5, 31
Virginia Louise Mining Co., 139
virtues of justices, viii
voting rights
    for African Americans, 44
    for women, 44, 99, 105–106, 113, 141
vulnerable, giving voice to, viii

W
Wade, Benjamin, 23, 26
Wagner, Sue, 170

Washoe City, Nevada, 45
Washoe County
   public offices, 106–107
   seat, first of, 45
Watergate, 169
Watson, Harry, 178
Weinberger, Caspar, 135
Whig party, 28, 64–65
Whitman, Bernard Crosby, 69, 69–72, 70
Whitman, Mary Elizabeth (Church), 69
Windle, J. H., 99
Wingfield, George, 102
Winnemucca (city), 99
Winnemucca, Sarah, 98
witnesses, corruption among, 2
women
   assault charges against, 98
   criminal convictions against, 46
   executions of, 96–97
   in higher education, 33
   suffrage, 44, 99, 105–106, 113, 141
Workmen's Compensation Act, 141
World War II
   Army enlistments, 157
   casualties, 191
   marines, 172
   navy enlistments, 177, 186–187
   soldier training, 163

Y

Young, Cliff, 155, 175

Z

Zenoff, David, 145, 159, *172*, 172–176

About the Author

DAVID A. HARDY WAS APPOINTED by Nevada governor Kenny Guinn to the Second Judicial District Court (Washoe County) in 2005. Since then he has presided over a variety of general jurisdiction cases and fulfilled many administrative roles, including chief judge of the district court and president of the Nevada District Judges Association. Judge Hardy received his undergraduate and graduate law degree from Brigham Young University and his MA and PhD from the University of Nevada. He has been adjunct faculty at the University of Nevada and was a frequent lecturer at the National Judicial College. His scholarship and publications focus on Nevada territorial history, judicial ethics, and legal issues involving the elderly.